W9-AFB-213

PENGUIN BOOKS

TO THE PROMISED LAND

David J. Goldberg is Senior Rabbi of The Liberal Jewish Synagogue, London, and is a leading spokesman for Progressive Judaism in the UK and Europe. He was educated at Manchester Grammar School, Oxford University and Trinity College, Dublin, and received his Rabbinic Ordination from the Leo Baeck College, London, in 1971.

He worked for a year on a kibbutz between school and university, and was a volunteer in the Six Day War of 1967. During the 1982 Israeli invasion of Lebanon, he spent three days in and around besieged Beirut. Increasingly involved over the years with the 'peace camp', Goldberg was one of the small band of Jews in Israel and the Diaspora who nurtured relations with Palestinians and their Arab supporters, even when contact with the PLO was officially prohibited under Israeli law. Their efforts eventually helped to pave the way for the Oslo Accords. He has contributed regularly on Jewish and Israeli topics in *The Times*, the *Guardian*, the *Independent* and other major newspapers and journals.

With his former colleague, Rabbi John D. Rayner, he co-authored *The Jewish People: Their History and Their Religion*, also published by Penguin.

DAVID J. GOLDBERG

TO THE PROMISED LAND

*A History of Zionist Thought from Its Origins
to the Modern State of Israel*

PENGUIN BOOKS

PENGUIN BOOKS

Published by the Penguin Group
Penguin Books Ltd, 27 Wrights Lane, London W8 5TZ, England
Penguin Books USA Inc., 375 Hudson Street, New York, New York 10014, USA
Penguin Books Australia Ltd, Ringwood, Victoria, Australia
Penguin Books Canada Ltd, 10 Alcorn Avenue, Toronto, Ontario, Canada M4V 3B2
Penguin Books (NZ) Ltd, 182–190 Wairau Road, Auckland 10, New Zealand

Penguin Books Ltd, Registered Offices: Harmondsworth, Middlesex, England

First published 1996
1 3 5 7 9 10 8 6 4 2

Copyright © David J. Goldberg, 1996
All rights reserved

The moral right of the author has been asserted

Set in 10/12pt Monotype Bembo
Typeset by Datix International Limited, Bungay, Suffolk
Printed in England by Clays Ltd, St Ives plc

Except in the United States of America, this book is sold subject
to the condition that it shall not, by way of trade or otherwise, be lent,
re-sold, hired out, or otherwise circulated without the publisher's
prior consent in any form of binding or cover other than that in
which it is published and without a similar condition including this
condition being imposed on the subsequent purchaser

For Rupert and Emily, as promised

CONTENTS

INTRODUCTION

Zionism is a unique national movement, in that it emerged among a scattered and disparate people who had little in common apart from religion and had not lived in what they regarded as their homeland for nearly two thousand years. It met none of the criteria by which nationalism and national movements are usually judged. It was brought to public notice and given political impetus by emancipated Jews of western Europe, who were anxious to solve the plight of the Jewish masses in eastern Europe by large-scale immigration to Palestine. The state which eventually came into being as a result of their initiative – Israel – has a population today of over four million Jews, but nearly 60 per cent of them are of eastern, not European, origin; they immigrated to Israel from Arab countries – just one of several differences between Zionism in theory and Zionism in practice.

The word 'Zionism' is undoubtedly one of the most emotive in the political lexicon of the last hundred years. Its opponents use it as a term of abuse, alongside Nazism or fascism; a 1975 resolution at the United Nations, subsequently rescinded, equated Zionism with racism. Its supporters compare it to idealistic liberation movements like the Italian Risorgimento and accuse its critics of being anti-Semites in disguise. The *theory* of Zionism – the books, pamphlets, speeches and articles that constitute Zionist thought – has received little of the sustained analysis accorded to communism, capitalism, socialism and other ideologies since the French Revolution, yet Zionism in practice – meaning the state of Israel – has been at the centre of controversy since it was established in 1948.

There have been numerous books about modern Israel and the history of Zionism. A public relations, propaganda and (mis)information industry has put the Arab or Israeli versions of their conflict to governments, the international media and the world public. Distinguished scholars, venal politicians, pen-for-hire journalists – all have entered the lists on behalf of the Zionist or the Arab cause. The academic and intellectual integrity of these mercenaries has been one of the casualties of an intractable dispute that has led to four major wars, two large-scale campaigns, many smaller engagements and tens of thousands dead and wounded since 1948. In such a bitter, passionate and tragic conflict, objectivity is wellnigh impossible, and truth is in the eye of the partisan beholder.

This is not yet another book to put the Zionist case. I have grown tired of the repetitive polemic, the endless rehash of stale controversies, the interminable arguments about who-did-what-when and where the blame lies, that surround discussion of Israel and the Middle East situation. My interest is in Zionism as a history of ideas – the intellectual, social and political currents that shaped individuals and their theories, and how those ideas were adapted and modified by application and experience: the translation of theory into practice. This book tries to analyse the major strands of Zionist thought, through pen portraits of the men who fashioned them. As such, it is the first full-length study of its kind that I know of, certainly in English, and its occasionally irreverent judgements may discomfort those who prefer to view the architects of Zionist thought – Herzl, Achad Ha-Am, Ber Borochov, A. D. Gordon et al – through the rose-coloured spectacles of 'official' Zionist texts and biographies. If Herzl, the flimsiest of the theoreticians, appears to receive disproportionate attention, it is because without his contribution the Zionist movement would not have come into being and Zionism would have faded as a wan fantasy.

I made use of the work of many authors in composing this book; they are acknowledged in the bibliography. But if any one work was in my mind while writing, it was the late Edmund Wilson's superb study of the socialist tradition in European thought, *To the Finland Station*. I can still remember my excitement when reading it at university over thirty years ago, and in conscious tribute to it, and in the modest hope that I may have invested Zionist ideology and its progenitors with a little of the verve and lively insight Wilson brought to Karl Marx and socialism, I chose the title of this book: *To the Promised Land*.

During the fraught and divisive decade of Likud government in Israel under Menachem Begin and Yitzchak Shamir, it was a tiresome necessity to have to parade one's Zionist and pro-Israel credentials before daring to criticize aspects of policy such as treatment of the Palestinians or the West Bank settlement programme. Those of us who felt compelled to do so were happier when Likud was replaced by a Labour government committed to the peace process; a process that accelerated in the months between prime minister Rabin's assassination and the May 1996 election that brought Binyamin Netanyahu to power. However, the habit of self-justification dies hard and prompts me to explain my personal interest in Zionism and Israel.

I spent a year in Israel in the late 1950s, between school and university. To an adolescent socialist *manqué*, the experiment of co-operative farming was appealing, so I tried kibbutz life. The first kibbutz I worked on had split from its neighbour over the issue of whether kettles should be allowed in members' quarters, or whether drinks, as other meals, had to be taken in the communal dining hall. Every Friday afternoon we went to the communal store to receive our allocation of clothes and toilet requisites for the coming week; the store foreman took any request for extra razor blades or another shirt as a violation of his personal property. From that kibbutz, too prosperous and staid for my taste, I went to a pioneering settlement in the heart of the Negev desert. S'deh Boker, with its barbed wire, bunkers and tank emplacements, on a newly built road linking Beersheba to Eilat, had all the excitement I could have wished for. It also had David Ben-Gurion, the prime minister, as its most illustrious member. His wife Paula Jewish-grandmothered me, and I had a couple of conversations with the hero of modern Israel in their dwelling, larger than the others and painted green, but wooden and spartan like the rest. I thought then, and still think over thirty-five years later, that Ben-Gurion was a great man; he made me feel guilty for long afterwards at not passing up an Oxford scholarship to become a pioneer of the new state.

Nine years later, as a volunteer during the Six Day War, I listened to the weekly communal meeting on another kibbutz that turned into a heart-searching examination of the generation gap, and the gulf in aspirations between older and younger members – all because some soldiers back from the front had hoisted the kibbutz secretary's car on to a roof for a prank. It was also on that stay, walking the streets of East Jerusalem and talking to Palestinians for the first time, that I recognized the falsity of propaganda stereotypes classifying all Arabs as enemies of the Jewish state. Since then, I have visited Israel many times, have family and friends living there like most Diaspora Jews, and have become more closely – and controversially – involved with those sections of

Israeli society and politics which sought a solution on the basis of mutual recognition and granting the same right of self-determination to Palestinians that Israelis had demanded for themselves.

To understand a conflict, one must know its causes, which led me into a deeper reading of Zionist literature rather than the sanitized snippets of school text books and government information packs. Zionist thinkers were a mixed and diverse group, and their ideology is eclectic, a fascinating blend of originality, borrowings from other systems, high moral intent and evasive obfuscation of the dilemma of asserting one's needs at the expense of another's rights. Its ideologues and theorists deserve attention from anyone wanting to assess the validity of Zionism's aims, its success in achieving them, and its role in twentieth-century Jewish history; hence this book.

It is always an author's pleasure to acknowledge those who encouraged him. In my case, I must thank my wife Carole-Ann for her steady support, my brother Jonathan for help when it was needed, and all those friends in Israel and England who offered advice and made suggestions. Any merit this book may have is due to them; its faults are mine alone.

DAVID J. GOLDBERG
London, 1996

PART ONE

DIASPORA

I

The Antecedents of Zionism

The spread of nationalism in Europe throughout the nineteenth century was a result of, or a response to, the ideals of the French Revolution. The spread of nineteenth-century Jewish nationalism – Zionism – was a result of, or a response to, a perceived failure to fulfil those revolutionary ideals.

The French Revolution broke up for ever the traditional structures of European Jewish existence, built on the twin foundations of rabbinic legislation and ghetto domicile. Before 1789, Talmudic scholarship and a rigorously observant lifestyle had been a palliative against oppression for most Jews, and the ancient wisdom of Jewish law and lore had barely been touched by the disquieting ripples of secular culture. All that changed. When French armies occupied northern Italy they abolished the ghettos. Napoleon's victories were enthusiastically welcomed by the Jews of the Rhineland, and France came to be regarded as protector and emancipator. Napoleon ruled his new Jewish subjects with firm efficiency and ensured that Prussia and the puppet kingdom of Westphalia undertook major reforms giving them civic equality.

Emancipation presented the Jew with options, from conversion or assimilation to neo-traditionalism, from radical socialism to entrepreneurial capitalism. Jewish religious and social history since 1789 has been a response to modernity and to the opportunities, challenges and dilemmas of confronting society beyond the ghetto walls.

In western Europe, the middle decades of the nineteenth century provided the Jews with steady progress towards civic equality. They achieved equal rights in Germany and Austria–Hungary, in Italy, Switzerland and Scandinavia. In 1858, the first Jew took his seat in the British House of Commons, and individual Jews rose to government rank in France, Holland, Italy, and the constituent assemblies of the German states. Although baptized at the age of thirteen, Benjamin Disraeli, who became prime minister of Britain for the first time in 1868, remained a Jew in the eyes of the public and, more equivocally so, in his own. Still more significant than this reassuring evidence of political acceptability was the enthusiasm with which Jews responded to cultural and commercial opportunities. A Jewish middle class emerged: taking advantage of the climate of toleration, they were prominent in business, industry, banking and relatively open professions such as journalism and the theatre. As restrictions were lifted, they streamed into secondary and university education; the grandsons of pedlars and street traders became physicists, mathematicians, doctors and lawyers.

The corollary of acculturation was a decline in religious observance. An important factor in the growth of the Reform movement within Judaism from the 1820s onwards was the wish of its adherents to minimize the differences from their Christian neighbours. New synagogues were built in the style of imposing civic edifices, and sermons were delivered in the language of the country, rather than Yiddish. The traditional liturgy was drastically pruned, particularly of references to the rebuilding of the Temple or the Ingathering of the Exiles in Zion. An organ accompanied the mixed choir, and decorous congregations imitated the dress and deportment of Sunday churchgoers. As the barriers to equality were dismantled, the pressure to convert – using the baptismal font as 'the entrance ticket to European culture' in Heinrich Heine's wry flippancy – grew less acute. Mixed marriages, on the other hand, became more frequent among the affluent upper-middle class.

Jewish life in western Europe had undergone an astonishing transformation in the half-century since Napoleon. Determined to secure and extend their newly won freedoms, the Jews were effusive in their declarations of loyalty and patriotism, nowhere more so than in Germany, where the Orthodox, the Reform and the secularists vied in denying the national and racial characteristics of Judaism and assuring cautious legislatures that the German homeland had long since replaced in Jewish affections the birthplace of their faith. It really did seem, at long last, that the prevailing liberal *Zeitgeist*, and their own adaptability, had combined to provide the Jews with a safe haven after centuries of persecution and exclusion. That, certainly, was the assumption of the greatest of Jewish historians, Heinrich Graetz, who noted with satisfaction in the Preface to the final volume of his monumental *History of the Jews* that, 'happier than any of my predecessors', he could express the opinion that 'in the civilized world the Jewish tribe had found at last not only justice and freedom but also a certain recognition. Now at long last it had unlimited freedom to develop its talents, not as an act of mercy but as a right acquired through thousandfold sufferings.'

Paradoxically, when the future had never looked brighter, the first eccentric suggestions of restoring a national Jewish homeland in Palestine were mooted. A disparate band of Orthodox rabbis, radical socialists, philanthropists and Judeophile Christians all began, independently, to propound their theories. No common ideology or shared experience of Jewish life united them. If any unifying factor can be detected in their emergence, it would be that all of them were witnesses to the nationalist eruptions which convulsed Europe in the mid nineteenth century. Nationalism was a reaction against the cosmopolitan and universalist values preached by the *philosophes* of the Enlightenment, and in Germany, especially, the French cultural assumptions about universalism, science and the progressive victory of reason over custom and prejudice were passionately rejected. The Germans, lacking a tradition of military or political hegemony, and self-conscious about their scant achievements in art, literature and science, compensated by discovering in themselves superior qualities of a moral and spiritual kind. In comparison with worldly and decadent French culture, German thinkers regarded themselves as young and energetic, the true harbingers of the future. To this vision of national destiny was added a nostalgic and romanticized evocation of the Teutonic past and its folk heroes.

The intellectual rationale for such concepts originated with the philosopher Johann Gottfried von Herder (1744–1803), who articulated the notion of the *Volksgeist* or national genius. According to von Herder, all nations, from the humblest to the most exalted, possess a peculiar and irreplaceable way of life and unique national destiny. 'Let us follow our own way . . . Let men say what they like, good or bad, about our nation, our literature, our language. They are ours. They are *us*. That is all that counts.'

Von Herder was the inspiration for the romantics of the Young German movement[1] and for oppressed minorities within the Austro-Hungarian,

---

1. A group of writers and thinkers who advocated the concept of a specifically German national culture, in resistance to the cosmopolitan values of the French Enlightenment.

Turkish and Russian empires. A vehement opponent of the cosmopolitanism of the *philosophes*, and no strident patriot but an advocate of
cultural pluralism, it was von Herder's perverse fate to be applauded as
the father of political nationalism. His contention that a fundamental
human need – as basic as food, shelter and procreation – is to belong to
identifiable communal groups, each possessing its own language, traditions and historical memories, appealed powerfully to Italians, Slavs and
Balts struggling for independence; it also appealed to some Jews.

Rabbi Judah Alkalai (1798–1878), the earliest proto-Zionist, who
spent his youth in Jerusalem, was appointed leader to the Jewish community in Semlin, the capital of Serbia, in 1825. There he witnessed the
efforts of Balkan minorities to throw off Ottoman domination; neighbouring Greece had recently won her independence, and dreams of
freedom and national restoration abounded.

But Alkalai was an Orthodox rabbi, steeped in Talmud and the
arcane mysteries of the Kabbalah. The Jewish redemption he yearned
for depended upon divine, not human, agency. The Ingathering of the
Exiles and rebuilding of Zion was a heartfelt petition on almost every
page of the Orthodox prayer-book, a plea to the Lord of the Universe
to look with compassion on the sufferings of his people Israel and deliver them, as He had done at the time of Egyptian bondage. To pre-
sume to hasten the work of redemption was impious interference in the
unfolding of the divine master-plan, which would be fully revealed
only at the end of days. He therefore approached his theme circumspectly, from within the boundaries of traditional Jewish theology, justifying his programme for Jewish colonies in the Holy Land by quoting
proof texts from the Bible and Kabbalah, not by appealing to the spirit
of the times. The notorious 1840 Damascus Affair, when the Jewish
community were accused of the blood libel that Gentile blood had
been used in the preparation of Passover unleavened bread, convinced
Alkalai that the Jewish people would find freedom and security only in
their ancestral homeland. He issued a series of pamphlets written in the
classical style of rabbinic legal decisions, known as Responsa literature,
with but a naive grasp of contemporary political realities. His writings
were addressed primarily to the wealthy and acculturated Jews of western Europe, men like the English philanthropist Sir Moses Montefiore
and the French politician Adolph Cremieux, both of whom had been
instrumental in resolving the Damascus Affair. Alkalai fancied that with

their financial and political support the sultan could be persuaded to cede the Holy Land to the Jews, just as Ephron the Hittite had sold the field of Machpelah to Abraham in Genesis.

Like many of his successors in Zionism's cause, Alkalai was received sceptically by Jewish notables, and travelled tirelessly to little avail. His combination of ascetic mysticism and half-baked practicality did not inspire confidence, least of all in plutocrats pestered to dig into their pockets to aid less fortunate Jews. A pietist and visionary rather than a man of action, Alkalai ended his days, as all devout Jews wished, in Jerusalem. He was a reclusive, soon-forgotten precursor of Zionism, a kabbalist who drew more from that poignant strand of redemptive yearning fuelled in the Jewish masses by the seventeenth-century false messiah, Shabbetai Tzevi, than from the intellectual currents of his own century. One significant fact ensured that his name would survive: among his tiny group of adherents was, for a time, the grandfather of Theodor Herzl.

A more influential rabbinic contemporary of Alkalai's was Tzevi Hirsch Kalischer (1795–1874). He too was born and lived in a strategically sensitive region: the buffer province of Posen in western Poland, which Prussia acquired in the second partition of that country in 1793. Nationalism was an issue that the large Jewish population of the region could not avoid, especially during the abortive revolts of 1830–31 and 1863, when it became a matter of political and military significance whether the Jews chose to regard themselves as Poles, Russians or a separate nationality. Like Alkalai, Kalischer viewed Jewish nationalism from the perspective of rabbinic teaching and messianism. He was a typical product of the ghetto educational system, a learned Talmudist of modest means, who could devote himself to serving without stipend as spiritual leader of the community in Thorn.

Men of his generation and background had only a peripheral interest in the non-Jewish world of ideas. They picked their way suspiciously through the new opportunities for emancipation, centuries of experience having bred a deep distrust of Gentile intentions. Sufferance was their badge and determination to protect traditional Judaism was more important than dabbling on the fringes of secular culture. The Reform movement within Judaism, not the competing claims of Germans or Russian sovereignty, posed the greatest challenge to Kalischer. Posen was on the border between the east European Jewish way of life, based on strict observance and ghetto conformity, and the new, disturbing milieu of western Europe, where Jews were avidly shedding their past to join the mainstream of society. It was as much to preserve the integrity of traditional Judaism from the lure of Reform and assimilation as to alleviate the poverty of the east European Jews that Kalischer became interested in the idea of resettling the Holy Land.

He began, in standard fashion, by approaching a wealthy co-religionist, head of the Berlin branch of the Rothschild family. 'The beginning of the Redemption,' he explained in a letter of 1836, 'will come through natural causes by human effort and by the will of the governments to gather the scattered of Israel into the Holy Land.' The response was not encouraging, and Kalischer sought consolation in rebutting the Reform movement's abandonment of the doctrine of the Return to Zion through a series of pamphlets which demonstrated his mastery of Talmudic legalism; he also wrote a treatise on Jewish philosophy, and commentaries on the standard code of Jewish law by the sixteenth-century rabbi and kabbalist Joseph Caro.

Kalischer appeared to lead the conventional, undramatic existence of a rabbinic scholar, preferring his study to the market place, engaging in polemics only when the norms of traditional Judaism were threatened. But colonizing the Holy Land was never far from his thoughts. Contemporary events in Europe encouraged his dream, and added a realistic dimension to his fancies. The Risorgimento and the national struggle of the Poles and Hungarians showed what could be achieved by courage and resolve; could not the Jews do likewise, especially when all the ancient authorities were adamant that living in the Holy Land was one of the foremost religious duties of a Jew? Jewish notables had the political and financial influence to establish agricultural settlements to provide a livelihood for the Jewish poor of Palestine; such settlements would also encourage the homeless Jews of eastern Europe to emigrate there, in fulfilment of religious precept. Kalischer even considered the problem of security for Jewish colonists. Would their property and harvests be safe from predatory Arabs? The two-fold reassurance he proposed was the formation of a Jewish military guard allied to pious confidence in the present pasha as 'a just man, severely punishing robbery and theft'.

In 1862 Kalischer encapsulated his musings in a pamphlet entitled *D'rishat Zion* (Seeking Zion). It was published in Frankfurt an der Oder by the Society for the Colonization of Palestine, a small organization of a few hundred members founded by a Dr Chayyim Lorje. Both the pamphlet and Dr Lorje had only ephemeral recognition, but their significance was more long-term than immediate. Lorje claimed descent from Rabbi Isaac Luria, 'the holy lion' and famed sixteenth-century master of the Kabbalah. Lorje was himself a dabbler in mysticism and a rare combination of observant Jew and German university graduate. His interest in Jewish nationalism had been fanned by the upheavals of 1848, which he saw as presaging the millennium and the days of the Messiah who would redeem Israel. He had, however, a practical, orderly side which existed uneasily with his vanity and propensity for charlatanism. He founded his colonization society, advertised its aims and recruited members in systematic fashion. A modest organization now existed, which could bring together those attracted to the notion of encouraging Jewish settlement in Palestine. Kalischer submitted his pamphlet to it for publication.

The Kolonisationsverein für Palastina had only a brief life. Dr Lorje was a secretive, autocratic director, whose pompous aspirations and vague book-keeping methods alienated his colleagues. They succeeded in transferring the society's office to Berlin, where it quietly folded in 1865, having failed to send a single immigrant to Palestine. Kalischer, however, had the satisfaction of persuading the Alliance Israélite Universelle to found an agricultural school on the outskirts of Jaffa in 1870 – an isolated achievement, and soured by the denunciations of devout Jews living in Palestine, who feared a decrease in the charity they received from Europe. They also argued that working the land would tempt the young from study and lead to heresy.

Both Kalischer and Lorje, like Alkalai, were from the mainstream of traditional Judaism. They looked at the world around them, and the nationalist fervour agitating Europe, for signs and portents which would corroborate ancient Jewish beliefs about the Ingathering of the Exiles, much as well-meaning Gentiles would quote scripture in support of their conviction that the time was ripe for rebuilding Zion.

Shortly after the Damascus Affair had been resolved, the British consul in Syria wrote to Sir Moses Montefiore and the Board of Deputies of British Jews, urging them to organize large-scale colonization of Palestine under the slogan 'Palestine is the national sanctuary of the Jewish people'. An anonymous German pamphlet of the same time proposed the American mid-west, because Palestine 'which had been the cradle of the Jewish people . . . could not be its permanent home'. Yet another pamphleteer, after gloomily surveying the prospects for Jewish acceptance in Europe, called for a neutral Jewish state to be established between the Nile and the Euphrates, to restore equilibrium among the eastern powers. Political considerations played their part in such proposals. The slow decline of the Ottoman empire had made 'The Eastern Question' an issue of perennial concern in Europe, and between 1839 and 1854 self-interest prompted the major powers to establish consulates in Jerusalem and affirm their concern for the holy places. The revived importance of the one city in the Holy Land where Jews (mainly pious hermits or impecunious artisans) were in the major- ity (5000 as against 4500 Muslims and 3500 Christians in 1840; half the total population of just under 20,000 by 1860) prompted the Turkish government to detach Jerusalem from the province of Beirut in 1854 and appoint a governor responsible directly to Constantinople.

Diplomatic opportunism alone does not explain the reason for this burgeoning sympathy for the idea of a Jewish homeland. Certainly Palmerston and the British Foreign Office, through their mouthpiece newspaper, the *Globe*, had reasons of policy for mooting a Jewish buffer state between Turkey and Egypt, but there were opportunities else- where for military and economic influence in the Levant. The enthusi- asm of these Gentile advocates stemmed from their background as devout Bible-readers who shared a conviction that it was their re- sponsibility to alleviate the suffering of God's Chosen People.

Benjamin Disraeli, in his novelist's incarnation, and George Eliot were two sympathizers who gave literary expression to the vision of a rebuilt Jewish homeland. In *Alroy*, *Coningsby* and *Tancred*, Disraeli paid tribute to his Jewish roots by extolling the qualities and potential of the Jewish people. His observation in *Tancred* that 'All is race; there is no other truth' anticipated anthropological theories which were later used by Jews and anti-Semites alike to argue that European civilization was inherently antipathetic to Semitic stock, and that the only solution was to encourage the Jews to find a land of their own. George Eliot's *Daniel Deronda* was frank and unabashed in its special pleading that the Jews, who took precedence of all nations in the ranks of suffering, had yet to fulfil their mission of rebuilding a national centre in Palestine. The novel's eponymous hero devotes his life to that goal.

From the 1840s onwards, there was a slowly growing endorsement of the cause of Jewish nationalism. A few Jewish advocates, mainly Ortho-dox, argued the case initially; some non-Jews, motivated by liberalism, religious sympathy or reasons of state also saw merit in the idea of a Jewish homeland. But there was as yet no substance to the schemes. They remained in the realm of chimera and religious yearning. The few Jews committed to the dream could not convince their co-religionists, most of whom were busily taking advantage of emancipa-tion in western Europe, while those in the heartlands of eastern Europe had neither the spirit nor the energy to see beyond the daily grind of existence. The acculturated Jews were sceptical, the pious ones bowed down by poverty and discrimination, for which their only palliative was a resigned trust in divine providence. The well-meaning Christian sympathizers also lacked realism. The notion of planting a colony of reluctant Jews in a forsaken corner of the Ottoman empire, dependent on the whim of an eastern potentate and the goodwill of distant Europ-ean powers, was about as plausible as the unworldly François Fourier's 'solution' for the disposal of refuse in ideal communities: little boys, who love playing in dirt, should be the refuse collectors.

Support for Jewish nationalism might have gone the way of a hun-dred other stillborn utopian ideas which washed over Europe in the middle decades of the nineteenth century. But an outside source gave new stimulus and fresh urgency to the dream.

2

Moses Hess – Returnee to the Fold

The term 'anti-Semitism' was coined by Wilhelm Marr, a venal journalist and the baptized son of a Jewish actor, in a pamphlet entitled *The Victory of Judaism over Germanism*, which went through twelve printings between 1873 and 1879. Such popularity for a shoddy essay confirmed that in the decades preceding its publication 'The Jewish Question' had become a major source of political, economic and scientific controversy in the liberal western European countries. A fresh animus against the Jews, cloaked in a veneer of anthropological respectability, had replaced the medieval Judeophobia encouraged by centuries of Church teachings.

The enthusiasm and avidity with which Jews had seized the opportunities offered in commerce, industry and the professions, and the speed of their transition from pariah to parvenu, provoked hostile reactions. Their mobility in pursuit of social betterment altered the demography of Jewish existence, and families streamed in from rural areas to urban localities. From former Polish territories they moved to Leipzig, Cologne, Frankfurt and Berlin; from Alsace to Paris; from Moravia and Galicia to Vienna. The Berlin Jewish community had grown from around 3000 in 1816 to 54,000 by 1854, and in Vienna the increase was sharper still. Whether as assimilated but still detectable members of the bourgeoisie, or as a distinctive grouping in the urban proletariat, the Jews of western and central Europe had come to the fore too fast, too *pushily*, for their detractors' liking. Populist agitators, jealous competitors, reactionary Junkers and disaffected intellectuals – all could point the finger at a scapegoat for their, and society's, shortcomings.

The typical Jewish response was to dismiss such prejudice as atavism, an irrational hangover from the Middle Ages. The Jews, as exemplary citizens, would convince anti-Semites of their loyalty and civic worth. In Germany, especially, Jewish apologists stressed the affinity between their universal values and the national spirit. No cultural symbiosis went deeper, they averred, than that of Judaism and Germanism. If anything, anti-Semitic manifestations accelerated the process of assimilation, so keenly did emancipated Jews empathize with German civilization. For those not willing to sever all ties with their heritage, the Reform movement offered a discreet, socially acceptable compromise. The prevailing ethos of German Jewry was to accentuate their similarities with, and minimize their differences from, the *Volksgeist*. In the bitter judgement of an Italian Orthodox scholar, Samuel David Luzzatto, these assimilated Jews were the monkeys of European society, aping the intellectual fashions of the age.

That Orthodox rabbis should condemn assimilation and any dereliction of religious duty was to be expected, but when the criticism came from Jews who had most keenly championed the benefits of universalism, it merited uneasy consideration. In their time, both Heinrich Heine and his equally celebrated Jewish contemporary, the essayist Ludwig Börne, expressed second thoughts about the advantages of assimilation. Theirs was disappointed idealism at the failure of society to become more tolerant; they had not been allowed to break out of what Börne once called 'the magic Jewish circle'. Lesser-known Jews echoed them.

None of these advocated Jewish nationalism as an alternative. And in 1862 the one man who did – who went furthest in his radical solution, who excoriated Jewish self-delusion most sardonically, who dissected inherent German anti-Semitism most prophetically, who grasped the significance of the east European Jewish masses most presciently – sold just 160 copies of the slim volume in which he summarized his ideas. A year later the publisher suggested that the author should buy his books back at a remaindered price.

Rome and Jerusalem by Moses Hess is nowadays regarded as the seminal work of Zionist literature. And it is with the life and career of Hess that any study of Zionist history usually commences.

The hard-to-translate Yiddish word *luftmensch* is used to describe any rootless, feckless, well-intentioned but insubstantial individual; in short, a Moses Hess. He was born in Bonn in 1812. When his parents moved to Cologne in 1821, beckoned by its business opportunities but regretting its lack of Jewish educational facilities, nine-year-old Moses was left behind, in the care of his rabbinically trained grandfather. The boy received a traditional upbringing, studying Bible, Talmud and rabbinic Codes. In a celebrated essay which did much to rehabilitate Hess's reputation, the philosopher Isaiah Berlin ponders what difference it might have made had Karl Marx, the younger contemporary and occasional colleague of Hess, been educated by *his* rabbinic grandfather instead of his father, who was a disciple of Voltaire's and had Karl baptized at the age of seven.

To judge from Hess's reaction, it would have made the founder of 'Scientific Socialism' even more vitriolic in his dismissal of Judaism. The precocious Moses confided in his diary that the Jewish religion was beyond revival. He joined his father in Cologne after his mother died in 1826, styled himself Moritz not Moses, and chose to study philosophy at the University of Bonn. He was active in the literary exchanges between the Young Hegelians during the 1830s and 1840s. Out of this cultural milieu emerged his first book, the bombastically titled *The Holy History of Mankind, by a young Spinozist*. Although acknowledging the excommunicated Jewish lens-grinder as his master, the work was replete with Hegelian influence and the contemporary vogue for historical philosophy. Hess wrote that the people chosen by their God must disappear for ever, to make way for a new, purer way of life. His father, by now a prosperous but still observant manufacturer, was little pleased, especially since his son showed small commitment to the family business but great facility at frittering his allowance. Their relationship cooled still further when Moses began to dabble in socialist politics. Two of his new friends were Friedrich Engels and Karl Marx.

During 1842–3, Hess was Paris correspondent for Germany's most radical newspaper, the *Rheinische Zeitung*, edited by Marx. He collaborated with Marx and Engels on two books of critical analysis of contemporary society, and was sufficiently prominent in the German revolution of 1848 to be sentenced to death and forced to flee into French exile. Yet in *The Communist Manifesto* of that same year, Marx derides his erstwhile revolutionary friend as one of those false socialists who merely translated French ideas into German: 'speculative cobwebs, embroidered with flowers of rhetoric, steeped in the dew of sickly sentiment, a Philistine, foul and enervating literature'.

Why was Hess the object of some of Marx's ripest vituperation? At the ideological level, Hess did not accept the concept of materialistic determinism. His socialism was predicated on purely moral premises and the choice of the conscious will, rather than the 'objective forces of history'. He had a naively optimistic view of human nature and its innate goodness. Yet that alone did not justify the barbs, just as his political theorizing did not merit lengthy refutation. Hess was too lightweight for that.

Something about his artless nature and transparent personality goaded serious people. He was one of Dostoevsky's holy innocents, impulsive, generous and open-hearted. The pain he caused his respectable, bourgeois father was not motivated by resentment at childhood deprivation, any more than his choice of a Cologne seamstress for a wife was made to humiliate him. Hess wanted, rather, to make a quixotic personal gesture of atonement for a society which exploited the lower classes. Such theatricality would have exasperated Marx, even as it precipitated the final rupture between Hess and his family. They hinted darkly that Sibylle, even worse than a seamstress, was a prostitute; few Jewish parents totally approve of their sons' marital choices. In the event, Sibylle cuckolded Hess regularly, but throughout their long married life of poverty and wanderings retained for him the warm affection he evoked from those who met him casually but were spared having to live or to work with him.

Like many Jewish radicals since — Rosa Luxemburg and Trotsky are two who come to mind — Hess subordinated any residual feelings of Jewish identity to the wider needs of mankind. He wrote about his reactions to the Damascus Affair, 'I wanted to cry out in anguish in expression of my Jewish patriotism, but this emotion was immediately superseded by the greater pain which was evoked in me by the suffering of the proletariat of Europe.'

In a book published in 1851 under the suitably portentous French title, *Jugement dernier du vieux monde social*, Hess gives two grim examples of peoples punished by history for clinging to their outworn institutions: the Chinese, 'a body without a soul, and the Jews, a soul without a body, wandering like a ghost through the centuries'. Now more-or-less permanently domiciled in Paris, Hess moved in the circle of German political émigrés and fellow socialists like Ferdinand Lassalle, writing the occasional article, holding a succession of menial jobs in order to eat. He followed with warm sympathy the struggles of Garibaldi and Mazzini for Italian independence. In 1852, changing tack in a manner that was typical, he forsook politics for the study of natural sciences, bringing to the new discipline all the bursting enthusiasm he had previously shown for Hegel or socialism. A decade later, in his fiftieth year, in a volte-face surprising even by his volatile standards, Hess wrote his paean of praise to traditional Judaism and the Jewish people.

What had caused the latest transformation?

There were one or two likely reasons. In 1853, the first text book of modern racism, Joseph Gobineau's *Essai sur l'inégalité des races humaines*, which adapted Darwin's theory of natural selection to divide humanity into superior 'Aryan' and inferior 'Semitic' species, was published to a positive reception. It was followed by the overt racial anti-Semitism of Richard Wagner in music, and of Georg von Schoenerer, founder of Pan-Germanism, in politics. The gauntlet had been thrown down to Hess and other idealists who proclaimed the universal brotherhood of man.

Secondly, Hess's father had died in 1851. The death of a parent, especially after a fraught, unresolved relationship, and coming when he was entering the second half of life, was bound to affect Hess and turn his thoughts inward. For once, he gave priority to personal concerns over global ones. There is much guilt and self-flagellation in his book. Whatever its creative spur, *Rome and Jerusalem* was completed quickly. One of its few readers who responded positively was Heinrich Graetz. Another was Dr Lorje, who wrote to complain that the author had made no mention of his Colonization Society. Hess sent a graceful apology and a subscription to join.

Otherwise, it fell on deaf ears. Written in the form of twelve letters and ten notes to a fictional lady, its artificial style militates against the urgency of its argument. Hess begins with a poignant personal confession:

After twenty years of estrangement I have returned to my people. Once again I am sharing in its festivals of joy and days of sorrow . . . A sentiment which I believed I had suppressed beyond recall is alive once again. It is the thought of my nationality, which is inseparably connected with my ancestral heritage, with the Holy Land and Eternal City, the birthplace of the belief in the divine unity of life and of the hope for the ultimate brotherhood of all men.

Having reaffirmed his links with the Jewish people, Hess breaks with his contemporaries of the left who regarded anti-Semitism merely as the dying twitches of the old, reactionary order. German racial antipathy for the Jews is something deeper, instinctive and irrational: 'German antagonism to our Jewish national aspirations has two sources, reflecting the dual nature of man . . . which are nowhere so sharply defined – and opposed to one another – as among the Germans.' That is why all efforts at religious reform, assimilation, or even conversion, are doomed to failure. 'The Germans hate the religion of the Jews less than they hate their race – they hate the peculiar faith of the Jews less than their peculiar noses. Reform, conversion, education and emancipation – none of these opens the gates of society to the German Jew; hence his desire to deny his racial origin.'

He is scathing about Jewish Uncle Toms, like the son of a convert who spent hours every morning at the mirror, comb in hand, trying to straighten his curly hair: 'Jewish noses cannot be reformed, and the black, wavy hair of the Jews will not be changed into blond by conversion.' He directs his sharpest invective against the Reform movement, as do many non-practising Jews today who may nevertheless feel uneasy about modifications to the marmoreal structure of Judaism. He regards as the greatest threat those who 'with their newly invented ceremonies and empty eloquence have sucked the marrow out of Judaism and have left only a shadowy skeleton of this most magnificent of all historical phenomena'. Yet when Hess insists that the divine teaching of Judaism was never completed, but 'has always kept on developing, always representing the typically Jewish process of harmonizing the sacred unity of life with the spirit of the Jewish people and of humanity', he is summarizing precisely the central tenet of the Reform movement. What he really objected to in Reform theology was its elimination of prayers for the restoration of the Jewish homeland and its derogation of the national character of Judaism.

For Hess, homelessness was the heart of the Jewish problem. The Jew was in exile, and his *ubi bene ibi patria* philosophy would earn him neither the respect nor the trust of the nations among whom he lived. The Jews needed to lead a normal national existence: 'Without soil a man sinks to the status of a parasite, feeding on others.'

Given the two basic assumptions of his dialectic, that Jewish identity is essentially national and that xenophobia of the German kind would always resist Jewish integration, Hess comes up with the only possible solution: a return to the land of Palestine. Economic and political conditions were propitious. The digging of the Suez Canal and the laying of a railway to connect Europe and Asia were encouraging portents. Jewish colonies would be supported by liberal, humanitarian France, out of enlightened self-interest. Hess recognizes that western Jews, keen to extend their hard-won civil rights and etiolated by assimilation, would not emigrate to a remote and barren country. It is the Jews of eastern Europe, the huddled masses of the Russian, Prussian, Austrian and Turkish empires, whose fidelity to their religion had kept them insulated from secularism, who would respond to the challenge. Whereas Marx had mistakenly assumed that the communist revolution would begin in the industrially advanced states of Europe, Hess correctly forecast the source of the main thrust and enthusiasm for Jewish nationalism. He was unusually and sympathetically responsive, for a western Jew of his generation, to the spiritual vitality of eastern Jewry, especially its populist Chasidic sects.

Typically, Hess overstates his appreciation, insisting that no fashionable dilution or adaptation of Judaism is acceptable. 'I myself, had I a family, would, in spite of my dogmatic heterodoxy, not only join an Orthodox synagogue, but would also observe in my home all the feast and fast days . . .' He derides those who would replace a single traditional observance with some abstract notion of a Jewish 'mission' to be a light unto the Gentiles. 'What I do not understand is how one can believe simultaneously in "enlightenment" and in the Jewish mission in exile, that is to say, in the ultimate dissolution and the continued existence of Judaism at one and the same time.'

Hess's practical proposals for colonizing Palestine demonstrate, in equal parts, his optimism about human nature and his political naivety. He notes that both Rabbi Hirsch Kalischer of Thorn and Monsieur Ernest Laharanne, an adviser to Emperor Napoleon III, had recently advocated just such a venture. The Turks would be willing, for a handful of gold tossed them by Jewish bankers, to admit large numbers of Jewish colonists. Marching together, the French and the Jews would regenerate the parched land and bring civilization to Asia. French democracy, Jewish genius and modern science would combine in a new triple alliance, to revive an ancient people in their homeland and ultimately usher in the age of universal brotherhood free of class and racial struggles.

That, shorn of its digressions and repetitions, is the essential message of *Rome and Jerusalem*. Addressed principally to German Jews, it provoked from the few who read it a predictable reaction. Abraham Geiger, a formidable leader of the Reform movement, sneered in an anonymous review that its author was 'an almost complete outsider, who, after bankruptcy as a socialist, and all kinds of swindles, wants to make a hit with nationalism . . . and along with the questions of restoring Czech, Montenegrin and Szekler nationality . . . wants to revive that of the Jews'. The *Allgemeine Zeitung des Judenthums* put forward the standard Hegelian argument of those Jews who preferred to describe themselves as Germans of the Mosaic persuasion: '. . . we are first and foremost Germans, Frenchmen, Englishmen and Americans, and only then Jews.'

After his brief foray into the field of Jewish nationalism, Hess's life resumed its characteristic course. He eked out a living as the correspondent of various Swiss and German journals; he joined the International Workingmen's Association, founded by Karl Marx, and was a member of the First International. Never an orthodox Marxist, he discerned no incompatibility between socialism and Jewish nationalism — for him both were based on the desire for social justice, the biblical morality he had acquired at his grandfather's knee. When the Franco-Prussian war broke out in 1870, he was expelled from Paris as a Prussian citizen, although he vociferously denounced German militarism. He eventually returned to Paris, and to his study of the natural sciences, and died there, obscure, impoverished and ignored, in April 1875. As he wished, he was buried with his parents in the Jewish cemetery in Deutz.

The events of the twentieth century have given posthumous validity to Hess's Jewish predictions. He foresaw, with chilling accuracy, the apocalypse that would overwhelm assimilated German Jewry; he correctly surmised that western Jews were too comfortably adjusted to emigrate voluntarily, whereas the Jews of eastern Europe knew both the internal cohesion and the economic deprivation which would make colonization of Palestine a serious proposition for them.

With justification, therefore, 'the communist Rabbi Moses', as Arnold Ruge[1] dubbed him, is regarded as a Zionist *avant la parole*, and has streets named after him in modern Jerusalem and Tel-Aviv. His overriding conviction that the search for Jewish acceptance in European society was a chimera, and that only statehood could solve the problems of a people without a national homeland, became the central plank of Zionist ideology.

1. German philosopher and political writer.

3

Leo Pinsker and Chibbat Zion

The process of Jewish emancipation and acculturation during the middle decades of the nineteenth century was a phenomenon of western European societies. In eastern Europe, where the bulk of Jewry resided, the pace of change was slower, more grudging, and marked by erratic swings, depending upon shifts of government policy. More than five million Jews lived under Russian rule, in the towns and villages of Lithuania, White Russia, Poland, Galicia and Romania. Whereas the demands for social change had altered other European states drastically, in Russia the tsar, a privileged nobility and the state Church resisted all pressure for reform.

Official policy was to limit Jewish habitation to the empire's western provinces, 'the Pale of Settlement'.[1] Only about 200,000 Jews – mainly bankers, prosperous merchants, university graduates and army veterans with twenty-five years of military service – were permitted to live in the cities of St Petersburg, Moscow and Kiev. Warsaw, with over 200,000 Jews, was the largest community in Europe, followed by Odessa with nearly 150,000. Few lived on the land, so the smaller cities like Vilna, Brest, Bialystok and Litovsk were predominantly Jewish. According to census statistics for 1897, fully 82 per cent of Russian Jewry lived in towns or cities, but since the places where they could reside were limited, it was not uncommon for Jews to make up 70–80 per cent of the total urban population.

Although Jewish influence was strong in the sugar and textile industries, the development of the railways and the grain and timber trades, for the most part the masses engaged in petty trades and crafts, leased distilleries and inns, or melted into the urban poor, desperate for any employment. Ethnically distinctive and traditionally pious, they provoked government suspicion and the hostility of the *lumpenproletariat*.

1. The 25 provinces of tsarist Russia in which Jews were officially permitted to reside. The system was instituted in 1791 by Catherine the Great, and officially abolished in March 1917.

Most professions, university enrolment and government service were barred or stringently limited. Army conscription for the standard twenty-five years, but preceded in the case of Jewish youth by six additional years in military schools, was a harrowing, ever-present threat, to be evaded, if possible, by bribery or the acquisition of a guild certificate which granted exemption.

Treatment of the Jews oscillated between repression and tentative attempts at liberalization. During the reign of Nicholas I (1825–55), no fewer than 600 legal enactments were promulgated against them, including book censorship, the prohibition of traditional dress and uncut side curls, and the abolition of the local self-government (*kehillah*) system. An attempt was made to replace the network of Jewish primary schools and *yeshivot* with a state system of education, to reduce Jewish 'self-isolation', but it foundered (as did so much of the legislation) on a combination of bureaucratic inefficiency and Jewish resistance.

Russia's poor showing in the Crimean War made manifest how far she lagged behind other European powers, both economically and industrially. Alexander II (1855–81) recognized the need for change, and the abolition of serfdom was followed by reformation of the judiciary and local government. Restrictive anti-Jewish legislation was either modified or allowed to lapse. Forced conscription was abandoned. Favoured groups such as merchants, university graduates, registered artisans and medical personnel were granted permission to live outside the Pale of Settlement; for the first time Jewish communities were established in St Petersburg and Moscow. Modest though such amelioration was, Alexander's reign came to be regarded as a golden age of Russian Jewry, a foretaste of freedoms to be hoped for in the none-too-distant future.

It was in this favourable climate that the Haskalah (Enlightenment) movement flourished, fashioned on the German model initiated by Moses Mendelssohn in Berlin seventy years previously. The Reform movement made little or no headway in eastern Europe, where emancipation had not been achieved, and traditional Judaism was not challenged, therefore, by radical alternatives; but Haskalah, with its goal of integrating well-educated, religiously aware, socially productive Jews into wider society, offered possibilities in Russia during the reign of Alexander II. The writers, essayists and intellectuals of the east European Haskalah differed widely in their analysis of the Jewish situation and recommendations to improve it; their only common ground was rejecting the stereotyped image of the downtrodden Jew seeking refuge in Talmudic learning and the stifling pieties of small-town communal life. Some advocated co-operation with the authorities; others – like the novelist and editor Peretz Smolenskin – looked for a revival of cultural nationalism. The young Eliezer Ben-Yehudah (later to publish the standard modern Hebrew dictionary which bears his name), was attracted by the aims of the Russian populist movement, the Narodniki, and the bomb-throwing nihilists. Moshe Leib Lilienblum flirted with the prospect of religious reform before coming under the influence of the Russian positivists Pisarev and Chernyshevsky, and devoting himself to the socialist class struggle.

What is significant about these Haskalah spokesmen and their less well remembered contemporaries is that they all accepted the *fact* of Jewish nationhood (the evidence of five million Jews living a separate, cohesive existence was all around them), but did not propose a Jewish homeland in Palestine as a solution to Jewry's woes. They had yet to go through the extravagant expectation and disillusionment which had dashed Jewish hopes in western Europe. Their turn came with the assassination of Alexander II in 1881. A wave of pogroms, tacitly condoned by the government, which suspected significant Jewish involvement in anarchist and socialist groups, swept over hundreds of Jewish communities. The widespread carnage, looting and destruction outraged western liberal opinion, especially in Victorian England, and devastated those Jews who had fought most keenly for Haskalah values and now concluded that there was no future for Jewry in Russia. The pain and shocked reappraisal occasioned by the disasters of 1881 is well caught in the diary of Moshe Lilienblum. He changed within weeks from being an ardent, atheist socialist into a passionate supporter of Jewish colonization of Palestine. His faith in the proletariat was replaced by the pessimistic realization that even after a workers' revolution the Jew would still play the role of scapegoat and lightning rod. His conversion was echoed in the reactions of other helpless observers of the violent mob anti-Semitism which raged throughout 1881.

The response of Leo Pinsker (1821–91), a respected Odessa physician, who belonged to the Society for the Spread of Culture, which taught the Russian language and secular subjects to young Jews, was typical. At a meeting in the summer of 1881 he announced his immediate resignation, as a protest against the irrelevance of discussing student bursaries when the whole Jewish people was under attack and in desperate need of leadership. Pinsker was too prim, tightly controlled and dry to provide it. The son of a noted scholar who had been the authority on the esoteric sect of Karaite Jews, Pinsker had, unusually, studied at a Russian high school and the University of Moscow. After returning to Odessa, he joined the staff of the city hospital, was highly regarded as a physician, and was honoured by the tsar for his services during the Crimean War. He was, in short, an exemplar of the 'enlightened' Jew breaking the shackles of the past and making his way in Russian society. And Odessa was an auspicious city in which to break the mould: a cosmopolitan seaport, as raffish as Marseilles, its large Jewish population had infiltrated most areas of the city's life, respectable or otherwise, as the vivid short stories of one of its most talented sons, Isaac Babel, demonstrate.

All the more shocking, therefore, was the outbreak of anti-Jewish violence there, although the authorities did move promptly and severely to quash it, arresting over 1300 rioters. Pinsker had been able to rationalize the pogrom of ten years previously, at Easter 1871, as a local aberration, but the scale and savagery of the 1881 riots made such rationalization otiose. He was shaken to his emotional and physical roots, a personal trauma which mirrored the blow to the central nervous system of Russian Jewry. He left Odessa in turmoil, to seek sympathy and understanding in western Europe for his new-found revelation that only a homeland of their own could provide Jews with security.

He was greeted with expressions of concern and polite scepticism. In Vienna, the city's foremost rabbi, Adolf Jellinek, told him that Jewry had invested too much, intellectually and morally, in the struggle for emancipation and acceptance to discard it for the artificial revival of Hebrew patriotism; he counselled Pinsker to take a rest cure in Italy, where ancient ruins would remind him that the Jews had survived Titus and Vespasian and would survive Russian anti-Semitism. The response everywhere was similar. In London, Arthur Cohen MP, President of the Board of Deputies of British Jews, diverted his querulous petitioner by murmuring that Pinsker's ideas were not without merit but should be put down in writing, for clarification. That is precisely what Pinsker did.

In Berlin, in September 1882, he published anonymously (Pinsker was a man who safeguarded his privacy, to the extent of never marrying) a pamphlet entitled *Auto-Emancipation: A Warning to His People by a Russian Jew*. He wrote it in German for two reasons: he was adamant that only western Jewry had the capacity, organization and influence to rescue the east European masses, and he was enlisting their support; secondly and practically, because his essay would not find its way past the Russian censor.

Auto-Emancipation is a faithful reflection of its author's personal strengths and weaknesses. Terse, clinical, it is acute in diagnosis but less assured about cure. Its tone is one of fastidious contempt for the morbid pathology of anti-Semitism, and caustic irritation at Jewish timidity and self-abnegation. The message hammered home on every one of its thirty-six pages is that Judeophobia is a hereditary, incurable disease, and that there is no individual salvation for the Jew, only a collective one, because 'a people without a territory is like a man without a shadow: something unnatural, spectral'. Pinsker examines the condition of Jewry using the metaphors and terminology of a doctor examining a patient – to remedy the sickness by getting at its roots. Having long since lost independence and fatherland, the Jews were to the world the frightening spectre of the dead among the living. They had ingratiated themselves, adopted cosmopolitan traits, renounced Jewish nationality for civil rights, but still remained foreigners. Living in a country for several generations no more changed their alien status than being emancipated implied their acceptance. Nomadic, evasive about their past and shifty about their future, the indelible stigma could not be removed by a poultice of legal rights. By the same token, it was a waste of time and energy to try to rebut anti-Semitism with rational arguments; Judaism and anti-Semitism were ineradicably linked, they had 'passed for centuries through history as inseparable companions'. The malign Gentile image of the Jew was fixed in perpetuity: 'For the living, the Jew is a dead man; for the natives, an alien and a vagrant; for property holders, a beggar; for the poor, an exploiter and a millionaire; for patriots, a man without a country; for all classes, a hated rival.'

There is no one so bitter as a disillusioned believer. Like Hess before him, Pinsker had been forced to renounce the aspirations of his adult life and career and flays Jewry for his disappointment. He derides the lack of dignity and self-respect, abandoned for the vain dream of acceptance, just as Hess mocked those Jews (like himself) who had changed their names. One is reminded of Arthur Koestler's comment that he became a communist out of hatred for the poor, and a political Zionist out of hatred for the 'Yid'.

And when it comes to remedies, Pinsker is even less practical and realistic than his mystical predecessors, rabbis Alkalai and Kalischer. The tragedy of Jewish pariahdom requires a territorial solution, *any* territory. Pinsker does not reject the idea of Palestine, nor does he advocate it vigorously. He speaks vaguely of a 'sovereign pashalik' in Asiatic Turkey as a possibility, although inclining towards a colony in the vast open spaces of North America. The great powers would be asked to guarantee this Jewish refuge, which would be a home for surplus unfortunates, those unable to maintain themselves in their countries of dispersion; he concedes that wealthy or emancipated Jews of western Europe would not be attracted. Apart from its political neutrality, he has little to suggest about the status, government and constitution of his autonomous Jewish region, or how the venture would be financed.

It would be unjust, though, to condemn Pinsker's pamphlet for these omissions and lacunae. Desperate situations require urgent remedies, and he was responding to the catastrophe of 1881. The pogroms abated somewhat, but continued until 1884. A series of harsh regulations, the May Laws of 1882, further circumscribed Jewish existence in the Pale of Settlement. Thousands of refugees fled the countryside to the greater safety of the cities, and those who could took ships from Odessa. This was the beginning of that mass migration in which, between 1881 and 1914, two and a half million Jews left the lands of the Russian empire for America, Britain, the British colonies, or elsewhere in Europe.

Predictably, *Auto-Emancipation*, addressed to the Jews of western Europe, received a muted response. Compassion for the plight of Russian Jewry could not be allowed to deflect communal organizations and opinion-formers from their determination to extend the gains of emancipation. The Jewish newspapers of Mainz and Bonn deplored current events in Russia, but regretted the anonymous author's failure to understand the thrust of eighteen centuries of Jewish history or the special nature of Judaism's universal mission by positing a non-existent 'national consciousness', as if the condition of the Jews was comparable with that of Romanians, Serbs and Bulgars. It was, they thought, dangerously reactionary – evidently the influence of pernicious Russian nihilism – to elevate Jewish nationalism above the goal of civic integration, which would come eventually even in Russia, despite the present distressing events.

In eastern Europe – although the pamphlet could only be reported not published in the Russian–Jewish press, and no text was available in Hebrew or more crucially in Yiddish for several years – the reaction was sharper and vociferously divided. The Orthodox objected to its excessively secular approach and lukewarm espousal of the Holy Land. Jewish magnates and their coteries in the big cities were affronted by its pessimism about Russian Jewry's future and the implication that their success was only transient. The Haskalah intelligentsia, on the other hand, welcomed it enthusiastically. *Auto-Emancipation* might say little new about the Jewish condition, but it had never before been expressed in such remorseless terms, and directed externally, in the German tongue, rather than internally, with the indulgent self-regard to which Russian Jewish writing was prone.

It was not long before the writer's identity became known. With the pardonable vanity of even the most reticent of authors, Pinsker sent his pamphlet, with covering note, to a select few, among them Moshe Lilienblum and Lev Osipovich Levanda, official expert on Jewish affairs to the governor-general of Vilna.

In response to the pogroms of 1881, a nucleus of small societies had sprung up in the towns and villages of the Pale, as Pinsker mentions in his pamphlet, dedicated to the aim of a return to Zion. One such group of Kharkov university students, calling themselves the Bilu association (from the Hebrew initials of verse 5 in Chapter 2 of the Book of Isaiah, 'O House of Jacob, come, let us walk' – but significantly omitting, as good socialists, the concluding words 'in the light of the Lord'), decided upon immediate emigration to Palestine, to establish a farming co-operative. Lilienblum persuaded Pinsker, by appealing to his stature and public eminence, to become titular leader of these proliferating Chibbat Zion (Love of Zion) societies. Pinsker's hesitation was characteristic: he had no predilection for Palestine over any other territory, and no leadership pretensions. He had noted in *Auto-Emancipation*, 'We probably lack a leader of the genius of Moses – history does not grant a people such guides repeatedly.' Eventually, his sense of duty prevailed.

A conference of Chibbat Zion was convened at Kattowitz in Upper

Silesia in the winter of 1884. The thirty-six delegates elected Pinsker as president, and in a subdued opening address he stressed the importance of a Jewish 'return to the soil' by giving aid to pioneering settlers. Initial euphoria soon gave way to dispiriting practicality, at Kattowitz and subsequent conferences. At its peak, the movement could claim 15,000 Chovevei Zion (Lovers of Zion) members, over eighty affiliated societies, and a plethora of ambitious colonization schemes; but it never raised more than 40–50,000 roubles a year to implement them, at a time when the estimated cost of settling a family in Palestine was 3000 roubles. About 20,000 Jews emigrated from Russia in 1881–2, but only a few hundred chose Palestine. Pinsker's fears about his leadership qualities were confirmed. He tried, ineffectually, to mediate between the religious factions, led by Rabbi Shmuel Mohilever of Bialystok, and their antipathetic counterparts, the free-thinking *maskilim*. Conference debates about setting up a permanent office in Palestine, or the best method of apportioning limited resources for land purchase, degenerated into angry exchanges between traditionalists who insisted the land be allowed to lie fallow every seventh year, as the Bible commanded, and the modernists, who had no patience with such notions.

More depressing still was the news from those pioneers who had made Aliyah (ascent) to Palestine. Enthusiasm had waned under the harsh reality of Turkish suspicion, rugged terrain, inhospitable climate and local Arab hostility – the last a factor blithely ignored in drawing up plans. The experience of the Biluim was symptomatic. They had hoped to attract 3000 cadres, but only about fifty reached Palestine. The initial group waited in Constantinople for a *firman* of authorization from the Ottoman government, which suspected a Russian plot to establish a bridgehead on its territory. Thirteen men and one young woman eventually sailed for Jaffa at the end of June 1882. Once in Palestine, they eked out a living as unskilled labourers at the Mikveh Israel agricultural school founded in 1870 by the Alliance Israélite Universelle in response to Zvi Hirsch Kalischer's promptings. Prodigal with high-flown schemes for organizing their model communities, but desperately short of farming knowledge or the money to buy basic equipment, the Biluim were saved from extinction by a grant from sympathizers in Minsk, which they used to purchase a tract of land south of Jaffa. On it they built Gedera, a solitary, forlorn testament to their socialist ideals, and a visible source of irritation to the Orthodox, who were scandalized at the impious and immodest behaviour of its few inhabitants.

Other settlements had been founded, but with no greater success. Petach Tikvah, Zichron Ya'akov, Rishon-le-Zion and Rosh Pinah are evocative place-names on early Zionism's roll of honour, but there was nothing glamorous about living there, or in Rehovot and Hadera, pioneered by a few dozen of the 20,000 Jews forcibly expelled from Moscow in 1891, when the tsar's residence was transferred from St Petersburg. Poverty and disease – especially malaria – were endemic. Friction simmered between 'veteran' settlers and newcomers, between the rabbis in Jerusalem and the secularists on the land. Relations with the parent Chibbat Zion organization were soured by mutual recriminations, impatience at lack of funding and the natural resentment of those in the front line at what they felt was patronizing advice from back home. Defeated by the conditions, debilitated by sickness, made abject by poverty, eroded by the defections of the faint-hearted back to Russia or to the lure of America, the settlers swallowed their pride and bowed to the inevitable. Cap in hand, they went to the rich Jewish philanthropists to bail them out. Baron Maurice de Hirsch made his support conditional on Russian Jewry raising 50,000 roubles towards the rescue scheme, and when that did not materialize he switched his interest to buying land in Argentina, to settle Jewish farmers.

Baron Edmund de Rothschild was more accommodating, but did not allow sympathy to affect his prudence or commercial judgement. He expected the settlements – 'my colonies' as he proprietorially called them – to be self-supporting, and put in agents to supervise them. Viniculture became their basic industry, as an extension of the baron's wine interests in France. Rothschild's brand of paternalistic capitalism was hardly to the liking of socialist Chovevei Zion idealists, but they had no choice; without his support their settlements would have gone bankrupt. During a twenty-year involvement with his colonies, Rothschild subsidized them to the tune of £1.5 million (in 1880s terms), whereas all the Chibbat Zion affiliates raised only 5 per cent of that amount. One ironic result of the baron's benevolence was that pioneers who had fled Russia partly to escape the taint of parasitism became, in the Holy Land, as much passive recipients of charity as were the devout poor in Jerusalem. Their initiative was sapped by knowing that in the last resort they could always rely on Rothschild for help: 'The baron will pay' became their wry catchphrase.

Pinsker died in 1891, ousted by internal wrangling from the presidency of an organization he had been dubious about leading in the first place. By now there were a score of colonies in Palestine, populated by perhaps 3–4000 settlers, but hardly the mass influx of five million souls Pinsker had envisaged. A young intellectual from Odessa, writing under the pen name of Achad Ha-Am (One of the People), had caught the mood of widespread complaint about settlement policy in the first of his critical essays from Palestine, entitled 'This is Not the Way'. In 1893, the Turkish government banned the immigration of Russian Jews into Palestine and any further purchase of land. But in any case America, not Palestine, was the preferred haven of the vast majority of migrating Jews. Although Chibbat Zion branches were in operation throughout Russia and Poland, and had finally been granted legal status in 1890, the favoured communities of western Europe remained stubbornly resistant to or oblivious of the colonizing efforts of their oppressed Russian brethren.

Man of few illusions that he was and schooled in disappointment, Pinsker would have conceded, as his life drew to its close, that the movement to resettle Jews in Palestine was dormant at best and, at worst, probably destined to peter out in recrimination and failure. The problem of Jewish homelessness was no nearer resolution. Yet within six years Zionist hopes, dreams, scant successes and abundant failures cohered in a serious political movement, due to the energies of its most remarkable and unlikely apostle.

4

Theodor Herzl – Founder of a Movement

In his delightful autobiography, *Memoirs of a Fortunate Jew*, Dan Vittorio Segre describes his arrival in Palestine before the Second World War as a refugee from Mussolini's Italy, and how the Jewish nurse at the reception centre '. . . almost choked when I, in turn, asked her who the bearded gentleman was looking at me with sad eyes from the wall. "Theodor Herzl," she growled, "the founder, the prophet of Zionism." '

Thus has been apotheosized the man who in 1894 had never heard of Pinsker and could not have named a single settlement in Palestine, was embarrassingly ignorant of Judaism and Jewish history, knew next to nothing about east European Jewry except to disdain it and, had the word been uttered in his presence, could not have said what 'Zionism' was. The term had been coined early in 1892, to describe the political process of establishing a Jewish state in Palestine, by Nathan Birnbaum, a prolific pamphleteer whose lurchings between socialism and nationalism, Hebrew and Yiddish, atheism and ultra-Orthodoxy made the career of Moses Hess appear staid. It was Herzl who through force of personality and compulsive energy transformed Zionism into a coherent national movement, who took under its umbrella all the disparate philanthropic, humanitarian, religious and political tendencies which had attempted to revive a Jewish homeland, who acted as the bridge-builder between western and eastern Jewry, who gave to the nascent Zionist organization its sense of purpose and to the watching world an impression of seriousness and credibility. The picture of Herzl, with his beard and sad eyes, adorns the walls of government offices, postage stamps and humble shops in the modern state of Israel, as if he were royalty. To his dazzled followers, it really did seem that a Jewish prince, some descendant of the House of David, had come among them.

Herzl was born in 1860, the same year as Anton Chekhov, and died in 1904, also the same year as the great Russian writer, and there is a certain similarity in their handsome, melancholy features. As a young man Chekhov walked past the Bolshoi Theatre in Moscow and vowed that his plays would be performed there. As a young man about Vienna, Herzl walked past the Hofburgtheater and made the same vow. It is not recorded that Chekhov ever expressed regret that he was not the founder of a state; it is on record that Herzl many times regretted not achieving major success in the theatre. His talents were essentially theatrical, the key to his impressive public image. Whether as dandy, aesthete, journalist or statesman-in-waiting, he adapted to his role convincingly and with the easy charm of a leading man. He was facilely gifted, excessively vain, overly sensitive, insecure. And he was sustained in times of crisis by the consoling knowledge that his father thought him wonderful and his mother utterly adored him. A Jewish prince indeed.

Herzl's family came from Budapest in the old Austro-Hungarian empire. His paternal grandfather had been a follower of Rabbi Judah Alkalai, so there was only a single generation between Theodor and the classic, observant Judaism of the east European ghettos, but that was the crucial emancipated generation. Jakob Herzl had left Semlin for Budapest, where he joined the Reform congregation, did well in the timber business, married, and gave his only son Theodor just enough Jewish education for him to undertake his *bar mitzvah* ceremony at the age of thirteen without shaming his pious grandfather. Theodor's mother Jeannette filled her son's imagination with dreams of greatness, as did other mid-nineteenth-century mothers. Perhaps these women were responding to the Promethean hero cult, popular in European literature and music of the time, and to their frustrations at being confined by society. *Madame Bovary* had been a *succès de scandale*, and Ibsen was soon to come.

Herzl grew up with a loyalty to the German language and culture and a fondness for chivalric heroism. He kept his diary meticulously from an early age. In it he noted that, given the choice, he would most like to have been a member of the old Prussian nobility. Chameleon fantasies were common among assimilated Jews who had been uprooted from their traditions and had still to find a place in their new environment. When Herzl's family moved to Vienna in 1878 after his only sister's death, he enrolled at the university to study law, and cultivated an elegant, dandified persona, consciously distancing himself from both the money-making Jewish stereotype and the east European refugees, who were flooding into Vienna to escape the 1881 pogroms.

For all its cosmopolitan pretensions as the empire's capital, Vienna was (as it still is) a conventional city. The bourgeoisie, Gentile and Jewish, were alarmed by the influx, and the working classes resented the competition or threat to their livelihoods. It was a fertile breeding ground for anti-Semitism, especially after the publication in 1881 of Eugene Düring's *The Jewish Question, as a Question of Race, Morals and Culture*, in which he asserted that the Jews, greedy, exploitative and bent on world domination, should be expelled from all governmental and educational posts and forbidden to intermarry, to avoid 'Judaization of the blood'.

Herzl's calculatedly serene response to the book was to endorse, with minor quibbles, its animadversions on Jewish character and morality and to condemn its thesis while praising its style '. . . so well-written, in such a deliciously pure and excellent German . . . '. He offered the counter-proposition that intermarriage was the best means of Jewish integration: 'Cross-breeding of the occidental races with the so-called oriental one on the basis of a common state religion, this is the great, desirable solution.' But in 1883, when his university duelling fraternity marked Wagner's death with a ceremony that had anti-Semitic undertones, Herzl felt compelled, as a point of honour, to resign.

The idea of voluntary conversion was one Herzl returned to ten years later in a draft plan about solving the Jewish Question, at least in Austria, once and for all. He – Herzl – would go to the pope and offer the free and honourable conversion of Jews to Christianity. It would take place on Sundays in St Stephen's Cathedral, with festive processions and the pealing of bells. The leaders of the Jewish community would escort their flock to the church threshold and symbolically hand them over, so that 'the whole performance was to be elevated by a touch of candour'. By now Herzl had a reputation as a deft essayist, so the scheme may have been intended as humorous fantasy, but the choice of the word 'performance' is revealing. For Herzl, life was one long bravura performance, to be played out with elegance and style. The only times his performance faltered in the years before his Zionist conversion were when he had to acknowledge that his young protégé Arthur Schnitzler was a more successful playwright, and that his arranged marriage was a miserable failure. But his literary gifts brought compensations. After he graduated in 1884, his proud parents rewarded him with a lengthy European tour, during which he wrote impressionist travel pieces for Vienna's leading newspaper, the *Neue Freie Presse*. He was invited to join the staff on his return, and built up his reputation as a gifted and able journalist.

In 1891 he was offered an enviable promotion, to become the newspaper's Paris correspondent, which also enabled him to disengage with propriety from his painful domestic situation. Henceforth, he and his wife Julie maintained the bare façade of marriage, with dire results for their three children, who were plagued for most of their lives by mental illness. Their eldest daughter, Pauline, committed suicide, as did their son on the twentieth anniversary of his father's death, having previously converted to Christianity. The youngest, Trude, died in a Nazi concentration camp. Herzl's diaries, so fulsome about his activities and impressions, are noticeably spare concerning his family.

Herzl took to Paris avidly: 'Paris conquered me and shook me through and through.' It was a breath of fresh air after staid Vienna, a city of stimulating variety, to which his press card gave him easy entrée. He matured, and imperceptibly became involved in a spiritual sea-change which he acknowledged he did not fully understand himself: a serious appraisal of anti-Semitism and his Jewish identity. Certainly, enough was going on to arouse his journalist's interest and latent Jewish anxieties. Anti-Semitism had surfaced in France after the humiliations of the Franco-Prussian war, to be manipulated by monarchists and clerics opposed to the Third Republic. Jews were prominently implicated in the Panama scandal, when the company formed to build the Canal was declared bankrupt after a decade of spectacular mismanagement and corruption. Edouard Drumont, author of the anti-Jewish polemic *La France Juive*, had founded a newspaper and was attracting a noisy following. In June 1892, a Jewish officer in the French army, Captain Mayer, was killed in a duel with a notorious anti-Semite, the Marquis de Morès. His funeral was a public event, at which the chief rabbi of Paris, Zadoc Kahn (later a cautious supporter of Herzl's), delivered an unctuous eulogy assuring France of the unswerving loyalty of her Jewish sons. Herzl reported the event for his newspaper.

Anti-Semitism was also on the rise elsewhere. Bismarck, the imperial chancellor, had given tacit support to anti-Semitic propaganda as he fought off liberal opposition. Agitators inveighed against Jewish 'control' of the press and the sinister conspiracy of Jewish 'international capitalism'. Anti-Semitic candidates captured sixteen seats in the Reichstag at the 1893 election. In Vienna, the democrat-turned-demagogue Karl Lueger was elected mayor on a crudely anti-Jewish platform. The Dreyfus Affair erupted shortly after Herzl had finished, in three weeks of frenzied creativity, what he considered his finest play, *The New Ghetto*. None of his theatre pieces has stood the test of time, and *The New Ghetto* is mawkishly sentimental where his other plays were brittle social comedies, done better by Schnitzler. But in it he at last deals seriously with Jewish characters, as if making recompense for the humour he had extracted at their expense. Before long, Herzl would use the epithet 'self-hating Jews' against those who resisted his Zionist schemes; until 1894, the barb could have been directed against him.

It would be the stuff of 1930s Hollywood 'biopics' (in which Paul Muni was invariably the star) to suggest that Herzl watched Dreyfus's public degradation on the parade ground of the École Militaire and rushed off instantly to begin feverish composition of his Zionist credo, *Der Judenstaat* (The Jewish State). Yet the suggestion has plausibility. It was a scene of enormous, poignant drama. Herzl would have watched with appalled fascination as the tiny officer was stripped of his epaulettes and drummed out of the gate in disgrace, while the crowd howled imprecations against the Jews. Dreyfus, whose family had moved from Alsace to Paris after the débâcle of 1870 to affirm their French loyalty, who had diligently made his way through the prejudiced ranks of the French army, stood there as the stripped, forlorn symbol of the Jew's perennial failure to gain acceptance no matter how far he bent to the mores of his host society. Which dramatist would not have been struck by the power of the scene!

It was now that Herzl divined his destiny: to be the saviour of his despised, rejected people. For those who doubt the suddenness of his metamorphosis, there are two clues in his writings. In a diary entry for June 1895, he notes that he has just learned about Shabbetai Tzevi, the seventeenth-century pseudo-messiah; his curiosity about Tzevi, and their similarities, stayed with him until the end of his life. A couple of weeks earlier, in another diary entry which he dated according to the Jewish calendar, contrary to all previous habit, Herzl confided that he was preoccupied with a project of great magnitude which saturated his being and would lead he knew not where. He must write it down. Perhaps it would become a memorial for mankind; if not, a major contribution to literature. Herzl concludes with one of those facile antitheses that were typical of his literary style, 'If the romance does not become a fact, at least the fact can become a romance. Title: The Promised Land!'

He did what everyone else with a scheme for Jewish salvation did; he importuned the money aristocracy. Baron Maurice de Hirsch heard him out with weary scepticism; Herzl, convinced of the rightness of his cause, became flustered and combative, alienating the grandee he had come to woo. His first effort at diplomacy ended in humiliating rejection. With the House of Rothschild he tried a different approach. In mid-June 1895 he prepared 'An Address to the Rothschilds', which summarized his views (in effect, a draft of *Der Judenstaat*), and wrote to Baron Albert, head of the Viennese branch of the family, grandly informing him that he would be in Vienna in July, when he wished to present his solution for the Jewish Question to the Rothschild 'family council', whose good offices he sought to gain an interview with the Kaiser. His presumption (well described by the Yiddish word *chutzpah*) was staggering, and can be explained only as the blithe insouciance of someone in the grip of an obsession. Which he was; he admitted in his diary that at times he thought he was going out of his mind.

When the baron ignored his letter, Herzl turned to lesser names for support. An early disciple was Max Nordau, a Hungarian Jew with something of a reputation as a journalist and social analyst — dismissed, accurately, by Chekhov in his short story *Ariadne* as 'a mediocre philosopher' — who shared Herzl's apocalyptic vision of rampant anti-Semitism. Moritz Güdemann, the chief rabbi of Vienna, was more guarded, given his delicate public position, but put Herzl in touch with Narcisse Leven of the Alliance Israélite Universelle, an important contact because through Leven he learned about Pinsker's pamphlet and the existence of the Chibbat Zion movement in eastern Europe. Leven also suggested that Rabbi Zadoc Kahn of Paris and Colonel Albert Goldsmid in England were influential sympathizers. But Herzl was impatient at his lack of concrete progress. He went to the two Jewish owners of the *Neue Freie Presse*, Moritz Benedikt and Eduard Bacher, to demand a regular column for discussion of the Jewish Question. His employers were appalled; such a request went against the grain of their carefully nurtured editorial credibility, but they gave him leave of absence to travel to Paris and London to study Zionism in depth.

At this point his father Jakob chipped in with sound advice. The Jewish magnates, he told his son, were unlikely to support any scheme for the mass exodus of Jews; their business philosophy was based upon integration. It was the little men, banding together like a mighty river, who would be attracted by the vision of building a Jewish homeland. To reach them would require a popular pamphlet whose arguments could be disseminated throughout the civilized world.

Herzl listened to his father. In February 1896, *Der Judenstaat* was published in Vienna, in an edition of 3000. It became as significant for Zionism as was *The Communist Manifesto* for socialism, but is, in truth, a disappointingly mundane document of some 30,000 words – the length of a typical novella. Herzl was trying too hard to establish his credentials as the sober, judicious Doctor of Law rather than the author of drawing-room comedies.

His tone is brisk, businesslike. He states his aim plainly in the opening sentence of the preface: it is to develop an old idea, that of restoring the Jewish state. He refutes at length the charge that such an idea is 'utopian', and makes a dig at another Austro-Hungarian writer, Theodor Hertzka (the similarity of name, and the possibility of its leading to mistaken identity, was irksome to Herzl), who in 1890 had published a popular utopian novel *Freiland*, about an ideal state established in equatorial Africa; such a scheme was fantasy, a 'joke', whereas Herzl is in grim earnest. His reality is the propelling force of the Jewish people and the fact that the 'world needs the Jewish state; therefore it will arise'. He then proceeds to analyse anti-Semitism, which he claims to understand. It is a confused, cursory analysis, predominantly economic and social, drawing upon his own and the western European experience as typical, castigating efforts to assimilate as 'not praiseworthy', even were host nations to allow the Jews to do so, because it is Jewish distinctiveness and cohesiveness that prompt anti-Semitism. The other factor – one which Herzl regularly returns to in his speeches and articles and which displays an unattractive intellectual arrogance – is the Jewish propensity for producing a stream of 'mediocre' intellectuals, which provokes jealousy and competition.

Where Pinsker was remorseless and unmitigatedly pessimistic in diagnosing anti-Semitism, Herzl wavers between the widespread belief of *fin-de-siècle* social critics in human progress hastened by the benefits of science ('To my mind, the electric light was certainly not invented so that the drawing rooms of a few snobs might be illuminated, but rather to enable us to solve some of the problems of humanity by its light'), and the contrary evidence of stubborn and deeply ingrained prejudice. As he remarks percipiently, 'folk wisdom and folklore both are anti-Semitic'. Because the Jewish question is not primarily social or religious but national, Herzl concludes that it should be regarded as an international political problem, to be solved in concert by the civilized nations of the world. It would be in everyone's best interests to find a solution. Those Jews, especially in France, who preferred assimilation to emigrating to the new Jewish state, would have satisfactorily proved their patriotism and be left in peace by the anti-Semites. Those dedicated Jews who emigrated would, on the other hand, free the proletariat in their host countries from the goad of Jewish competition.

Ideologically, *Der Judenstaat* is a conventional tract of its times, assuming underlying compatibility of national interests and social forces once dispassionate reason has shed its light on them. Not that Herzl was immune from mundane human foibles. He loftily dismisses previous efforts at Jewish colonization as well-meaning but picayune, diffident attempts at infiltration in contrast to his great scheme. 'A small enterprise may result in loss under the same conditions that would make a large one pay. A rivulet is not navigable even by boats; the river into which it flows carries stately iron vessels.' He cannot resist a side-swipe at Baron de Hirsch for having snubbed him: 'No human being is wealthy or powerful enough to transplant a people from one place of residence to another. Only an idea can achieve that.' Later, Herzl would be willing to consider the baron's colonies in Argentina as a possible locale for his new Jewish state.

Having made his case and outlined the problems in the preface and first chapter, Herzl reiterates them in the rest of the book. His restatement of the Jewish Question and recapitulation of anti-Semitism's causes add nothing new by way of analysis, and have only the occasional value of a writer's imaginative *aperçus*. He notes, for example, that the stock exchange may have replaced medieval money-lending but not the traditional hostility towards its Jewish exponents, and that in the class struggle Jews stand most vulnerably between the capitalist and socialist camps. He perceives that anti-Semitism is an outgrowth of Jewish emancipation, which it would be 'contrary to the spirit of our age' to rescind; but the new social mobility and economic fluidity of the Jews only deepens hatred of them. That in turn provokes an extreme reaction: 'When we sink, we become a revolutionary proletariat, the corporals of every revolutionary party; and when we rise, there rises also our terrifying financial power.' The result is inevitable: 'We are one people – our enemies have made us one whether we will it or not.'

And so to Herzl's grand design, which appealed to Jews and anti-Semites alike, and had the merit of brilliant simplicity to make it generally comprehensible. 'Let sovereignty be granted us over a portion of the globe adequate to meet our rightful national requirements; we will attend to the rest.' That involved setting up two agencies, the first a political body called the Society of Jews, to assume responsibility for Jewish national affairs, treat with governments and administer the newly acquired territory; the second a commercial enterprise, the Jewish Company, modelled after the great trading associations, to supervise the Jewish exodus and provide an industrial and commercial infrastructure for the influx of immigrants. It is to the scope and activities of this Jewish Company that Herzl devotes the longest chapter of *Der Judenstaat*, and in which he reveals his second-hand quality as a social theorist, the ideas worthily progressive, intellectually à la mode, and almost totally devoid of originality. The Jewish Company was to be a joint stock company established in London, with a capital of £50 million. It would liquidate the migrants' assets in their countries of domicile, and provide land, housing and employment in the new territory. A seven-hour working day (symbolized by the seven golden stars on a pure white backcloth of the new state's flag), enlightened concessions for women workers, a school system 'conducted on the most approved modern methods' and model workmen's dwellings, each with its little garden, designed by architects whose sensitivity to local landscape enabled them always to site their conurbations within visibility of a synagogue, 'for it is only our ancient faith that has kept us together' – all this would be implemented by the Jewish Company.

Immigration to this proto-Milton Keynes would be similarly controlled and effortless. The poorest would go first, to lay the foundations. Their efforts would stimulate trade, which in turn would create markets, thus attracting new entrepreneurial settlers to the frontier that had opened up; an evocation, whether conscious or not on Herzl's part, of the migration westwards that had attracted thousands of east European Jews to the United States since the pogroms of 1881. Next would come the middle classes, led by those 'intellectual mediocrities' who tried Herzl's patience so sorely but for whom he had now created a purpose.

Government would be by a limited monarchy or an aristocratic republic. Herzl did not trust the Jews, any more than other nations, with universal democracy. An orderly hierarchy would percolate from the upper strata, everyone knowing his place and not presuming beyond it, the priests remaining within their temples just as the army would remain within its barracks. As neutrality would be the political stance of the administration, the army was mainly for decorative purposes, as were the impressive robes of the clergy. Anxious to prevent the emergence of a professional civil service, Herzl airily proposed that the stipends for his neutered warriors and public officials should come from the dowries of 'our wealthy girls'. Freedom of faith, creed and nationality, and equality before the law would be the civic cornerstones of this transplanted Arcadia.

As to its location, Herzl leaves the options open, to be decided by the Society of Jews. On the one hand, the vast open spaces and temperate climate of Argentina were attractive, once the republic had been persuaded that large-scale Jewish immigration was in its interest. On the other hand, Palestine 'is our unforgettable historic homeland'. Its very name was a potent rallying cry. Furthermore, were the sultan to cede Palestine to the Jews, they could provide competent management of Turkey's finances as part of Europe's defensive wall in Asia, 'an outpost of civilization against barbarism'. A strongly tilted neutrality indeed, but inevitably so, since the European powers would have to guarantee the state's existence. In return, the Jews would internationalize the holy places of Christendom and mount a guard of honour over them, as symbolic recognition that the Jewish Question had been settled after eighteen centuries of affliction.

Finally, Herzl rehearses yet again the objections to his scheme and his refutations. To do so, he is forced to modify the premise of universal reason and enlightened self-interest leading nations to act together in peaceful concert, on which his argument has been based. It will be to the advantage of Jews and anti-Semites alike to set up a Jewish homeland, even though that will create one more barrier between peoples. But universal brotherhood is an impracticable dream: 'Conflict is essential to man's highest efforts.' Nietzsche and Wagner (Herzl's only recreation while writing his pamphlet was listening to *Tannhäuser*), not the apostles of secular liberalism, have become his mentors. Jewish need demanded a state; aided by the benefits of technological progress, doughty Jewish fighters would eventually establish one. 'And what glory awaits the selfless fighters for the cause! Therefore I believe that a wondrous breed of Jews will spring up from the earth. The Maccabees will rise again. Let me repeat once more my opening words: The Jews who will it shall achieve their State.' In this peroration, and there alone, Herzl signals a radical departure from all previously expressed yearnings – religious, nationalist or utopian – for a return to Zion. The Jew would enter the arena of politics to fight for his cause. He would become master of his destiny, like a Nietzschean superman. The will-to-power would inspire him, where previously there had been only the negative urge to survive.

Such a drastic inversion of the Jewish stereotype, as potentially shocking to a whole range of Jewish sensibilities as it would be alarming to those inimical to Jewish aspirations, caused Herzl to have second thoughts. He did not want to scare off Jews and Gentiles alike, so he concludes *Der Judenstaat* with the somewhat lame assurance of a pious universalism: 'And whatever we attempt there for our own benefit will redound mightily and beneficially to the good of all mankind.'

There is medical evidence to confirm that Herzl was going through a psychosomatic crisis at this time. In March 1896 his family doctor examined him and diagnosed 'a heart ailment caused by excitement'. The excitement was in his mind, rather than as a result of *Der Judenstaat*'s reception, which had been lukewarm. He had offered himself, by implication, as the commander of a Jewish army, but there were not enough troops to form a battalion. 'Here in Vienna,' he wrote to his English supporter Colonel Albert Goldsmid, 'the essay I have published has gained me the greatest of hatreds and the warmest of friendships. The Zionists of Vienna and Berlin have proclaimed their enthusiasm for my plan. The money-men praise and denounce me in the sharpest possible way. The anti-Semites treat me fairly. At all events, the discussion is now open and, it seems, will soon reach the parliaments.' The hyperbole of vague generalization became Herzl's trademark for the rest of his brief career.

In reality, the Zionist circles in Vienna, Berlin and Cologne had welcomed the addition to their ranks of a modestly celebrated *littérateur*, but were suspicious of his sudden conversion and irritated by his dismissal of existing efforts at colonization in Palestine. Diverse individuals, including Colonel Goldsmid, responded warmly to the pamphlet, but Jews in positions of public visibility were studiedly non-committal, or hostile. 'I have read your *Judenstaat* with lively interest,' wrote the chief rabbi of Paris. 'You have posed a question of the highest importance . . . The future will show whether it is practical.' The chief rabbi of Vienna, Moritz Güdemann, who had provided Herzl with a list of contacts, changed tack sharply. He denounced the mirage of Jewish nationalism; belief in the One God was the unifying factor for Jews, and Zionism was incompatible with Judaism's teachings.

It was in eastern Europe that Herzl's publication had the sharpest impact. He was still ignorant of the reservoir of manpower, talent, organization and experience that existed in Russian Jewry, but was a quick learner and soon realized that troops were more likely to come from the ranks of east European Jewry than from the acculturated 'upper Jews' (as he liked to call them) of western countries. His belated discovery of the poor Jewish masses, and their faith in him, was a profound personal experience. But in the spring of 1896 his knowledge of the Chibbat Zion network in Russia and neighbouring states was sketchy, and filtered through the perceptions of individual Zionists like Menachem Ussishkin, or Professor Tzevi Belkovsky of Odessa, who had troubled to respond to *Der Judenstaat*. Herzl did not know that the leading Russian Jewish newspapers had all commented adversely on his scheme, none more so than the Russian-language *Voskhod*, whose reviewer had dismissed his 'utterly naive' programme and inquired sarcastically whether it was the author's intention to become the 'Jewish envoy to the royal court in Vienna'. Nahum Sokolow, a prominent Zionist and literary figure in Warsaw, opposed a Yiddish edition of the pamphlet, on the ground that its half-baked ideas would mislead credulous people. The *Neue Freie Presse* maintained a Trappist silence. The *Jewish Chronicle* of London judged that the scheme's lack of a religious perspective rendered it 'cold and comparatively uninviting'. Aristocrats like the Rothschilds and Baron de Hirsch may have had private feelings about the presumptuous essayist, but did not comment publicly. The fair treatment from anti-Semites that pleased Herzl seems to have been a solitary reference to Ivan von Simonyi, a Hungarian editor, who had reacted positively to the notion of large-scale Jewish emigration. But the general public, and their representatives in the parliaments, showed conspicuous lack of interest in the author's hoped-for debate.

One unabashed enthusiast was Max Nordau, who became the

Engels to Herzl's Marx. He wrote glowingly that 'this single pamphlet would assure you of a permanent place among the heroes of all times'. And he noted, as one fecund word-painter to another, what a heroic act it had been for 'an artist in love with style to have dispensed with all verbal glitter' in favour of concision. Warming to his theme, Nordau compared Herzl's boldness in honesty with that of Luther at Worms – not, perhaps, the most felicitous of comparisons to make.

The papal nuncio in Vienna, Mgr Agliadi, dutifully keeping abreast of political or religious stirrings to report to the Vatican, agreed to meet Herzl, who noted in his diary that he entered the nuncio's residence as furtively as a man visiting a house of ill repute. He inferred from their brief discussion that 'Rome will be against us'. A more bizarre Christian interlocutor was William Hechler, chaplain to the British embassy in Vienna. He was one of those cranks who predicted, on the basis of 'proofs' drawn from biblical texts, the restoration of the Jewish homeland, and had set 1897 as the date for the great event. Herzl's pamphlet was timely confirmation of his prophecy, and Hechler made haste to contact its writer. The amiably eccentric cleric had formerly tutored the son of the grand duke of Baden and, although suspicious of his motives ('an impecunious clergyman with a taste for travel'), Herzl was quick to recognize Hechler's potential for useful introductions.

He then found a second dubious sympathizer to steer him through the *demi-monde* of diplomatic contacts. Philipp de Nevlinski was a similar type to the notorious Major Esterhazy, who was playing out his shady role in the unfolding Dreyfus Affair. A minor Polish nobleman whose estates had been confiscated by the Russians after the 1863 rebellion, congenitally extravagant and perennially in debt, Nevlinski sold his services to the highest bidder, at various times the Austrians, the Russians, the Turks, the Serbians, the Bulgarians and the Romanians. When Herzl met him, he was running a small news agency specializing in Near Eastern affairs, as cover for spying activities on behalf of whoever would pay him. Most did, except the British, who rightly suspected him of being a Turkish agent.

Herzl was entranced by him: the most interesting figure he had met since taking up the Jewish cause, he wrote in June 1896. Here was the man to open the door to the sultan himself. For his part, Nevlinski milked the aspiring Jewish statesman with practised ease, taking regular subventions in return for unfulfilled promises, tantalizing his dazzled paymaster with glimpses of what might be achieved in Constantinople. Even after Nevlinski's death in April 1899, when some of his duplicity came to light (including the fact that he had never transmitted Herzl's messages to the elusive sultan, but had, on the contrary, offered to spy on him), Herzl was surprisingly generous in his diary assessment of a sleazy adviser. He blamed Nevlinski's faults on the company he kept; to judge more severely would have been to admit his own gullible vanity, and Herzl was already furbishing his reputation for posterity. Had he known more of Jewish history, he might have reflected that his relationship with Nevlinski bore curious affinities to that between David Reubeni and Solomon Molcho, two pseudo-messiahs of the early sixteenth century, whose dangerous habit of encouraging each other's fantasies led to an audience with the Holy Roman Emperor, Charles V, and prompt imprisonment.

Herzl was more concerned with making history than reading it. For a brief time, he and Sigmund Freud, unknown to each other, lived on the same street in Vienna. One wonders what the father of psychoanalysis would have made of Herzl, in the grip of his obsessive vision. His nervous energy, for one of a basically lackadaisical disposition, was astonishing, as he went about his self-appointed mission as saviour of the Jewish people. The strong streak of narcissism in Herzl's personality was given full rein while he set up appointments, wooed supporters, addressed Jewish audiences and sought introductions to the wealthy and influential. He savoured the role of messiah–king, conscious that his impressive beard and melancholy eyes contributed to the effect. Appearance was as important to him as to any matinée idol, a careful blend, as one swooning acolyte described it, of 'spirit and courage and kindness, strictness, softness and humility . . .' The Anglo-Jewish writer Israel Zangwill also fell under his spell: 'A majestic oriental figure . . . stands dominating the assembly with eyes that brood and glow – you would say one of the Assyrian kings whose sculptured heads adorn our museums.'

Through Hechler, Herzl met the grand duke of Baden in April 1896 at Karlsruhe. The nobleman listened to Herzl with ducal affability, but was noncommittal about furthering his scheme with the Kaiser. Nevertheless, Herzl judged that his first foray in external diplomacy had been a success, certainly more so than his efforts the year before with Jewish notables. It was the parvenu's revenge, to be taken seriously by the

Gentiles where his own people had been dismissive. Herzl was thrilled at becoming a player in the game, which was more exciting than the result, especially since his objectives were so vague and varied according to whom he was talking at the time. To Germans, he implied that the proposed Jewish territory would become an outpost of Berlin; to the British, that it would seek colonial status; to the Turks, that Jewish capital would alleviate their chronic economic situation; to the Jewish bankers, that it only required their loans for everything to fall into place. There was no consistent strategy; simply the lurchings of his febrile imagination. But then, no one knew better than Herzl that his grand design was a confidence trickster's sleight – dependent upon a hint here, a word there, the dropping of famous names and the confidential intimation of secret assurances from the powerful.

Constantinople was the *fons et origo* of Herzl's dreams. He travelled there in June, having first sent Nordau to intercede with Edmund de Rothschild in Paris. The baron was immovable. He considered Herzl's initiative foolhardy, especially when the Dreyfus case was fomenting anti-Semitism in France, saw no point in investing money in the sultan's worthless promises or alarming him with the threat of increased Jewish immigration, and resented competition to his own philanthropic settlements in Palestine. Herzl was unperturbed. 'We shall pass over him,' he noted grandly in his diary, and made arrangements for his journey, advised by the assiduous Nevlinski. The Orient Express stopped in Sofia, where a crowd of Chovevei Zion greeted him with flowers, speeches and cries of 'Next year in Jerusalem'. He arrived in Constantinople on 17 June, and stayed for twelve days. Two hundred and thirty years earlier, Shabbetai Tzevi, who had arrived in the Turkish capital in his guise as the messiah to confront the sultan, had his ears boxed, and was clapped in gaol. Treatment of unwelcome visitors had improved; Herzl was given an elaborately polite run-around instead.

He was hopelessly at loss in the labyrinth of Turkish politics. The ramshackle Ottoman empire functioned through intrigue, venality, subtle nuances of authority delicately entwined to enmesh and exasperate the most experienced foreign diplomat and an all-pervading inertia. Presiding with melancholy fatalism over the languishing vestiges of former glory was Sultan 'Abd al-Hamid, who had acquired in a twenty-year reign survival instincts to match his innate shrewdness and tenacity. The sultan had no intention, as successor to the Prophet, of relinquishing voluntarily Muslim control over any part of Palestine. He kept his own counsel, playing off his advisers and the great powers against each other. That Herzl came bearing no gifts of substance, and represented no one but himself, was quickly recognized. The bad news was conveyed with uncharacteristic alacrity at the end of his first day in Constantinople: no audience with the sultan, absolutely no negoti-ations about Jewish immigration to Palestine. Nevertheless, he was passed from one official to another, even reaching the grand vizier, but only on the strength of his credentials with the *Neue Freie Presse*. Turkey's harsh treatment of the Armenians was being unfavourably reported in European newspapers, and more balanced coverage would not come amiss; also, perhaps Dr Herzl could arrange a £2 million loan with the English banker and MP Sir Samuel Montagu, whose name he had recklessly put forward (on the basis of a brief meet-ing in London) as guarantor of recompense for ceding part of Palestine for Jewish settlement.

It eventually dawned on Herzl, despite Nevlinski's assurances of progress and his euphoria at treading the shabby corridors of Ottoman power, that he was being baited as a possible lead to Jewish money, with little chance of serious concessions in return. This stung his vanity. A token was needed to enhance his credibility with those monied Jews on whose behalf he claimed to act. Through Nevlinski he asked, 'with reluctance and secret shame', for a decoration. It arrived on his final day in Constantinople: the Cross of the Order of the Medjidje, Second Class, a bauble handed out as freely as Turkish delight.

Herzl's Constantinople adventure was emblematic of his career as a diplomat. 'The earth floats in mid-air. Similarly, I may be able to found and stabilize the Jewish State without any firm support. The secret lies in motion,' he had written in his diary for 7 May. He was in perpetual motion for the rest of his life, his list of appointments a social climber's dream as he floated from one important contact to the next, usually making a favourable impression with his charm, dignity and fervour, but emerging with nothing more significant than expressions of polite interest or, at best, a minor decoration. He sustained himself on hope, the applause of the downtrodden and the conviction of his manifest destiny.

And so to London, rejecting the opportunity of a second audience with the grand duke of Baden on the way – 'I don't need [him] at the moment'. In London he was treated to an Anglo-Jewish variant of the Turkish wild-goose chase. The important people were unavailable or unconvinced. Colonel Goldsmid, a baptized Jew who had introduced himself to Herzl on his previous visit with the sibylline utterance 'I am Daniel Deronda',[1] was away in Wales, inspecting his regiment. Simeon Singer, a fashionable rabbi, and Israel Zangwill were discouragingly evasive. Two distinguished representatives of the Anglo-Jewish Association, Claude Montefiore and Frederick Mocatta, listened to Herzl's plan for the Society of Jews, and poured cold water over it. Most frustrating of all, Herzl discovered that the seriously rich feel safe only in the company of those equally endowed. Sir Samuel Montagu received him in the imposing splendour of the House of Commons, where he made clear that any financial support would be dependent upon great power agreement to Jewish immigration to Palestine under Turkish sovereignty, the £10 million legacy of Baron de Hirsch (who had died in April) being available for the project, and Baron Edmund de Rothschild joining the executive committee of the proposed Society of Jews. Given the improbability of the first two conditions being met, the third was a calculated put-down. More fundamentally at issue than a debate about the wisdom or otherwise of large-scale Jewish colonization was a power and class confrontation; the monied aristocracy was not about to cede authority over European Jewry to a suspect publicist who evoked recollections of Shabbetai Tzevi.

Herzl's one palpable triumph in London confirmed the mutual antagonism. On the evening of 12 July, he addressed a huge gathering in a workingmen's club in Whitechapel with hundreds on the street outside. Using German rather than stilted English for his predominantly east European and Yiddish-speaking audience, Herzl was touched with inspiration. Here was his natural constituency, and he preached his vision of a Jewish renaissance with a simplicity, force and sincerity that was irresistible. It was one of those epiphanies occasionally experienced by a great artist, sportsman, or actor, and drew comparisons with Moses and Columbus from his enraptured listeners, who cheered him to the echo. Herzl pondered on his transformation: 'As I sat on the platform of the workingmen's stage on Sunday I experienced strange sensations. I saw and heard my legend being born. The people are sentimental, the

1. Protagonist of George Eliot's last novel, published in 1876. See p. 10.

masses do not see clearly. I believe that even now they no longer have a clear image of me. A light fog is beginning to rise around me, and it may perhaps become the cloud on which I shall walk.' But since he wrote his diary with one eye on publication, he prudently dispensed with further reveries on self-deification and reverted to the solemn thoughts appropriate in a leader. He was 'the man of the little people', not some 'clever deceiver or impostor', and would strive 'to become ever worthier of their trust and affection'. He had found among the masses the nucleus of his army, and 'the lukewarm and hesitant rich', as he described them, were alarmed. Colonel Goldsmid, so enthusiastic the year before, wrote to warn Baron de Rothschild that a dangerous visitor was on his way to Paris.

The confrontation with Edmund de Rothschild finally took place at the baron's office in rue Lafitte on 18 July. It was a frosty encounter. Herzl was touchy and aggressive, the baron aloof. He dismissed Herzl's offer of the leadership of the embryonic Zionist movement – an offer that had been painful to make – and reiterated his concerns about upsetting Turkey, or giving ammunition to anti-Semites by hoisting the flag over a building for which the land had yet to be provided. And who, himself apart, would succour the 150,000 Jewish *schnorrers* (beggars) emigrating to the new territory?

Herzl had been rebuffed but was not displeased. If the family name synonymous with every major Jewish enterprise of the last hundred years had disdained involvement, there was now no one to challenge his leadership. The old order would be changed. 'I consider the house of Rothschild a national misfortune for the Jews,' he wrote to the French chief rabbi. The idea of Herzl versus the Rothschilds spurred him on; his answer would be to convene a general assembly of Zionists. 'There is only one reply to this situation,' he wrote on 21 July to Jacob de Haas, a young London supporter, 'let us organize our masses immediately.' Correspondents in Vienna, Paris and Sofia received similar instructions. A year later, the first Zionist Congress met in Basel.

Although Herzl would enjoy subsequent propaganda coups, such as being received by the Kaiser and, eventually, the sultan himself, his feat in masterminding the first Zionist Congress for more reporters and spectators than attending delegates was his most spectacular piece of public relations theatre. It was the production of a man possessed, working himself beyond exhaustion. The tiny Zionist coterie in Vienna dutifully submitted to his leadership, and letters of encouragement arrived from as far apart as Jerusalem, Galicia and Johannesburg. But in eastern Europe, the intellectual élite remained hostile, motivated in part by resentment at the condescending assumption of an assimilated western Jew and, more importantly, by the ideological divide which had opened between Chibbat Zion supporters and Marxist-inspired socialists, who condemned Zionism as dangerous romantic bourgeois nationalism diverting the Jewish masses from their role in the proletarian struggle. At the same time that Herzl was trying to get his Zionist assembly off the ground, the General Union of Jewish Workers in Lithuania, Poland and Russia (the 'Bund') was being formed to raise the level of Jewish political consciousness and allying with the Russian labour movement. Herzl's pilgrimage around the capitals of Europe was sedulously reported in the Russian–Jewish press, but under the quotidian threat of censorship opinion formers were careful not to offer favourable comment.

The frustration of no tangible progress plunged Herzl into frequent bouts of gloom, and he suffered the common reaction of self-appointed national guardians: the people were not worthy of him. 'The Jews do not deserve that I should go to pieces trying to help them.' Even those who did his bidding were only out to promote their own careers. At his bleakest he composed, as befitted a romantic hero, his own epitaph. 'My name will grow after my death . . . I am conscious today, as I have always been, that I have used my pen like a man of honour. I have never sold my pen, never used it to mean ends, never made it an instrument for the promotion of friendships. This last testament may be published.' There was not even the frisson of meeting celebrities. Through Nevlinski he had obtained an audience with the recently elected and tenuously enthroned Prince Ferdinand of Bulgaria, and had kept in desultory contact with the Turkish ambassador to Vienna, but that was scant consolation for failure to reach either the Kaiser or the British prime minister, Lord Salisbury. At his nadir, Herzl even clutched at the straw that Sir Samuel Montagu and Edmund de Rothschild might temper their opposition. 'I am no raging agitator,' he hastened to assure Zadoc Kahn, when the French chief rabbi mooted the possibility of a confidential meeting of Jewish representatives to consider Herzl's scheme. As the year drew to its close, Herzl's mood was of lassitude and despair. 'It is a vicious circle,' he wrote to de Haas in London, 'no funds no propaganda, no propaganda no funds.' And in his diary, 'the general torpor of the movement is gradually getting into my bones'.

But sudden fluctuations of humour are the mark of many mystics and visionaries. On 3 January 1897, Herzl matter-of-factly informed de Haas, 'I intend to call a general assembly of Zionists in Switzerland this summer,' and asked him to prepare advance publicity. By February he had decided on the venue (Zurich) and a probable date in late August; he became absorbed in the technicalities of the spectacle, and what role the Russian Jews would play in it. The nucleus of a production team fortuitously came forward in early March when a delegation of Berlin Zionists met with Herzl in Vienna. The Berliners were experienced philanthropists, in regular touch with existing settlements in Palestine and chary of grandiose manifestos rather than practical projects. Their number included Nathan Birnbaum, who resented Herzl's cavalier appropriation of his neologism 'Zionism', Willy Bambus and Hirsch Hildesheimer, two long-standing Chibbat Zion members, and Moritz Moses, who had attended the Kattowitz conference of 1884. They were vastly more knowledgeable about Zionist affairs than Herzl, but he smoothly won them over in two days of friendly talks. The Berliners went home reassured about the flamboyant Dr Herzl's conference plan, rescheduled for Munich, and he was elated at having at last found serious allies.

'If you will it, it is no dream' was the motto that Herzl would give to his utopian novel *Altneuland* (Old-New Land), published in 1902. He willed the first Zionist Congress, and it came into being. By stating often enough that it would take place, he turned a possibility into controversial reality. After years of journalism, he knew how to 'plant' a story and watch it take a life of its own. Within days of the March meeting, the *Jewish Chronicle* had received a preliminary agenda, and invitations had been despatched to the notables of western Jewry, complete with a personal letter from Herzl, registration details, and a summary of aims — 'a glorious demonstration to the world of what Zionism is and of what it wants' was his description to a London sympathizer, Herbert Bentwich.

The response was predictably negative from Sir Samuel Montagu (who was opposed to the Jews acting 'internationally on political matters') and Zadoc Kahn (who assured Herzl of his close interest, but begged him to appreciate that, as state officials, the position of French rabbis was 'extremely difficult'). Edmund de Rothschild was given no chance to decline; Herzl had no intention of inviting him. More demoralizing was the reluctance to commit themselves of those who could be considered allies. Colonel Goldsmid and the British Zionists, wary of hostile public reaction, would have nothing to do with the Congress. Bambus and Hildesheimer, alarmed by the adverse publicity Herzl was generating, and annoyed that their preference for an assembly meeting in closed session had been discarded for Herzl's choice of a public rally, disassociated themselves. The executive of the Association of German Rabbis, representing the Jewish communities of Berlin, Frankfurt, Breslau, Halberstadt and Munich, denounced the 'efforts of the so-called Zionists to create a Jewish National State in Palestine' as contrary to the 'prophetic message of Judaism and the duty of every Jew to belong without reservation to the fatherland in which he lives. Religion and love of the fatherland, no less than our regard for the welfare of Judaism, lay upon us the duty to repudiate the aims of Zionism and to ignore the call to the Congress.' Herzl's reply to the 'Protest Rabbis', as he sarcastically dubbed them, contained some of his ripest invective. He mocked their patriotic but shaky command of the German language in *Die Welt*, a Zionist weekly which he had launched with his own and parental funding. The first issue appeared on 4 June 1897, printed on provocative yellow paper – the colour of the medieval badge of shame, which would transmute into a badge of honour.

The tiff with the 'Protest Rabbis' is an apt illustration of Herzl's genius for building bricks without straw. They had fallen into his trap by responding seriously to the phantasm of a Jewish state, thereby giving credence to a rumour. His passionate excoriation of their timidity fuelled public interest and was printed in a newspaper which claimed to speak for the Jewish people on the march, yet which, despite a large-scale promotion campaign, had fewer than fifty initial subscribers.

Munich had been chosen for the Congress on the assumption that its kosher restaurants would cater for observant east European delegates, whereas the Russian government would look askance at a venue like Zurich, haven of anarchists and revolutionaries. But since the Munich community had vociferously declined the honour, bland Basel became second choice. Giving orders to a small band of loyalists – his entourage in Vienna, a handful of students in Berlin and Paris, faithful de Haas in

London, Max Bodenheimer and David Wolffsohn of the Chibbat Zion group in Cologne — Herzl girded himself for a final mighty effort to bring the Congress to realization.

He was now blessed with the luck that Napoleon looked for in his generals: the Russian Zionists, after agonized equivocation, decided to attend. Herzl had made the psychological breakthrough from unsuccessful suitor of western Jewry to champion of the eastern masses. At least, as the dubious Menachem Ussishkin wrote to congenitally sceptical Achad Ha-Am, Herzl and his friends 'have hopes, but they have a programme too, while we have hopes, but do not know what to do'.

Only belatedly had Herzl recognized the need to woo the mass constituency on whose behalf he, and western Jews generally, expressed so much patronizing concern. Flitting between the European capitals, he was as irritatingly elusive to Russian Jews, restricted for permission to travel, as the millionaire grandees had been to him. A further complication was that ideology had polarized around conflicting views of the *nature* of the Zionist mission. The more distant people are from realizing their political goals, the more vehemently they argue about theory, and the Russian Chibbat Zion societies had splintered into nuanced, competing tendencies, passionately advocating different versions of the Zionist millennium.

Mercifully unaware of such hair-splitting, Herzl contacted Russian Zionists across the ideological spectrum, his only concern that they should advance the cause of his Congress. He invited the leading religious Zionist, Rabbi Shmuel Mohilever of Bialystok, in a specially composed letter in Hebrew, urging his attendance and that of other sages 'who know the spirit of our people and our Holy Law' and whose advice would be invaluable in Basel. That secured the acceptance of the Orthodox Mizrachi movement. Next, he sent an unctuous invitation to Moses Lilienblum, and dangled the carrot of becoming a correspondent for *Die Welt*. Menachem Ussishkin was approached, as was Sokolow in Warsaw, on the principle that it was wiser to flatter their vanity than risk their journalistic ire. The tactic did not work with Achad Ha-Am, who responded with tight-lipped pedantry, veiled criticisms and the assurance that he was *not* offended at having been invited *after* Mr Lilienblum. Herzl and Achad Ha-Am were instinctively antagonistic in outlook, style, temperament and vocation. It flustered Herzl that Achad Ha-Am was impervious to charm or flattery, and it riled Achad Ha-Am, the dry schoolmaster, that his rival moved through life with such easy grace.

Herzl clinched Russian representation at his Congress – vital to its credibility – with a bold personal initiative. He despatched Yehoshua Buchmil, a Russian student of agriculture at Montpellier University, on a support-raising mission to Russia. Buchmil visited Zionist groups in Odessa, Kiev, Bialystok, Kishinev and two dozen other towns and cities, while another adherent, Moritz Schnirer, undertook a similar journey to north Russia and Lithuania. Young, outspoken, impatient with the timidity of their elders, Herzl's ambassadors compelled their audiences to face the issue of whether or not to attend the Congress, which they insisted was the most important decision to confront Russian Jewry since the 1881 pogroms. The tactic worked, but it was a close-run thing. Not until the end of July did a group of influential Chibbat Zion personalities, meeting in Carlsbad, give their blessing to Russian participation, subject to three provisos: that the debates in Basel should not offend Rothschild susceptibilities; that the Turks should not be alarmed; and that the tsarist government should not be the butt of criticism.

A jubilant Herzl gave the necessary assurances. Nevertheless, the Russians were uneasy, sensing that their programme of modest settlement in the Holy Land was about to be usurped. As S. P. Rabbinowitz, one of the organizers of the 1884 Kattowitz conference, said in a circular letter to Chibbat Zion societies, 'It would have been a great deal more convenient if the Congress had never been convened at all, but now that it has . . . we must make every effort to sweeten the pill . . . to prevent any harm being done to the *Yishuv* [the existing settlement in Palestine] as it presently stands, and to our future activities.' Achad Ha-Am gloomily relished playing the spectre at the feast. 'Perhaps, after all, I too shall be there. It is possible that I shall be of some small use, for it is painful to see everything put into the hands of young people whose enthusiasm is greater than their understanding.'

A month later, on Sunday morning, 29 August 1897, the first Zionist Congress opened in the concert hall of the Basel casino. Herzl had travelled to Switzerland in advance to stage-manage all the arrangements: a bureau was staffed by secretaries who spoke the necessary languages, including Yiddish; the agenda had been printed, and delegates received a badge of accreditation depicting a Lion of Judah encircled by the

Star of David, with the inscription THE ESTABLISHMENT OF A JEWISH STATE IS THE ONLY POSSIBLE SOLUTION TO THE JEWISH QUESTION. The press had been alerted, and a special edition of *Die Welt* printed. Herzl called on the president of the Canton of Basel, and persuaded him to attend one of the conference sessions. On sabbath morning, 28 August, Herzl made a rare visit to the local synagogue, and laboriously recited the Hebrew benediction he had memorized parrot fashion, in anticipation of being called for the reading of the Law.

Like all theatre people, he suffered first-night nerves; he also recognized the fragility of his production. On his way to Basel he had confided in his diary, 'The fact is – which I conceal from everyone – that I have only an army of *schnorrers*. I am in command only of youths, beggars and sensation mongers.' The fear of failure enervated him. He had fashioned a Congress for the Jews, and now it was up to them: 'As for myself, there are times when I have had more than my fill of the whole thing.'

In the event, his Congress was a triumph once last-minute details – such as insisting that delegates attend the opening session in formal white tie and tails – had been ironed out. Some 250 delegates from twenty-four localities, outnumbered by press reporters, spectators and specially invited guests, stood while Dr Karpel Lippe, a Chibbat Zion veteran from Romania, recited the opening benediction. Not even Lippe's propensity for platitudinous loquacity could mar the occasion. When, finally, he came to the purpose of his address and proposed a message of gratitude and devotion to the sultan, Herzl took his place on the podium.

How magnificently he looked the part! One excitable delegate from Odessa was swept off his feet. 'Before us rose a marvellous and exalted figure, kingly in bearing and stature, with deep eyes in which could be read quiet majesty and unuttered sorrow. It is no longer the elegant Dr Herzl of Vienna; it is a royal scion of the House of David, risen from the dead, clothed in legend and fantasy and beauty.' Euphoria swept the hall. The delegates clapped, cheered and waved their handkerchiefs for fully fifteen minutes. Zionism was crowning its undisputed leader, a king who, four years previously, had barely heard of the movement he now commanded. Herzl deliberately played down the sweet moment, 'so as to keep the business from the outset from turning into a cheap performance,' as he noted in his diary.

When quiet was restored, he delivered his speech, which was, inevitably, an anti-climax: an elegant résumé of the arguments he had been rehearsing for two years, designed for internal reassurance and external effect. He defined the task of the Congress in a ringing but vague generality, 'We are here to lay the foundation stone of the house which is to shelter the Jewish nation.' He paid court to Jewish tradition by declaring that 'Zionism is the return of the Jews to Judaism even before their return to the Jewish land'. The next step was to harness and organize this great popular movement, bringing its aspirations into the public arena of international discussion. Not for Zionism the covert and conspiratorial methods of socialism; its open and declared aim was the revival of Jewish national consciousness. Herzl explicitly rejected the Chibbat Zion philosophy. Commendable though previous efforts at colonization had been, they could go no further, because they lacked legal recognition. Only a negotiated agreement with the powers concerned could advance the task: 'The basis can only be that of recognized right, and not of sufferance. We have had our fill of experience with toleration and the protected Jew.' He reminded his audience of the watching world. Their deliberations were pregnant with destiny and the greatness of a cause more urgent than the whims and ambitions of the assembled individuals. The eyes of hundreds of thousands of Jews were fixed on them in hope and expectation. 'Today we meet on the soil of this friendly nation. Where shall we be a year from now?'

It was a measured, statesmanlike performance, but the next speaker, Max Nordau, stole the show. He spoke extemporaneously on 'The General Picture of the Condition of Jewry at the Close of the Nineteenth Century' and rose to the theme with a powerfully flamboyant oration, contrasting the daily, grinding, physical poverty of the eastern masses with the moral impoverishment of their western brethren, who had cut adrift from their roots in forlorn pursuit of emancipation's rewards. The result was insecurity, suspicion, neurosis; the western Jew had become 'an inner cripple'. Thus spoke the worldly *littérateur* who had changed his name from Südfeld. It was a magnificent speech. Men in the audience cried unashamedly. Herzl clasped his friend's hand and told him he had made the Congress. The first day had exceeded his most optimistic expectations.

Herzl started the second day by announcing that telegrams, petitions and letters of support were arriving from all over the world; but the high drama of the opening could not be sustained as the delegates settled down to discuss practicalities and endured a succession of reports on the situation in Palestine and on the revival of Hebrew, and the reading of a lengthy message from Rabbi Mohilever of Bialystok. Procedural niceties took an inordinate time, as fussy speakers claimed their moment in the spotlight. Constitutional proposals were picked over with Talmudic precision before it was agreed that the Congress should be the supreme organ of the movement, the right to vote in its elections acquired by payment of a small annual fee, the 'shekel'. But Herzl, who had been elected president of the Congress as an act of homage, did not have things all his own way; the demography of the delegates ensured that. Taken together, they were an assembly of the articulate middle classes, in business, the professions, industry and higher education. Liberal men of letters rubbed shoulders with a disproportionate number of rabbis, due to Herzl's touching belief that rabbis held the key to the hearts of the people. More than half the delegates came from Russia or eastern Europe, and shared loyalty to Chibbat Zion's gradualist philosophy of settlement in the Holy Land. Meeting Herzl in the flesh for the first time, they were sceptical about his aims while recognizing his gifts.

The tension in debate was between the tried, piecemeal method of colonization favoured by Chibbat Zion and its wealthy underwriters and Herzl's brash new vision of political action. Three lengthy, excitable and acrimonious sessions were required before an acceptable statement of the Zionist programme was achieved. Herzl, as chairman, negotiated a skilful course between the impatient radicalism of those like Nordau and Leo Motzkin, and the ingrained caution of old school representatives on the steering committee, to arrive at a formula which the Congress accepted with acclamation.

The crucial preamble stated: 'Zionism aims at the creation of a home for the Jewish people in Palestine to be secured by public law.' It went on:

To that end, the Congress envisages the following:
1. The purposeful advancement of the settlement of Palestine with Jewish farmers, artisans and tradesmen.
2. The unification and organization of all Jewry into local and wider groups, subject to the laws of their respective countries.
3. The strengthening of Jewish national feeling and consciousness.

4. Preparatory steps towards obtaining the consent of the various governments necessary for the fulfilment of the aims of Zionism.

Herzl had his mandate. Henceforth, he would travel and barter as the official spokesman for the Jewish national movement. Zionism was now on the agenda, with all the other political and nationalist trends of modern Europe. Certainly the watching diplomats thought so. The Austrian legation reported to Vienna that the scheme for a Jewish homeland in Palestine had been hatched by radical German socialists. The French consul in Basel ironically dismissed the dream as the brainchild of Jewish journalists. In the margin of a lengthy and detailed report from his Berne legation, the Kaiser scribbled, 'I am all in favour of the *kikes* going to Palestine. The sooner they take off, the better. I shan't put any obstacles in their way.'

As the third day of debates drew to a close, Max Mandelstamm, a Russian Zionist from pre-Pinsker days, expressed the fervent gratitude of those present to 'that brave man who was primarily responsible for the gathering of Jews from all countries taking counsel on the future of our people'. More cheering and applause, a modest acknowledgement from Herzl: 'I believe that Zionism need not be ashamed of its first Congress', and the proceedings terminated on the same high note as they had opened. Herzl was exhausted but jubilant. He returned to Vienna and penned his diary entry for 3 September, famous for its prophetic accuracy, 'Were I to sum up the Basel Congress in a word – which I shall guard against pronouncing publicly – it would be this. At Basel I founded the Jewish State. If I said this out loud today, I would be answered by universal laughter. Perhaps in five years, and certainly in fifty, everyone will know it.'

5

Herzl – Paying Court to the Powerful

Herzl had less than seven years to live. Never again, despite temporary successes and brief hopes, did he enjoy the rapturously uncritical adulation of his first Congress. His career acquired a melancholy grandeur, and in his declining years life and art coalesced, to produce an authentically tragic hero. Not Shabbetai Tzevi, but Moses, who viewed the Promised Land from afar, became a more apt comparison with Herzl. Certainly *he* fancied the resemblance, jotting down notes for a biblical drama about the hero who 'becomes inwardly weary, while retaining his will to the full', a leader despite himself, who 'must urge others for ever forward'.

Setting up a Jewish Colonial Bank to finance the proposed exodus was his next scheme. Herzl despatched David Wolffsohn, the only man in his entourage with any experience of banking, to the bourses of Europe in search of subscribers and underwriters; the only company to show any interest was the non-Jewish German firm of Schaffhausen. Herzl detected the malign influence of the House of Rothschild, and vented an outburst of paranoia against 'the world menace that this octopus constitutes'. A sketch of his in *Die Welt* of October 1897, entitled '*Mauschel*' (the kike), would have gladdened the hearts of Nazi anti-Semites thirty years later. He excoriated Jewish opponents of Zionism as a degenerate strain, 'mean', 'repellent', interested only in 'dirty business', bent on subversion. Zionists, holding a second arrow in reserve like William Tell, would finish them off. 'Take care, *Mauschel*! Friends, Zionism's second arrow is aimed at *Mauschel*'s breast.'

That year, significantly, the usual Christmas tree was replaced in the family drawing-room by the nine-branched Chanukkah candelabra. Herzl gave his children a history lesson on the Maccabean revolt, and penned a whimsical fable, entitled 'The Menorah', about an assimilated Jewish artist returning to his roots. January 1898 provided two further distractions from the dispiriting task of trying to raise money for a Jewish bank. *The New Ghetto* was finally produced on the Viennese stage, in the hope of capitalizing on its author's notoriety. Despite the nervousness of the police censor, who feared a public disturbance and insisted on cuts, the play drew a lukewarm reception. When it transferred to Berlin, it was panned. Rejected once again in the sphere where he craved acceptance, Herzl went into deep depression, and asked Nordau to take over as leader of the Zionist movement.

Herzl was grateful for his refusal when it was announced later in the month that the Kaiser would make a pilgrimage to the Holy Land. The diplomatic potential of such a visit reawakened his appetite, and he convened a meeting of the Zionist executive to organize a second Congress. The twenty-two members gathered in Vienna on 22 April. They were sceptical of Herzl's plan, fearing that fewer delegates would, or could, come again so soon after the triumphant first Congress, and that ideological differences about colonization were bound to surface. Herzl was eloquent in rebuttal. A second Congress would have even more impact than the first, especially if the bank launch could be announced. To Leon Kellner's reproach that the movement was all *noise*, he retorted, 'Yes, of course. But noise is everything . . . All of world history is nothing but clamour: clamour of arms, clamour of ideas on the march.' He persuaded them, and the second Zionist Congress was scheduled, again in Basel, for 28 August.

Directing political theatre was his consolation for stage failure. Once again, he oversaw every detail. The symbols of statehood – flags, heraldry, architecture – became an issue of supreme importance. If he postdated Garibaldi in his awareness of the flag's symbolic potency (and of a leader's virility emphasized by a flowing beard), he preceded Mussolini in his grandiose architectural schemes, wanting to create a 'neo-Jewish style' that anticipated Milan's railway station. He asked the architect Oscar Marmorek to design a congress building as a permanent landmark in Switzerland. Financing the Colonial Bank was harder. By August, initial subscriptions amounted to only £100,000 of the required £3 million. With characteristic bravura, Herzl decided to launch it at the Congress, anyway, turning it into a popular bank, rather than one dependent on reluctant Jewish capitalists.

The second Congress was indeed larger than the first, with 360 delegates and nearly 500 observers. The attendance of Bernard Lazare, the radical French socialist and new convert to Zionism, caused a ripple of excitement. Of more lasting significance was the presence of an obscure chemistry student from Russia, Chaim Weizmann, who would beget the Balfour Declaration and become first president of the state of Israel. In the intervening year, the Zionist organization had grown to 913 affiliates world-wide. The stage-managing of their conference had improved correspondingly. No squabblings about formal attire or proper accreditation, as the black-tie delegates, elected by their constituencies, took their seats to the music of *Tannhäuser*. The Aryan motif – a calculated genuflection to the Kaiser and his forthcoming Holy Land pilgrimage – was reiterated in the art nouveau souvenir postcard, depicting an armoured Siegfried against an oriental background.

A happy augury before the conference began had put delegates in optimistic mood. As the Zionist flag was being unfurled from the balcony, a group of passing Swiss students, celebrating a local saint's day, had shouted 'Long live the Jews!' The watching Zionists were moved, none more so than Nordau, the Hungarian sentimentalist, who retired to his room in tears. Herzl alluded to the incident in his opening speech. Did it presage the coming of better times for the Jews? His words were drowned in applause, as was every other sentence in a banal address. Its main theme was the winning over of Jewish communities to Zionism, despite opposition from 'Protest Rabbis' and other communal agencies. He also lauded the Kaiser as 'the most modern ruler of the inhabited earth', while reassuring the 'indestructibly resilient', 'brave' and 'magnanimous' Turks that their country would benefit immeasurably from the addition of Jewish enterprise and industrial know-how.

But the delegates, for all their applause, had not come meekly to do Herzl's bidding. Once again, the Russian caucus outnumbered any other, and if its members were united in one thing, it was their ambivalence about Herzl. His abiding impression from the First Congress had been of the vitality, cohesiveness and inner strength of the east Europeans, whose rootedness in Jewish tradition he envied, and whose attainments in a diversity of disciplines he admired. Their image of him was of a rootless, assimilated west European *luftmensch*, a smooth talker more at ease in café society than in Jewish culture. 'I cannot pretend that I was swept off my feet' was young Weizmann's reaction to meeting the leader whose travels, deeds and sayings were so avidly followed by the Jewish masses. Dissent focused, inevitably, on the colonization issue, whether as main text or hidden agenda. The apparently straightforward resolution to found a Colonial Bank became bogged down in a four-hour semantic debate, because the Russian Zionists, suspicious – with justification, as events proved – of Herzl's commitment to Palestine, re-fused to accept a first draft which mentioned its sphere of activities as being in 'the Orient'. Not until the words 'and especially Palestine and Syria' were added was the resolution passed. Debates on colonization in progress revealed overt disagreement. It was easy enough to criticize the Rothschild settlements, but a dangerous division emerged between those who supported existing immigration stratagems and Herzl, who was adamantly opposed to 'the smuggling in of settlers' instead of a formal understanding with the Ottoman court.

Underlying some of these apparently trivial differences of emphasis was a major ideological confrontation, as yet hardly articulated, be-tween the 'political' Zionists, led by Herzl, and the 'cultural' Zionists, whose spokesman was his formidable, absent rival, Achad Ha-Am. A bland paper delivered by the elderly Max Mandelstamm, which called for a synthesis of political action, culture and nationalism, was the first of many attempts at future congresses to paper over the dialectic cracks.

Absorbed in contemplation of their doctrinal navels, the delegates listened with little comment and no concern to a report from Leo Motzkin, recently returned from Palestine, which stressed the 'estab-lished fact that the most fertile parts of our land are occupied by Arabs . . . 650,000 souls, but this figure is not verified'. A random stat-istic, and passing reference to 'innumerable clashes between Jews and incited Arabs', did not yet disturb the standard Zionist image of Pales-tine as barren, sparsely populated terrain – 'a land without a people for a people without a land' – whose few Semitic inhabitants would welcome the Jewish settlers as emissaries of European culture in the backward East.

As Herzl brought the second Congress to a close on 31 August 1898, he was satisfied, as he put it in his peroration, that 'We have set out.' His authority, diffidently queried in some of the sessions, was confirmed by a standing ovation. And soon after the delegates had dispersed, two intriguing messages were conveyed to him: the first, from the sultan, graciously acknowledged the generous sentiments expressed about Palestine's ruler by the Congress; the second, via the eccentric

Hechler, invited him to visit again the grand duke of Baden, uncle to the Kaiser. The final act of Herzl's drama was about to start.

It began with a visit to the summer residence on Lake Constance of the grand duke, which offered boundless promise. Friedrich of Baden was one of those passé political figures who delude themselves, by dropping indiscreet gossip, that they still have a role to play. He confided that his nephew's forthcoming eastern pilgrimage had a diplomatic rather than a pious motive: to extend German influence in the Ottoman empire. Having broached the matter *personally* with his nephew, he could assure Herzl of the Kaiser's sympathetic interest in Zionist colonization under German tutelage. It required only an audience with Count Philip von Eulenburg, the German ambassador in Vienna, and through him to Prince von Bülow, the foreign minister. Fortuitously, the German diplomatic corps was in Vienna, awaiting the Kaiser's arrival for the funeral of Emperor Franz Josef's wife Elizabeth, assassinated in Geneva by an anarchist. A meeting was immediately arranged with von Eulenburg. The ramrod-stiff Prussian nobleman, his iron impassivity a mask for homosexuality, took to Herzl; this Jew was a pleasing change from the pedlar types. Herzl spoke with skill and subtlety. Apart from incidental advantages, such as weaning Jewish youth away from revolutionary politics, assuring Wilhelm II's role in history and guaranteeing the diffusion of *Kultur* throughout the Near East, a German protectorate over the Zionist colonies would obviate the need to approach other sympathizers – for example, England. The count got the drift and agreed to raise the matter with the Kaiser.

Herzl was in Amsterdam with Wolffsohn, wooing a young banker, Jacobus Kahn, who had shown interest in the Jewish Colonial Trust, when a letter arrived from von Eulenburg, informing him of the Kaiser's 'full and deep understanding for your movement'. He was thrown into a panic; with his bank stillborn, he would be revealed as having no clothes (he had recently discovered, and liked to quote, Hans Christian Andersen's fable). Wolffsohn and Kahn reacted coolly when Herzl imparted his news. They agreed that launching the bank was absolutely crucial, and gave added urgency to their London trip, planned for the following day. Their calming influence succeeded only partially. On his first night in London Herzl suffered a mild heart attack. Nevertheless, he went ahead with a speech in the East End's Great Assembly Hall which attracted an audience of 10,000 inside the building and on the pavements outside. They cheered him fervently. The success lingered sweetly in his reveries as he journeyed to Berlin for an appointment with von Eulenburg.

Von Eulenburg assured him that both the Kaiser and his foreign minister were won over to Zionism, and Herzl chose to assume that a German protectorate was in the bag. So he exulted in his diary, and to Wolffsohn he wrote, 'It is an extraordinary thing, which few human beings have experienced. A dream suddenly comes to realization.' The dream become reality meant, for Herzl, the consummation of nineteenth-century German Jewry's most fervent and pathetic illusion – a symbiosis of Judaism's heritage and Aryan culture. 'Life under the protectorate of this powerful, great, moral, splendidly administered, firmly governed Germany can only have the most salutary effects on the Jewish national character . . .'

It was foreign minister von Bülow who poured cold water over Herzl's gossamer fantasy. He received him with Prince Hohenlohe, the imperial chancellor, and Herzl wilted before their Junker anti-Semitism. They waved away any knowledge of royal approbation for Zionist schemes, and begged to doubt that the Jews would abandon their stock exchange to follow Herzl eastwards rather than flooding westward, as was their wont. Herzl conceded the stock exchange gibe ingratiatingly, but was confident that the poor Jews of Berlin – was it in the east or north of the city that they lived? – would emigrate to buy land at fair prices from the mixed multitudes of the orient who owned Palestine. The money was available. There was, to name but one example which he recklessly plucked out of the air, the Baron Hirsch Trust of £10 million. Mention of Jewish moneybags won him a reprieve. 'See you in Constantinople, Herr Doktor,' said von Bülow. Herzl had his audience with the Kaiser. Assembling an impressive Zionist delegation to accompany him at short notice was trickier. Eventually, he scraped together Wolffsohn, Max Bodenheimer, president of the German Zionist Federation, Dr Moses Schnirer, a Viennese physician, and Josef Seidener, an engineer and the only member of the party actually to have visited Palestine.

On 13 October they boarded the Orient Express, buoyed by the receipt an hour before departure of 6000 gold francs from a Russian supporter. As befitted their aspirations, the group took over the entire second floor of the Hotel de Londres in Constantinople; the first floor was occupied by visiting royalty. Nervous anticipation dissolved over three days of Turkish inertia and heel-kicking frustration. The German ambassador disclaimed any knowledge of a Dr Herzl or his delegation, and had no time to grant an interview. Court contacts from Herzl's previous visit to the Ottoman capital were unavailable, police agents hovered ostentatiously, and their mail was tampered with.

Meanwhile, on the morning of 18 October, the Kaiser's yacht sailed up the Golden Horn to a cannon salute. The Zionists' nerves frayed. They were due to embark for Palestine the following day. A resourceful Herzl rose to the occasion, the Wagnerian hero keeping his appointment with destiny. He despatched Wolffsohn with a letter requesting a private interview with His Imperial Majesty, and the meek timber merchant from Cologne discovered in himself reserves of daring to bluff his way past suspicious guards and deliver it personally to the Kaiser's court marshal. The response came after lunch. Herzl was to present himself at four-thirty. His pulse was racing, but he refused a sedative, fussing instead over the details of his toilet and choosing gloves in a becoming shade of grey. He and Wolffsohn took a hackney cab to Yildiz Kiosk, where his Sancho Panza was detained in the forecourt, while he was kept waiting in a guardroom for two hours, brooding morbidly.

At last he was summoned. He checked his trouser creases, then climbed the staircase to the Kaiser's suite, bowing as he passed the empress, who stood with von Bülow behind a marble column. She smiled graciously. The Kaiser, in hussar uniform and high boots, greeted him at the door, a would-be Achilles who spent his adult life trying to hide his withered left arm behind dazzling accoutrement and flashing charm. The two dandies assessed each other and took note of their most practised trademark: their eyes. 'Truly imperial eyes. I have never seen such eyes. They show a remarkable, bold, inquisitive soul,' Herzl recorded in his diary. The Kaiser was as complimentary in his memoirs about Herzl's 'expressive eyes, idealism, and noble way of thought'.

After such favourable first impressions, the audience was bound to go well. The Kaiser exuded easy magnetism, and Herzl's admiration for the very model of a modern, technologically aware warrior king stayed the right side of obsequiousness. They got along famously, von Bülow keeping discreetly in the background. Between them, the Kaiser and Herzl divided up the Near East in bold, easy strokes, eliminating the Turkish debt with Jewish money in return for a chartered land company under German protection to colonize Palestine. The sultan would be sure to accede to the wishes of his new imperial paymaster. It was settled. The Zionist delegation should present its formal petition to the Kaiser in Jerusalem.

'That is a monarch of genius' was von Bülow's enigmatic comment as he escorted Herzl down the stairs. Herzl was in no condition to detect ambiguities; he, a Jew, had been received seriously by the ruler of Germany, the sweetest triumph of his career. 'Overwhelming!' was the only word he managed for poor, agitated Wolffsohn, and back at the hotel his nervous reaction suggested a heart attack. Nevertheless, he struggled over the text of the petition that he had promised von Bülow would be delivered by the morning. Working intermittently through the night, he had it delivered just half an hour before their steamship was due to depart.

After such a diplomatic coup, the Holy Land itself was something of a let-down; Herzl thought it dirty, hot and impoverished. In 1898 there were about four thousand Jewish settlers living in sixteen new colonies, thirteen of them maintained by Edmund de Rothschild. Jerusalem was beautiful but decayed, the 'musty deposits of two thousand years of in-humanity, intolerance and filth lying in the foul-smelling alleyways . . . If ever we get Jerusalem . . . I would begin by cleaning it up.' At the Wailing Wall, last remnant of Herod's Temple, Wolffsohn and the others wept, but Herzl, offended by the clamouring beggars, could not feign such emotion. A fever had racked him since their arrival in Jaffa. Devout Orthodox Jews berated him for travelling on the sabbath, while local community leaders avoided him, for fear of Turkish displeasure, and Rothschild's administrators suspected his motives. At the Mikveh Israel agricultural training school, he had a second encounter with the Kaiser's entourage, on its way to Jerusalem. The emperor, fetchingly attired in grey uniform and spiked gold helmet, reined in his white stallion to exchange a few sentences about the heat and lack of water. Herzl judged the amiable pleasantries a good omen for their forthcoming formal audience in Jerusalem.

As in Constantinople, there was an anxious wait of several days before the imperial summons came for the afternoon of 2 November. Herzl checked every sartorial detail of his delegation, but refused, 'for the sake of history', to let them calm their nerves with a bromide before they set off under the noonday sun in top hats and evening dress for an appointment which, according to Herzl's diary entry, 'will live on forever in Jewish history, and possibly may entail world consequences'.

It did not, and a month later Herzl was characteristically comforting himself with the reflection that the Kaiser's change of heart was a benefit to Zionism's cause, because 'we would have had to pay the most usurious interest for this protectorate'. The audience had been brief and noncommittal. Herzl read out his petition, heavily edited by von Bülow, for a German protectorate in the land sacred to Jewish memory. The Kaiser thanked him for its sentiments but said the matter required further investigation, and delivered a homily on the agricultural needs of Palestine, which plentiful Jewish money could doubtless provide. He avoided any reference to a charter or a protectorate. 'He said neither yes nor no' was the consolation Herzl derived from a disappointing interview, but the reality was bleaker. Whatever passing interest the Kaiser had shown in Zionism was secondary to the purpose of von Bülow and his Foreign Ministry officials in cementing an alliance with the sultan against England, and securing the concession to build a strategic railway to Baghdad. 'These people have no money,' von Bülow explained to a journalist after his master's also less-than-successful pilgrimage to the orient. 'The rich Jews don't want to participate, and with the lousy Jews of Poland you can't do a thing.' The official German communiqué put it more tactfully: it expressed Kaiser Wilhelm's benevolent interest in all endeavours aimed at improving the agriculture of Palestine for the welfare of the Turkish empire and in full recognition of the sultan's sovereignty.

After eleven days, Herzl and his deputation slunk furtively from Palestine, at breaking point from disillusionment, constant Turkish surveillance and the paranoid fear of assassination. Their trip had been a fiasco, undertaken, Bodenheimer hinted, on the basis of Herzl's unwarrantedly euphoric report of his first audience with the Kaiser in Constantinople. Even the loyal Wolffsohn expressed reservations. It was a recriminatory and bad-tempered return journey to Europe, but Herzl already was working out an authorized version of his mission to give to the readers of *Die Welt* and supporters in Europe and America. 'The results surpassed all expectations,' he informed Nordau and others, 'the achievement is simply colossal.'

His reaction to the rebuff was a typical oscillation between still more grandiose designs and despair. He tried, and failed, to arrange an audience with the tsar. When attempts to meet again with the Kaiser were turned down, he offered the protectorate of the Palestine colonies to the grand duke of Baden, who was happy to entertain the notion, subject to approval from Berlin. So diminished was his influence, however, that the powerful Deutsche Bank ignored his letter of recommendation to act as receiving agent for shares in the stillborn Jewish Colonial Bank.

Diary entries provide a guide to Herzl's melancholia: 'Everything is bogged down. Something has to happen' . . . 'Days of despondency. The tempo of the movement is slowing down. The slogans are wearing out' . . . 'The well is running dry.'

In the meantime, the Third Zionist Congress, scheduled for mid-August 1899 in Basel, was approaching. After the expectation engendered by his Palestine trip, and his carefully orchestrated allusions to promising dialogue with the Kaiser, Herzl needed something tangible to set before the curious and the sceptical. He decided – a gambler's throw of the dice – to dispatch Nevlinski once more to Turkey in an attempt to reach the sultan. Nevlinski, a terminally ill man, set off for Constantinople with his wife and a physician. He wrote to Herzl that he had an appointment with the sultan for the following day, and promptly succumbed to a stroke. His widow cabled for money to bring the corpse home.

The Third Zionist Congress provided a foretaste of the divisions that eventually overwhelmed Herzl's leadership of the movement. Ostensibly, there were positive things to report. The number of Zionist societies had grown from 913 to over 1300; membership in Russia alone had increased by nearly one-third. Herzl was duly re-elected, to a standing ovation. But his performance was stilted and weary, and despite his request that the Jerusalem journey should not be debated lest it jeopardize a sensitive relationship with 'that genius, the Kaiser', who had bestowed his benevolent attention on their national idea, critical delegates reminded him of his rash promise the year before that the exodus would soon begin. They accused him of failure to consult the international executive, and suspiciously scrutinized the official budget, which had more than doubled but was vague about money distributed to agents in Turkey and elsewhere.

The year 1899 marked a watershed for Herzl. Zionism was in stasis, his marriage beyond repair, his capital and Julie's dowry bleeding away on an elegant lifestyle, travel expenses and financing of *Die Welt*, and his editors on the *Neue Freie Presse* were adamant about denying him further leave of absence. Once again, he tried literary creativity as the palliative. Two new light comedies were performed and received derisory reviews, due, Herzl persuaded himself, to hostility to his Zionist involvement; in reality, sympathizers were pained that the leader of the movement should demean himself with such shallow offerings. His listlessness continued into the new year and the new century. 'No, I wasn't sick,' he explained to Nordau, 'but I am greatly troubled for our cause. We need success like a bite of bread.' He had an altercation with Kahn, and a furious row with his loyal subordinate Wolffsohn. Herzl suffered a black-out that was diagnosed as brain anaemia; premonitions of death perturbed him. Physically he had deteriorated, little of the once-handsome dandy apparent in the stooped, grey-bearded forty-year-old, whose eyes had sunk deep into their sockets. The sterility of his domestic situation was made manifest in a revised will, which appointed his parents as sole heirs, his children after them, and Julie excluded.

A visit to England on bank affairs, and an introduction to a personality infinitely more exotic and effective than the lamented Nevlinski, lightened Herzl's accidie. In England, at war with the Boers, he spent a happy country weekend with Alfred Austin, the poet laureate, and promptly became enamoured of the English gentry. 'How well I understand them, the assimilated Jews of England. If I lived in England, I too might become a jingoist!' The new personality was Arminius Vambery, like Herzl a Hungarian-born Jew but now a professed atheist, having tried four religions in between, two of them as an ordained priest. Currently professor of oriental languages at Budapest University, Vambery's career had begun as a café singer in Constantinople, speedily advancing to that of French tutor of the royal harem and adviser to the grand vizier. He had written a popular account of his adventures in central Asia, was regularly consulted about Turkish affairs by interested governments, and spoke twelve languages fluently, including an earthy Yiddish. Nordau had arranged his introduction to Herzl.

The two kindred spirits from Budapest delighted each other. Vambery was dressed like a pasha, and confessed to Herzl that his professorial chair was a cover for secret agent activities on behalf of Sultan 'Abd al-Hamid – 'a foully conceived bastard and a madman' – and

Great Britain. Refreshingly, Vambery declared that he did not require payment for his good offices, having amassed a substantial fortune. He would help Herzl because he liked him, but cautioned that it would take time to get to the sultan. It did, nearly twelve months, but Vambery was almost as good as his word, and Herzl added another flamboyant courtier to his retinue.

The Fourth Zionist Congress was held that August in London, 'for we had outgrown Basel', and went deceptively smoothly. It was the largest yet, with four hundred delegates, and the familiar criticisms were muted, partly because the large Russian caucus from the towns and villages of the Pale of Settlement was overawed at being in the capital city of the world's greatest empire. Herzl had switched his hopes from Berlin to the new venue, as his opening address signalled: 'England, great England, England the free, England commanding all the seas – she will understand us and our purpose.' Otherwise, he was wan, repetitious and still suffering high fevers; it was Nordau's annual survey of the condition of European Jewry, with its sombre warning that anti-Semitism was on the rise and would get worse, that drew greater notice.

Back in Vienna, murky haggling resumed with alleged representatives of the sultan. Vambery seemed a more promising intermediary, but it transpired that he worked on commission. Herzl told him that he was waiting for some tangible sign to demonstrate Zionist gratitude. In the meantime, in February 1901, the Turkish government published new restrictions on Jewish immigration to Palestine. Herzl, whose legal training had always preferred a guaranteed charter to the clandestine infiltration favoured by Russian Zionists, detected a ruse. Was it not, he wrote to Vambery, simply a question of the whore raising her price before she eventually yielded? Vambery agreed. From Constantinople he apprised Herzl that the sultan expressed himself quite differently in private: his real concerns were gold and power.

Still, nothing moved, a galling impasse for Herzl, whose credibility depended on flurries of action and attendant publicity. On 2 May 1901, his forty-first birthday, he noted in his diary, 'It is almost six years since I started this movement which has made me old, tired and poor.' But a few days later the outlook changed. Vambery cabled the thrilling news. The sultan would see Herzl. Herzl dashed to Budapest to meet his successful intermediary, who milked the situation for all it was worth. He foul-mouthed the lunatic sultan and exaggerated the obstacles he had surmounted to gain the prized audience. After the good news came the caution. The sultan would not receive him as leader of Zionism, but in a private capacity, as a prominent Jew and influential correspondent of a leading Viennese newspaper. Nothing deterred, Herzl entrained for Constantinople in a state of febrile excitement, accompanied by Wolffsohn and Oscar Marmorek.

In all, Herzl was to visit the Sublime Porte, as the Ottoman court was officially known, five times between 1896 and 1902. He became adept at bazaar haggling, grew familiar with the toadies and hangers-on at the Yildiz Kiosk, fed enigmatic rumours to fellow journalists, distributed thousands of francs in *baksheesh*, afflicted his digestion with innumerable cups of black coffee and lukewarm, repulsive dishes, expansively offered to liquidate the Turkish national debt or regulate her finances with non-existent Jewish money in return for the right of Jewish settlement in Palestine. He came away with two ceremonial decorations, effusive protestations of respect and interest, and a bag of gold coins from the sultan, who worked on the principle that one must sow in order eventually to reap. In a world of serpentine cupidity, stratified venality and conjuror's illusion, Herzl was fleeced and discarded more lingeringly and totally than in any other of his diplomatic dealings.

Summoned to the royal palace on 18 May, Herzl was accorded the rare favour of a seat in the shade while the procession of pashas, eunuchs, ladies of the harem and dignitaries passed by, and was offered (again) the gift of the Order of the Medjidje, Second Class, which he firmly declined; the Grand Cordon of the order was then bestowed upon him. He was ushered into the audience chamber. Sultan 'Abd al-Hamid was a small, frail man, with a dyed red beard and a reedy voice. He introduced himself as an avid reader of the *Neue Freie Presse*, a surprising achievement for one who spoke no German, and inquired after the Emperor Franz Josef's health, which Herzl, with matching ingenuousness, confidently diagnosed. The pleasantries over, they settled to business through an interpreter, Herzl steering carefully clear of any mention of Palestine or Zionism, but expatiating on the fable of Androcles and the Lion. The thorn in the lion's paw was Turkey's chronic indebtedness, which Herzl and his monied friends would remove in return for a public measure friendly to the Jews.

The common ground had been defined and they trod it for two hours, then three further days. Herzl–Androcles played his role,

immune to reality. When the sultan outlined a scheme to consolidate
the state debt and realize – perhaps – a profit of £1.5 million, Herzl
pooh-poohed it as too modest, and asked for a full audit of the state
finances on which to make effective recommendations. Back came the
sultan's men with a counter-proposal. Herzl and his Jewish friends
should take over the financing and exploitation of all Turkey's mines,
oil fields and state monopolies, in return for £4 million which the
sultan needed to pay for some warships he had ordered. Would it be
possible to raise that sum quickly? Of course, replied Herzl, but naturally it would depend on the sultan's attitude towards the Jewish investors, experts and colonists who came to settle in Turkish territories.
The sultan sent word that Jewish settlers would be welcome, provided
that they became citizens, served in the army and established themselves discreetly – a few families here, a few there. No problem,
answered Herzl on their behalf, but would it not be more efficient to
set up a land company under Ottoman law in some uncultivated area –
Palestine, for example? The sultan intimated his receptivity, and asked
for a definite proposal to be submitted within four weeks.

Herzl departed from Constantinople in good humour. He exulted in
his diary, 'We have actually entered upon negotiations for the charter.
All it takes now to carry out everything is luck, skill, and money.' He
was deluding himself. The Turks were using him as bait, to extract
better conditions from a French consortium led by the former cabinet
minister, Pierre Rouvier. But Herzl, the hook between his gills, threw
himself into the task of raising money, with no more success than
before. In Paris, Edmund de Rothschild, and the Baron Hirsch Trust
with its tempting £10 million capital, remained impervious. In London,
he enjoyed a social triumph with Jewish and Gentile high society, but
nothing more; Cecil Rhodes could not be bothered to meet him.

Once again, Herzl could blame wealthy Jews, especially the Rothschilds. 'In fifty years their graves will be spat on,' he wrote to Mandelstamm. 'I almost concluded with the sultan, but could not raise the
filthy money.' Evidently the sultan had reached the same conclusion;
he did not acknowledge Herzl's carefully composed letters. The scepticism of close associates like Nordau was a further irritant, and the
encouragement from eccentrics like Vambery increasingly bizarre. In
answer to Herzl's appeal that he should earn his commission by interceding once again with the sultan, the seventy-year-old professor of

oriental languages wrote back that he was ready to stage a *coup d'état* in Constantinople.

It was in a state of suspended animation, his health poor and forebodings of an early death recurring, that he presided over the Fifth Zionist Congress in the last days of 1901. It had returned to Basel against his wishes, a boring venue after London but more accessible for east European delegates. In his opening address he made the ritual obeisance to the monarch presently being wooed, this year the sultan, whose 'kindliness and cordiality . . . justify the highest hopes. The attitude and the language of His Majesty gave me the feeling that in the ruling caliph the Jewish people has a friend and protector.' Such bland generalities no longer silenced his critics. The young, mainly Russian, opponents were derisory about bourgeois posturings that produced a few headlines but no facts, and scandalized by the amounts being frittered on bribes. Marshalled around Chaim Weizmann and Martin Buber, but with Achad Ha-Am as their guiding spirit, the thirty-seven delegates of the Democratic-Zionist Faction vented their frustrations over the seemingly innocuous issue of Jewish culture. A procedural clash with Herzl led to their collective walk-out.

The rift between Herzl and the cultural Zionists is usually presented as one between 'west' and 'east', between Jewish universalism and Jewish nationalism or, by Herzl, as he tried jocularly to defuse the tension, between a lively young faction and a staid older group. The divide went deeper. It was the failure of understanding between two antithetical experiences of Jewish history. Herzl was the product of Jewish emancipation, while his critics were conditioned by the restraints of their hostile environment. Buber was to say later of Herzl, 'We venerated him, loved him, but a great part of his being was alien to our soul.'

Herzl was summoned twice more to Constantinople, in February and July 1902. The negotiations became increasingly surreal, the cost for consolidating the national debt being raised to £32 million, in return for large-scale Jewish immigration to Mesopotamia, Syria, Anatolia — anywhere but Palestine. Not having the money, Herzl could afford to be reckless in his offers but firm about insisting on a charter for Palestine. His true evaluation by the Turkish authorities was humiliatingly revealed when they tried to buy him off with a large bribe to make the *Neue Freie Presse* more 'understanding' of the sultan's difficulties in Armenia. The paradox of his situation was that he had achieved nothing in the diplomatic arena, whereas his literary reputation, which he really cared about, was that of a second-rate journalist. This mournful self-assessment was occasioned by an invitation to appear in London before a Royal Commission on Alien Immigration, at the same time that he was putting the final touches to *Altneuland*. For twenty years, Russian and Romanian Jews had been pouring into England to escape persecution, and this influx of cheap labour had aroused public concern. Nathaniel Meyer, Lord Rothschild, the only Jewish member of the commission, shared his family's antipathy to Zionism, and had been hostile to calling Herzl as a witness, but was overruled. Herzl welcomed the opportunity of trying to win over the 'Lord of Banking Hosts', and travelled to London in June 1902.

Shortly after his arrival, he suffered a devastating psychological blow. His father was ill, and died before Herzl could reach Vienna. He was racked with guilt at not having been there in time: 'He stood by my side like a tree. Now that tree is gone.' Only his mother remained to offer adoring, uncritical support against a hostile world, but her carping relationship with the daughter-in-law she judged inadequate complicated the domestic situation that Herzl coped with only by escape. So he fled back to London, after a month's remorseful mourning, to the eagerly anticipated meeting with Rothschild. It turned out to be a sweet success. The wealthiest of all the Rothschilds, paternalistic leader of British Jewry, an English aristocrat to his fingertips and as prosaically unimaginative as all that breed, Lord Rothschild was won over to promote Herzl's cause once he felt reassured that a cautious espousal of Zionism would not fan anti-Semitism or threaten the delicate balance of being an Englishman first and a Jew second. Herzl played skilfully on his sense of philanthropic *noblesse oblige*, his vanity as a man of vast influence and his patriotic concern to further British interests while helping to relieve the suffering of east European Jews, without raising the (for Rothschild) dread spectre of the Jewish state. It was Rothschild who first mentioned Uganda as a site for a Jewish colony, and promised to have a word with Joseph Chamberlain, the colonial secretary. It was the Uganda offer which, thirteen months later, destroyed Herzl at the Sixth Zionist Congress, and precipitated his death.

In the meantime, he was summoned for his final, futile visit to Constantinople. Humiliation there intensified his courtship of London, using the same arguments but changing the names that he had vainly tried with the Kaiser. He wrote to an English supporter, 'It must be made clear to the British government that we are ready and able to serve as pioneers of the British interests . . . to stop the spread of French influence in Syria and Palestine.' Leopold Greenberg, a future editor of the *Jewish Chronicle*, became his chief contact in London; Rothschild was now regretting his earlier enthusiasm. 'I should view with horror the establishment of a Jewish colony pure and simple. Such a colony . . . would be a ghetto, with the prejudices of the ghetto; a small, petty Jewish state, Orthodox and illiberal [Rothschild was president of the Orthodox United Synagogues, and knew whereof he spoke], excluding the Gentiles and the Christians.' Herzl reprimanded Rothschild: the commonwealth *he* was endeavouring to create would deserve none of those epithets. For three years he had been working on a novel to allay such fears. It was entitled *Altneuland*, and due to be published shortly; he would send Lord Rothschild one of the first copies.

We do not know what, if any, was Rothschild's reaction to the literary gift. We do know that it provoked the bitterest controversy yet with the cultural Zionists, and marked the beginning of the end of Herzl's undisputed leadership of the movement he had largely created. His pen was mightier than his sword, but destructively so.

6

Herzl – Literary and Diplomatic Failure

The genesis of *Altneuland* came on Herzl's return from Palestine in the summer of 1899. Its title was suggested by the Altneuschul, the oldest synagogue in Prague. Worked on intermittently between flurries of diplomatic activity, it grew ever more ambitious in design, the definit-ive statement of Herzl's ideas about human progress embodied in Zionist achievement. What was intractable in life would be reconciled in art. Will and dream would fuse in the pages of a utopian romance, albeit briefly, because the all-pervasive melancholic Zeitgeist of turn-of-the-century Vienna overwhelmed Herzl with the despairing realiz-ation that everything was evanescent. 'If you will it, it is no dream,' was his novel's frontispiece motto. His postscript is less positive, more allusive. 'But if you do not will it, then it remains a dream which I have recited. Dream and action are not as widely separated as many believe. All the acts of men were dreams at first and become dreams again.'

The plot is simple, banal. A fabulously rich Prussian nobleman, Kingscourt, and a young Jewish lawyer, Dr Friedrich Loewenberg, soul-mates in their weariness and disgust with European society, retreat to an island in the Pacific at the close of 1902, on their way passing a few days in 'the ancient homeland of the Jews', which, in its decay, mirrors the decay of the Jewish people. The Prussian aristocrat and the Jewish intellectual spend twenty years in arcadian bliss – natural, uncorrupted men as conjured by Rousseau or Tolstoy – before returning on Kingscourt's yacht to inspect the world they had left behind. Their first stop is Palestine, so transformed that they cannot believe their eyes. Zionism has become a reality, the Jews have returned to their birthplace, anti-Semitism has evaporated in Europe, and Pales-tine is an ideal society to be emulated by the rest of mankind.

In an allegory such as this, where every character and incident has symbolic significance, the temptation is to overlook the narrative for the pleasure of psychoanalytical interpretation. Kingscourt is clearly a personification of Herzl's Junker hero-worship, with the additional

74

virtues of his new role model, the English gentry. Friedrich Loewenberg in his unregenerated state is an amalgam of the author, Heinrich Kana, a student friend who had committed suicide, and every footloose Jewish intellectual who had discarded his national heritage for the hope of advancement in rotten Viennese society. The leader of the new Palestine (based on David Wolffsohn) is named David Littwak (i.e. from Lithuania), who lives in a villa called Friedrichsheim, a haven for the young Loewenberg–Hertzl but also a gracious tip of the hat to his patron, Friedrich II, Grand Duke of Baden. Ultimately, Kingscourt stays on in Palestine as protector and guardian of Littwak's infant son, an audacious example of wish-fulfilment, given Prussian anti-Semitism and Germany's increasingly hostile response to the east European Jews flocking across her borders. The redeemed Loewenberg, who has become 'a tree of a man' during his island idyll, breaks off his engagement to the beautiful but shallow Ernestine (Julie), cuts his ties with Viennese Jewish society, and in the new land marries Littwak's sister Mirjam (modelled on his dead sister Pauline), surely to signify the fusion of eastern and western European Jewry, rather than, as some critics have inferred, incestuous longings on Herzl's part.

For all the satisfaction of identifying the real-life personages behind their fictional disguises, and despite the frequent instances where the reader is struck by Herzl's prescience in anticipating how the Jewish colony in Palestine will develop, *Altneuland* amply confirms his shortcomings as a creative writer; it is static, posed, artificial, a succession of staged tableaux rather than an unfolding narrative.

The main features of Herzl's new society are voluntary economic co-operation ('mutualism') and advanced technology. Mutualism was the middle ground between capitalism and collectivism, avoiding laissez faire exploitation on the one hand and socialist levelling on the other. Voluntary associations abound in this mutualist society; land and the major industries are publicly owned; newspapers belong to their readers; the opera and the telephone service are owned by their subscribers. Agriculture is organized into a system of co-operative farms, and grocery stores are run by the consumers. Petty trade, the bane of Jewish existence in Europe, has been abolished by mammoth, state-controlled department stores. Enlightened employers sell shares in their companies to the workers. Membership in this extended cartel of co-operatives is not automatic, but is earned by two years of service to the community, when it is open to all, Jew and non-Jew, male and female alike, who benefit from free education, equal rights, a seven-hour working day, and accident, sickness, old age and life insurance.

This society, relying on statistical and managerial techniques for optimum efficiency, is not coercive in its control of citizens. It is a 'free community', dependent upon the voluntary adherence of its members to the association's laws. Wrongdoers are not locked away, but given vocational training on model farms. Individual liberty is safeguarded by guiding human activity in the desired direction, encouraging people to utilize their freedom. This is a far cry from the benevolent oligarchy that governed in *Der Judenstaat*. But in the years between, at Zionist Congresses, Herzl had been subjected to every Jewish variant of the Marxist dialectic, to French anarchist thought, syndicalist ideals and the national socialism of Ferdinand Lassalle. Intellectual magpie that he was, and looking for a polity that would satisfy radical Russian Zionists while not scaring off the liberal Jewish bourgeoisie, the model he came up with was the contractual state founded on mutualism.

This healthy community, created without the hereditary afflictions of European society, so that there are Jewish artisans and Jewish farmers, but no Jewish pedlars, is bolstered by the latest achievements of science, and Herzl is at his most persuasive when writing about the power of technology to ameliorate the human condition. For a book published at the turn of the century, his vision is impressive. The streets are lit by electric lamps, there are automobiles, and in Haifa an electric monorail. At the Dead Sea there are chemical industries, while a system of underground tunnels from the Mediterranean to the Dead Sea provides hydroelectric power and replenishes the water level used to irrigate the now-fertile Jordan Valley. A rail network unites the country and links up Europe and Africa, since the Old-New Land is at the crux of the world's commercial routes. Its cities are architectural showpieces, with spacious family housing planned around boulevards, parks, department stores and places of education and entertainment. Jerusalem has been cleaned up, scrubbed down and repaved. The ancient heart of the city is left to houses of charity and religious devotion, but round about them a great metropolis has sprung up, 'a world-city in the spirit of the twentieth century'.

Leaving religion to its atavistic preoccupations, while people flock to the secular modern Jerusalem, is an apt image for the place of faith in

Herzl's new society. Religion is there for those who want it, but is excluded from influence on public life. There is, indeed, a rebuilt Temple, with organ, in the style of a Viennese Reform synagogue, but it is a symbol of ethical humanism: an expression of the Almighty's presence 'throughout the universe as the will to good'. The sabbath and festivals are observed as general days of rest, and Hebrew is used for liturgical purposes, but if there is a common language it appears to be German, with Yiddish for the lower orders. The villain of the novel is the rabble-rousing, narrow-minded Orthodox Rabbi Geyer – the personification of every 'Protest Rabbi' who had opposed Zionism – who is comprehensively defeated in the presidential election by the forces of liberalism.

The new society is open, pluralistic and tolerant; it fulfils the Jewish mission to be 'a light unto the nations'. The last words of the dying president, Eichenstamm (Mandelstamm) are, 'The stranger must feel at home among us.' So the new society takes and adapts all that is superior in wider *Kultur*. Its schools are run on German lines but teach the English sports of cricket, football and tennis. The hotels are English and Swiss, the spas continental, the Sea of Galilee a Riviera resort. At the theatre and the opera, for which proper dress is obligatory, a selection of Jewish and general productions are on offer. David Littwak and his sister Mirjam, prototypes of the new Jewish identity, are proud of their heritage but exquisitely refined and acculturated, able to converse in easy equality with an English noblewoman and causing Loewenberg to rejoice, 'now we can even manage a modest appearance in society'. Walking in the new Jerusalem, planned on American urban designs, through an English-style park with a German health clinic, Kingscourt, betraying his creator's weakness for epigrams, says to Loewenberg, 'I now understand everything in Old-New Land. It is a mosaic – a Mosaic mosaic.'

Thus, for Herzl, the role of a Jewish state is not to segregate Jews from the rest of the world, but to integrate them into it. The charter of the Jewish Academy in Jerusalem, whose forty members sit in conscious imitation of the Académie Française, commits them to work for 'the highest goals of humanity'. The composition of its membership precludes exclusivist chauvinism, since they came from many different cultures with the common aim of benefiting mankind. In their button-holes the academicians wear a yellow insignia – a constant reminder of past Jewish persecutions and a warning not to gloat in their present good fortune. As befits the experiment in Jewish emancipation which was blighted in Europe but under Zionist tending has reached full, universal flowering, this society is open to all. Reschid Bey, a Palestinian Arab, is the articulate spokesman for the native population whose existence Herzl had perforce to acknowledge on his Palestine journey. The Arab disposes of Achad Ha-Am-style lucubrations about native hostility to Jewish settlement: 'For us it was a blessing.' Everyone has gained from Jewish expansion, says Reschid Bey – the landowners from higher land prices, the peasants from regular employment and welfare benefits. But Kingscourt presses him in the voice of concerned liberal opinion. Even so, he asks, are not the Jews resented as 'interlopers'? The grateful recipient of Zionism's material and social benefits disagrees. 'Would you think of someone as a robber, who does not take anything from you, but rather brings you something? The Jews have made us prosperous, why should we be angry with them? They live with us as brothers, why should we not love them?' Game, set and match to wishful thinking.

But Herzl should not be accused of inconsistency or hypocrisy. For him, a child of his time, the white man's colonial burden and the Jewish mission coincide; they are joint bearers of enlightened progress for the less fortunate. The Eichenstamm Ophthalmic Institute in Jerusalem is seeking a cure for blindness in North Africa and Asia. The bacteriologist Steineck (Oscar Marmorek) wants to conquer malaria, to make Africa safe for colonization by surplus Europeans, with the added bonus of enabling black Americans to 'go home' and thus, at one fell swoop, solving the 'Negro Problem' too. Having rescued themselves and regained their pride, the Jews can now undertake, in a modern, secular, humanitarian manner, the task for which they were originally 'chosen': to be messengers of civilization to the nations of the world.

On this optimistic note, *Altneuland* ends. Herzl offered it to his Jewish constituency confident that his formula for success would meet with approval. Instead, it provoked a chorus of dissent, spearheaded by Achad Ha-Am in an acidulous review. Where, he inquired, was any specifically *Jewish* identity in Herzl's novel? The so-called Jewish Academy busied itself with general issues and, unlike its French counterpart, did not even speak the national language. In pandering to non-Jews and anti-Semites, Herzl had stressed the value of tolerance and the debt the new state would owe to European culture; in this supposedly Jewish society, there was no distinction of nationality or religion. Brotherly love between Jewish settlers and native Arabs whose land they had taken was a pipe dream. And where would the glorified Viennese Temple be rebuilt, given that the Mosque of Omar stood on the site of the former one, and nowhere else was religiously acceptable? Herzl's cosmopolitanism, devoid of a single quality of the Jewish *Volksgeist*, goaded Achad Ha-Am to his sharpest sarcasm. He seized the solving of the 'Negro Problem' to point out that any black renaissance basing itself on Herzl's Zionist ideals would end up with a black *Altneuland*. 'To copy others without showing a spark of original talent; to avoid "national chauvinism" in such fashion as to leave no trace of the character of one's own people or of its literature and spiritual creations; to gather oneself together and retreat into a corner merely to show others that we are tolerant, tolerant to the point of wearisomeness — that can be done by the Negroes too.' Herzl's book, he concluded contemptuously, was redolent of the atmosphere of 'slavery within freedom' characteristic of western thought.

Such a savage attack, echoed by Buber and other of Achad Ha-Am's disciples, called into question Herzl's fitness to lead the Zionist movement and could not pass unanswered. The confidant of the sultan and European statesmen did not respond personally, but asked his lieutenant, Max Nordau, to fire the bullets. The garrulous Hungarian did so with a vengeance. He accused Achad Ha-Am of wanting to impose Russian values on the new Zionist society: 'the guidelines of the Inquisition, the customs of the anti-Semites, and the anti-Jewish laws of Russia'. Achad Ha-Am was just another Protest Rabbi in secular garb, who abused the platform political Zionism had afforded him to propagate his ideas. Furthermore, although he might be capable of writing good Hebrew, he had nothing to say in it. Buber, Weizmann and Berthold Feivel organized a letter of protest at Nordau's broadside, signed by many prominent Zionists, and printed it in a new magazine, *Ha-Z'man*. A fierce debate ensued in the Hebrew press, which boosted sales of the book but widened the rift between Herzl's supporters and the cultural wing of Zionism. Instead of providing the consolatory tale which Herzl had intended, and unifying eastern and western Jewry in pursuit of a shared vision, *Altneuland* became the text of their ideological differences. In literature as in life, Herzl was losing the ability to sway the Jewish people into accepting his will.

Shortly after its publication, he returned to London for his meeting with the colonial secretary. Joseph Chamberlain was a new kind of Englishman for Herzl – a self-made pragmatic imperialist of driving energy, who assessed every situation from the profit-and-loss perspective of a Birmingham businessman. His sentiments about Jews, or Zionism, were immaterial, nor was he moved by Herzl's plea that he had come on behalf of the starving Jews of the Pale. Chamberlain wanted to know, What was in it for the British empire? He brusquely dismissed any idea of Cyprus; its Greek and Muslim communities would not accept Jewish colonization. Sinai was more promising. A Jewish settlement in the unpopulated El Arish region might be viable, provided the Egyptians did not object to a Zionist influx. Herzl responded with one of his witticisms: 'No, we shall not go into Egypt: we have already been there!' If England would lease the vacant Sinai Peninsula, she would reap increased power and the gratitude of ten million Jews. Chamberlain was interested, subject to Foreign Office consent and the imprimatur of Lord Cromer, officially the British consul-general, unofficially the most powerful man in Egypt. He arranged for Herzl to see the foreign secretary, and closed the interview with a little joke at his own expense about his difficulties in South Africa: 'Reassure Lord Lansdowne that you are not planning a Jameson Raid from El Arish into Palestine.'

The following afternoon Herzl was listened to sympathetically at the Foreign Office as he proposed the establishment of a Jewish Eastern Company, with a capital of £5 million, to be granted a concession for the development and settlement of the Sinai Peninsula, leading to semi-autonomous status under the British Crown. The foreign secretary was careful not to commit himself before consulting Lord Cromer, but Herzl was sufficiently charmed by Lansdowne's courtesy to tell his diary that it had been 'a great day in the history of the Jewish people'. He now despatched Leopold Greenberg to Cairo, to approach Lord Cromer. Encouraged by Greenberg's positive report of their discussions, Herzl began to plan the huge industrial complex he would set up on the Sinai coast, and had a furious argument with Leon Kellner of the Actions Committee, who tried to tell him, quietly but firmly, that the whole project was impossible because of lack of water. Herzl charged Kellner with being an unimaginative pedant.

The British government's reply to Herzl's memorandum outlining his proposals for the Sinai scheme lifted his spirits to their highest pitch since meeting the Kaiser. The Foreign Office recommended that a small commission be sent to investigate conditions in the Sinai Peninsula, although from information he had received Lord Cromer feared 'that no sanguine hopes of success ought to be entertained'. However, pending a favourable report, and subject to agreement on certain details regarding taxation, maintenance of a defence corps, adoption by incoming settlers of Turkish citizenship under Egyptian law and a satisfactory definition of what was meant in Herzl's memorandum by 'the guaranteeing of Colonial rights', the Egyptian government would look helpfully on Jewish colonization in Sinai for as long as the British occupation continued.

Herzl was jubilant. At long last he had a document, 'a historic document', which – however provisionally – recognized him and the Zionist movement as serious negotiating partners. He had the proof to wave at sceptics. 'We are about to emerge from the realm of dreams and set our feet on solid ground,' he wrote to a distinguished new supporter, and in such a mood of elation, day-dreaming was permissible. He imagined a flourishing 'Egyptian Province of Judea', protected by Jewish soldiers under the command of Anglo-Egyptian officers, with its own elected Jewish governor.

Selecting the Jewish members of the commission and supervising every detail of their expedition was the best tonic for Herzl's deteriorating health. The seven-member commission, preceded by its scout Leopold Greenberg, and with Colonel 'Daniel Deronda' Goldsmid as its quartermaster and liaison officer, embarked for Egypt in January 1903. On 11 February, mounted on camels and escorted by a retinue of servants, cooks, water carriers and runners supplied by Thomas Cook, the expedition crossed the Suez Canal and headed north-east towards El Arish. Greenberg stayed in Cairo to negotiate with the Egyptian government, and Herzl wrote to Lord Rothschild: 'I hope that the expedition will return safe and sound in just a few weeks and soon afterward I shall be in possession of the charter.' But dealing with Egyptians was no more straightforward than bargaining with Turks. Worse still, Greenberg seemed to have become as slippery and elusive as the natives. Fretting in Vienna, Herzl received contradictory information from his agent, who was showing too much personal initiative for the leader's liking. It did not sit easily with Herzl to be an anxious onlooker rather than the puppet master. The last straw was a message from Greenberg that Lord Cromer had warned against Dr Herzl's involvement, which would wreck everything. The two men had a frosty meeting in Vienna, at which Greenberg presented the fruits of his diplomacy: a document from Boutros Ghali, the Egyptian prime minister, offering municipal rights to Jewish settlers in El Arish, but making no mention of the Zionist movement – or of Herzl. Totally meaningless, declared Herzl, and booked a berth for Egypt the following day, to take charge of negotiations himself.

It was an unfortunate decision. Lord Cromer preferred dealing with his English Jews, who at least spoke the language. He did not take kindly to being pressured by a pushy Viennese. Be careful of Herzl, he was later to warn the Foreign Office, 'He is a wild enthusiast.' The antipathy was mutual. 'Lord Cromer is the most unpleasant Englishman I ever faced,' Herzl jotted in his diary. The more Herzl ferreted, the more Cromer insisted that everything had to await the commission's survey. The expedition returned to Cairo three days later, its members sun-tanned and in high spirits; it had been good sport. Like the twelve spies, they extolled the excellent prospects of the land, before unveiling their caveat. Under present conditions, the country was quite unsuitable for European settlers; on the other hand, if adequate water resources could be found, it would support a sizeable population.

Herzl was sick at heart, his adversary smugly confirmed in his reservations but willing to give a little in victory. Cromer allowed Herzl to engage a local Belgian lawyer to draft a contract for leasing Sinai from the Egyptian government. He made clear that everything would hinge on the final decision of Sir William Garstyn, chief of works, who would be returning from home leave in May. And he intimated that in the meantime Colonel Goldsmid would be a happier choice to represent Zionist interests. Herzl left Egypt on 4 April. He went by way of Paris, to try to drum up, yet again, financial backing from French Jewry.

On 19 April, Easter Sunday, a government-sanctioned pogrom broke out in Kishinev, the capital of Bessarabia. While the police stood by, awaiting orders from the governor, a mob murdered forty-five Jews, injured a further eleven hundred, raped, pillaged, looted and razed fifteen hundred houses. The censored Russian press gave no details of the atrocity, but the reports of foreign journalists began to appear in western newspapers towards the end of April.

On 23 April, Herzl was cordially received in London by Joseph

Chamberlain, who regretted the unfavourable Sinai report which lay on his desk, but mentioned that on his recent travels in Africa he had seen exactly the country for Dr Herzl, were he to give up his sentimental attachment to Palestine. Herzl waved the bait aside. The national base had to be in or near Palestine. Uganda could be settled later; there were Jewish masses ready to emigrate, but for the present they needed El Arish.

On 30 April, Herzl returned to Vienna, where Julie, who had been under psychiatric care for some months, suffered a nervous breakdown.

On 1 May, Goldsmid cabled from Cairo that the irrigation experts were still conducting their surveys. Herzl urged him to press ahead; Chamberlain and Lansdowne could be relied upon.

On 11 May, a telegram from Goldsmid reported that the Egyptian government was rejecting the Sinai plan. Confirmation of the failure came a day later, and on 13 May a detailed letter from Goldsmid explained that Sir William Garstyn had pronounced against the plan; his computations concluded that five times as much water would be needed as was available, so Lord Cromer had recommended its abandonment.

On 16 May, Herzl wrote in his diary, 'I thought the Sinai project so certain that I would not buy a family vault in the Döblinger cemetery, where my father is provisionally laid to rest. Now I consider the plan so hopeless that I have been to the district court and have acquired vault 28.' When his father's body was exhumed and transferred to its new resting place, Herzl murmured, 'Soon, soon I too shall be lying down there.'

On 20 May, Joseph Chamberlain repeated his offer of a territory in East Africa, and Herzl accepted.

It is only by noting the proximity and cumulative pressure of these events, each one of major significance and affecting Herzl deeply as husband, son, Zionist leader and Jew, that one can begin to understand his astonishing and fateful about-turn over Uganda. His whole life, private and public, was coming apart at the seams. Herzl's erstwhile friend and rival, the playwright Arthur Schnitzler, once said of his characters, typical of Vienna at this time, that a sense of the end of their world envelops them, and that the end of their world is near. It is no accident that psychoanalysis, based on the exploration of ambivalence, hysteria and neurosis, originated in Vienna. That 'in the midst of life we are surrounded by death' was an awareness shared, among others, by

Freud, Schnitzler, Rilke, Brahms, Mahler – and Herzl. We do not know, at this distance, whether the venereal disease he had contracted as a young man was a factor in his physical deterioration. But more and more he begins to sound like Oswald Alving in Ibsen's *Ghosts*. The death wish was taking over.

After Kishinev, it was natural for him to imagine it encompassing his people too; he had been forecasting the catastrophe for years. The quest for a shelter became all-consuming. He instructed Greenberg, strategically placed in London and therefore forgiven his presumptuousness in Cairo, to pursue links with the British government. The upshot was Greenberg's meeting of 20 May with Chamberlain, who again refused to consider Cyprus and declined to interfere against Cromer's wishes concerning Sinai, but elaborated on his previous suggestion of a territory in East Africa, with a good climate, favourable conditions, and room to accommodate at least one million settlers, who would be granted self-administration and, naturally, a Jewish governor. The implications were so contentious that Greenberg kept his counsel, absolving himself by sending a detailed memorandum of the conversation to Herzl, and awaiting instructions. Herzl jumped at the offer and the London solicitors George, Roberts & Company (whose senior partner, Lloyd George, would be prime minister when the Balfour Declaration was issued) were instructed to draw up a draft charter to place before the next Zionist Congress in August.

Uganda was only one piece of a feverish mosaic Herzl was trying to construct, playing 'the politics of the hour' as he thought, but in fact concocting schemes that bore the hallmark of disordered reason. At one and the same time he was trying to revive the Sinai project, putting out feelers to the Belgian government about a concession in the Congo, to Portugal about Mozambique, and to Italy about Tripoli. He wanted to create half-a-dozen Jewish colonies in Africa, to be used as training bases for the eventual conquest of Palestine. Even Izzet Bey, the sultan's secretary, was reactivated with the promise of a bribe should the Mesopotamia offer be renewed. When Nordau (made privy to the Uganda proposal because Herzl wanted him to deal with the migration question at the Congress) pointed out the devastating consequences of substituting Africa for Zion, Herzl replied with a rambling, incoherent letter. Had Nordau lost faith in his judgement? Like Moses, he was leading the people to their goal via an apparent detour. When he could have acquired Palestine from the sultan, the Jews did not give him the money. So be it, Uganda would be where they broke ground, their first political colony. Nordau could guess his meaning – a miniature England in reverse.

Herzl's next move smacked of megalomania. He would go to Russia, over the anguished protests of Russian Zionists, to negotiate directly, if not with the tsar then with the loathed Wenzel von Plehve, minister of the interior, who had turned a blind eye to the Kishinev massacre. Herzl was impervious to counter-argument. The needs of the hour – and the figure he would cut at the Sixth Zionist Congress – demanded that he should intercede for Russia's Jews. On 5 August, Herzl set out for St Petersburg.

As it happened, there was a convergence of interest between Herzl's Zionist aims and the Russian government's reading of its perennial Jewish problem. He was, understandably, to find the greatest en-couragement for Jewish emigration from the country which had systematically discriminated against its five million Jews since the reign of Tsar Nicholas. The oleaginous von Plehve received Herzl cordially, and insisted that he was an ardent supporter of Zionism as a means of removing an alien and revolutionary element from Russian society. It distressed him that recently the Russian Zionists had been talking less about Palestine and more about culture, self-defence and national autonomy within the tsarist empire.

They were, said Herzl, like Columbus's sailors before land was sight-ed. If help were given to reach the shore, their grumbling would cease, likewise their addiction to socialism. It only required the Russian gov-ernment to convince the sultan to grant a Zionist charter for Palestine, to facilitate emigration with subsidies raised from the taxes paid by its Jewish subjects, and to allow banned Zionist societies to operate freely within the terms of the Basel programme, for the exodus to commence. An accord was struck, once it was understood that the Kishinev pogrom would be skirted discreetly at the forthcoming Congress. From von Plehve, Herzl went on to the equally accommodating minister of finance, Count Serge Witte, who proclaimed himself a friend of the Jews despite their involvement in pimping, usury, socialism and other ugly pursuits. Witte agreed to lift the ban on the purchase of shares in the Jewish Colonial Bank.

From a political perspective, Herzl could be pleased with his achievements in St Petersburg. The ban against Zionist organization and fund-raising was lifted; an assurance was given of government support for Jewish emigration and of interceding with the sultan; the carrot of an audience with the tsar himself – after the Congress – had been dangled. That was why, at a banquet in his honour arranged by the St Petersburg Zionists, he warned them against flirting with radical politics; there would be time enough for that when they were in their own land. Not everyone agreed; there were murmurings, to grow in volume at Basel, that by consorting with the likes of von Plehve and Witte, Herzl had pardoned the butchers of Kishinev.

His journey homewards through the Ukraine took on the trappings of a royal progress, a dying king receiving the homage of his people. As keenly as in 1896, on his first visit to Constantinople, Herzl responded to the vitality, the resilient fortitude and the sustaining faith of the Jewish masses who turned out to greet him. In Vilna, the police beat back the crowds with truncheons and ordered the cancellation of all public meetings and a luncheon for Herzl in the town hall. He was presented with the community's most precious possession, a Torah scroll, as 'the greatest son of the Jewish people', and barely held back his tears. That evening he paid a secret visit to the nearby ghetto, where the poverty shocked him, but he rejoiced in 'good ghetto talks' – he who had spent his life trying to eradicate in himself any trace of the ghetto. His train was due to leave after midnight, but a vast throng waited at the station for a glimpse of him. The police arrived, and brutally dispersed them. To the few communal representatives allowed on to the platform, Herzl cried, 'Gentlemen, do not lose courage. Better times are coming. That is what we are working for.' The leader who had nothing in common with his east European followers, save an intuitive compassion for their suffering, bade them his last farewell.

After just a day's rest in a mountain resort with his family, he proceeded to Basel for what he anticipated would be a stormy Congress. While in Vilna, he had received from Greenberg the definitive offer of a territory in East Africa for Jewish colonization from the British government, interested, in the choice phraseology of Sir Clement Hill of the Foreign Office, in 'any well-considered scheme for the amelioration of the position of the Jewish race'. But when Herzl laid the proposal before members of the Actions Committee on 21 August, their cool reaction led him to note bitterly that his efforts in England and

Russia had not 'merited so much as a word, or a smile of thanks'. The next day, the sabbath, after attending service at the synagogue, Herzl invited a few of his reliable subordinates to consider the British proposal, while he absented himself so as not to inhibit their discussion. After four hours of debate, their decision was that the offer should be submitted to the Congress.

This Herzl did in his opening address. The initial response was all he could have wished; emotion, prolonged applause, excitement among the 592 delegates. But once the euphoria had abated, a cooler mood of critical appraisal, led by the Russian faction, dominated speeches from the floor. Herzl had been careful to reaffirm ultimate priorities. 'Zion this certainly is not, and can never become. It is only a colonizational auxiliary or help — but, be it noted, on a national and state foundation.' All he asked for was support for a resolution to send a commission of experts to the proffered region. Nordau, wanting to back Herzl although his feelings were ambivalent, delivered a speech that did more harm than good when he described Uganda as a *Nachtasyl*, an overnight shelter, where persecuted Jews would learn the political arts to apply later in Palestine. But those persecuted Jews, among them the delegates from Kishinev, were the most vociferous against deviation from a national home in Palestine. Herzl stayed aloof from the debate, suffering heart palpitations and trying to win over support in private conversations. When the vote was called, 295 delegates declared in favour of the resolution, 175 against, with 99 abstentions. Pandemonium broke out. The Russian members of the Actions Committee left their seats on the rostrum and marched from the hall, followed by their supporters. Outside, they keened and wailed like Orthodox mourners at a funeral — mourning a dead Zion. Leon Trotsky, watching from the press gallery, predicted the inevitable collapse of the Zionist movement.

Late that night, the secessionists, or 'Zionists for Zion', as they were labelled, were still meeting in demoralized caucus. They had locked themselves in a room of the congress building. Herzl went to plead with them, but they would not let him in; someone shouted, 'Traitor.' When they unlocked the door, Herzl admonished them in the biblical tradition of Moses or Samuel chastizing the stiff-necked Children of Israel. He reminded them of his labours in the Zionist cause, despite their ingratitude, criticism and failure even to give financial support. He had remained loyal to the Basel platform, but if they would not now show trust in his diplomatic moves, he would happily step down for the tranquillity of private life. Shame-faced, the rejectionist caucus yielded and agreed to return to their seats for the morning session.

After such emotional upheaval, the last two days of the Congress passed in a wan spirit of exhausted catharsis. Only three delegates voted against Herzl's re-election as president of the movement. In his closing speech, which was intimate and conciliatory, he performed perhaps his most consummate dramatic gesture. Slowly raising his right arm, he declaimed in Hebrew the words of Psalm 137, 'If I forget thee, O Jerusalem . . .'

But the semblance of unity had been restored at too great a cost, as Herzl realized. The Uganda controversy had decisively split Zionism, and the division passed through him. In his hotel room, utterly exhausted, he told his friends, Israel Zangwill, Nordau and Cowen, what the consequences would be. Whether or not the Uganda expedition reported favourably, by the time of the Seventh Congress he would have obtained Palestine or would admit the futility of further efforts. In either case, he would resign.

The remaining eleven months of his life were a melancholy reprise of what had gone before: high-level audiences that signified nothing, worsening health and intensified acrimony over East Africa. Even that offer was wavering; British settlers were outraged at the prospect of their territory becoming 'Jewganda' and launched a protest campaign in *The Times* and other newspapers. Julie nearly died of appendicitis aggravated by pneumonia, and Herzl suffered another heart attack. They were, he wrote to Wolffsohn, 'fearful days of horror'. In October, eight Russian Zionists, summoned by Menachem Ussishkin, met secretly in Kharkov and voted to present Herzl with an ultimatum. Either he gave up his authoritarian method of decision-taking, and renounced in writing the East African project, or they would organize an alternative Zionist representation. It was a calculated attempt to overthrow Herzl, fuelled by a mixture of principle and personal vendetta. Ussishkin, a stocky barrel of a man, fiercely committed to Palestinian colonization since his Chibbat Zion days, had been on a visit to the Rothschild settlements during the Basel Congress. He gave notice of the intended putsch in an open letter to *Die Welt*, which announced that he would not be bound by the resolution to send an expedition to Uganda.

Herzl published a withering reply alongside the letter. He condemned Ussishkin's meddling in Palestine, and explained condescendingly, as though to a simple peasant, that land purchase without the shield of a protective charter would do serious damage to the Zionist cause. Herr Ussishkin, a worthy man but blinkered by the prejudice felt against the educated by the ignorant, did not seem to understand that there was a vast difference between private and national acquisition. He could buy up every plot of land in his native Ekaterinoslav, but politically the area would still belong to the ruler of Russia. How unfortunate it would be if the purchase of land in Palestine were left to one so inept and obtrusive. It was an offensive rebuttal, but Herzl no longer cared. He had already drafted his proposed resignation letter to the Jewish people. When two hapless representatives of the Kharkov rebels turned up in Vienna to present their ultimatum, Herzl treated them with patrician disdain: 'I kicked them out with superb politeness.'

In December, at a Chanukkah ball in Paris, a deranged Russian student fired two shots at Nordau, shouting, 'Death to Nordau, the East African!' Herzl awaited a similar act, the pistol to be loaded, he was convinced, in Russia. At the year's end he sent a confidential letter to members of the Actions Committee acknowledging the collapse of the Ugandan initiative. Still he went through the motions — writing letters, establishing diplomatic contacts, floating schemes. In January 1904 he visited Rome, to meet the pope and King Victor Emmanuel III. The pope could not approve of Zionism, because the Hebrew people had rejected the Saviour. If they settled in Palestine, the Catholic Church would be ready to convert them. The conversation with the king was more affable. Victor Emmanuel revealed that an ancestor of his had attached himself to Shabbetai Tzevi, and quizzed Herzl about messianism. Herzl explained that in Palestine he had been careful not to ride a white donkey or horse, to avoid being taken for the Messiah.

A few weeks later, the writer Stefan Zweig met Herzl in a Viennese park, and expressed shock at how ill he looked. 'It was my mistake that I began too late,' Herzl replied, '. . . one cannot buy back lost years.'

On 11 April, he convened an extraordinary session in Vienna of the Actions Committee. Zionist leaders from ten European countries and the United States, including Ussishkin and the Kharkov rebels, attended. The patriarch of the clan was gathering his truculent sons around him for his blessing. He overlooked attacks on his leadership and appealed for unity. Congress decisions had to be obeyed. Before him, Zionism had been a loose federation of ineffectual groups; he had shown them the path to the objective, through organization of the people with Congress as its forum. Originally, he had supported the idea of a Jewish state anywhere, but in the course of time and learning about the Jews, he now understood that only in Palestine would they find a solution to their problem. Yet whatever their differences of principle and political expediency, maintaining the unity of the movement was essential. He reminded them of Solomon's judgement: 'The one who was prepared to cut the baby in two was not the real mother.' It was Herzl's swansong as Zionist leader; his critics went home with effusive expressions of harmony and reconciliation.

At the end of April, his doctors diagnosed myocarditis, and he was ordered to Franzensbad for a cure. On 2 May, he celebrated his forty-fourth birthday, and wrote fondly to his wife. When facing imminent death, the misunderstandings of fifteen years of unhappy marriage did not loom so large after all. To a Russian visitor he said, 'Let us not fool ourselves. With me, it is after the third curtain.' He returned to Vienna, before trying the recuperative qualities of Edlach on the Semmering. Briefly, his condition improved; he even managed walks in the garden. But he relapsed irrevocably, and the family gathered; his mother's presence gave him great comfort. His last days were spent in feverish hallucinations, switching between memories of Palestine and addressing the Zionist Congress in Basel. On the afternoon of 3 July he died.

His death prompted an effusion of grief, tinged with guilt, throughout the Jewish world. More than 6000 mourners followed his coffin to the Döblinger cemetery, where he was to be laid beside his father 'until the day when the Jewish people transfer my remains to Palestine'. The *Neue Freie Presse*, which had avoided any mention of Zionism during his lifetime, devoted two sentences to it in an obituary. In all the outpourings of public and private desolation, it was the London *Jewish Chronicle* which captured the symbolic potency of Herzl's career and early death.

. . . It is hard to believe that this imposing and picturesque figure, who seemed to personify the romance, as well as the travail of his people, has passed into eternity. His restless personality, moving from Jewry to Jewry, with its glowing message, 'A flag and an Ideal!', had grown to be an omnipresent and active element in Jewish life . . . When Dr Herzl began his formidable task, he had against him the indifference of his people, the heterogeneousness of their composition, and the overpowering facts of the political situation . . . Yet this Vienna journalist, unknown beyond a certain limited area . . . welded the utterly diverse Jewries of the world into a compact and homogeneous force; he obtained the ear of the press, as well as of the proudest courts in Europe, and most wonderful of all, he kept his army and his own leadership intact from the day he took up his great parable to the tragic hour of his death . . . Dr Herzl led a great movement; or rather, he voiced a great despair. At a moment when the Jews of Eastern Europe had abandoned hope of justice from the nations, he came forward boldly to give tongue to their feelings and conduct them to the only alternative goal, as he conceived it – a separate existence in their ancient home . . . Above all, he made the peoples of the earth realise that there was a Jewish Question to be solved. Never before had that baffling problem occupied the serious thoughts of Christendom to the extent that it does today . . . His greatest purpose of all, however, remains unachieved. He has barely been privileged to set eyes on the Promised Land, towards which his steps were steadily set. Cut down in the flower of manhood, and after efforts all too brief, he leaves the bulk of his people still in bondage, and with the gates of their home relentlessly barred against them.

Moses, Shabbetai Tzevi, 'the Parnell of the Jews'[1] – the comparisons came easily, each with its element of truth. Like only a handful in history, Herzl had transcended the prosaic details of his individuality to take on mythic resonance as the personification of his people. A precursor of the twentieth century in his awareness of the power of publicity, public relations and technology – of making bricks without straw – he coaxed and inveigled Zionism into the forefront of public attention. A rootless Jewish cosmopolitan, the damaged offspring of the decline of Austro-Hungarian culture, he was, first and last, a man of the theatre. His implacable critic Achad Ha-Am, resolutely earth-bound, suspicious of gesture, understood that. In a grudging eulogy, he wrote, 'He died at the right time. His career and activities during the past seven years had the character of a romantic tale. If some great writer had written it, he too would have had his hero die after the Sixth Congress.'

1. Charles Stewart Parnell (1846–91). Irish politician and nationalist leader.

7

Achad Ha-Am – Zionism for the Elect

After the first Zionist Congress in 1897, Herzl, by nature not prone to modesty, had declared, 'At Basel I founded the Jewish state.' After the same congress, Achad Ha-Am, by temperament not prone to humour, noted, 'At Basel I sat solitary among my friends, like a mourner at a wedding feast.' The disparity between their respective reactions went deeper than differences of personality, to the nature of the Jewish nationalist project that divided Zionists long after both had died.

Born near Kiev, in the Ukraine, in 1856, Asher Ginsberg (he signed the pen-name Achad Ha-Am, 'One of the People', to his first essay published in 1889) came from the ghetto aristocracy. His father was a rabbi and tax farmer, and his family were closely connected to the Chasidic Chabad movement. We learn from autobiographical snippets that his education was so pious that his teacher was forbidden to instruct him in the letters of the Russian alphabet, for fear of heresy; nevertheless, he read Russian by the age of eight, from deciphering the signs on shopfronts in his town. At eleven, he became absorbed in algebra and geometry, which provided some compensation for having been forced to give up smoking, on doctor's orders. By mid-adolescence, Ginsberg was regarded as a considerable Talmudic scholar.

In 1868, his family moved to a country estate leased by his wealthy father. Showing no interest then or later in nature and the countryside, the young boy shut himself in his room and began to read the works of medieval Jewish philosophers, particularly Moses Maimonides. From there, it was a short step to the scandalous writings of the modern Hebrew Enlightenment, and then the 'forbidden' books of secular literature and philosophy in Russian and German. He discovered the positivist thinkers, Comte and D. I. Pisarev, and lost his religious faith. A compulsive autodidact, he also mastered English and Latin.

The years until 1886, when his family moved to Odessa, were painful, and marked Ginsberg for life. Trapped from the age of twenty in an arranged marriage to an ailing wife with whom he had little affinity,

Ginsberg made feeble attempts to study in Vienna, Berlin and Breslau, but after a few weeks self-doubt and stirrings of duty forced him home. The move to Odessa was dictated not from choice, but because of a new government ukase forbidding Jews to lease land. It was a blessing in disguise for Ginsberg, opening up intellectual horizons after the suffocating constraints of rural existence. He joined the Odessa branch of Chibbat Zion in 1886. Three years later, he published his first article in the Hebrew literary journal *Ha-Melitz*, 'This is Not the Way', a critique of the settlement policy of the movement. His argument was that those who had gone to Palestine had been ill-prepared, materially and spiritually. The prime task of the Jewish national movement should be to imbue its followers with zeal for cultural regeneration – a mission that could not be accomplished within a year or even a decade.

The tenor of his philosophy was already set, strongly influenced by the evolutionist theories of Herbert Spencer, to whose writings he had been drawn after immersing himself in the British empirical tradition of John Locke, David Hume and John Stuart Mill. He signed the article Achad Ha-Am, 'to make clear that I was not a writer, and had no intention of becoming one, but was just incidentally expressing my opinion on the subject about which I wrote as "one of the people" who was interested in his people's affairs'. Such posed self-deprecation was characteristic, and carping came more naturally to him than approval. Another, younger Odessan, the short story writer Isaac Babel, said of himself that he had 'spectacles on his nose and autumn in his heart'; this was a fitting description of Achad Ha-Am too.

'This is Not the Way' was critical not only of Chibbat Zion but by implication of Pinsker's leadership of it. It won him instant notoriety, and a secretive coven of like-minded intellectuals gathered around him, calling itself B'nei Moshe (Sons of Moses), with the aim of putting his ideals into practice. Exclusive, conspiratorial, dedicated more to keeping undesirables out than broadening its appeal, B'nei Moshe never numbered more than one hundred members, and fell apart after the First Zionist Congress. Its history, and Achad Ha-Am's involvement in it, encapsulated his future role on the fringes of the Zionist movement, declining public office because he doubted his capacity for leadership, but finding it easier to damn with faint praise from the study. His fastidious, donnish manner and the spare, lucid style of his Hebrew prose won him respect, and even love, any expression of which would have sorely embarrassed him. He was, wrote the poet Chaim Nachman Bialik, the star around which the lesser planets revolved, mentor and doyen to a galaxy of talented younger admirers which included Martin Buber and Chaim Weizmann; but, as with many a prim dialectician, not above pique, spitefulness and a sense of unappreciated worth, especially when faced with glamorous crowd-pleasers like Herzl.

In 1891, Achad Ha-Am paid his first visit to the new Jewish settlements in Palestine. His dispirited appraisal provided the basis for an important essay, 'The Truth from the Land of Israel'. He approved of the attempt to create Jewish villages by daily work on the ancient soil, but deplored the land speculation which, unless stopped, would leave an indelible mark on the economic and social fabric of the new society. The pervasiveness of traditional Orthodoxy appalled him:

I went first, of course, to the Wailing Wall. There I found many of our brothers, residents of Jerusalem, standing and praying with raised voices – also with wan faces, strange movements, and weird clothing – everything befitting the appearance of that terrible Wall. I stood and watched them, people and Wall, and one thought filled the chambers of my heart: these stones are testaments to the destruction of our land. And these men? The destruction of our people.

In other words, religious petrification had all but destroyed the Jewish spirit. The paramount task of Zionism was not to indulge the fantasy of mass immigration to Palestine, but to prepare for a Jewish spiritual revival, slowly and selectively. Achad Ha-Am was a cultural élitist, his Palestinian colony for the chosen few who would express the new Jewish *Volksgeist*. He picked over this theme endlessly in his subsequent writings.

What distinguishes 'The Truth from the Land of Israel' from the gushing accounts of other visitors to the Zionist enterprise is the sober – one might almost say malevolent – realism he brings to the problems. High among them is the question of the indigenous Arab population. He says at the outset that it is an illusion to imagine an empty country: 'We tend to believe abroad that Palestine is nowadays almost completely deserted, a non-cultivated wilderness, and anyone can come there and buy as much land as his heart desires. But in reality this is not the case. It is difficult to find anywhere in the country Arab land which lies fallow . . .' The behaviour of Jewish settlers towards the Arabs disturbed him. They had not learned from historical experience as a minority within a wider population, but reacted with the cruelty of slaves who had suddenly become kings, infringing Arab boundaries, resorting to violence and treating their neighbours with contempt. The Arab, it was true, respected the language of strength, but not if it was applied un-justly. 'The Arab, like all Semites, has a sharp mind and is full of cunning . . .' He knew full well what Zionist intentions were in the country, as did the seemingly inert Turkish government, and 'if the time should come when the lives of our people in Palestine should develop to the extent that, to a smaller or greater degree they usurp the place of the local population, the latter will not yield easily.' Upsetting the balance of national forces in Palestine would inevitably lead to a clash.

Achad Ha-Am, the philosophical observer rather than the man of action, was better at tracing the moral dimensions of a situation than suggesting solutions. He has no answer for the confrontation he fore-sees, except to imply that a change of Jewish attitude might lessen Arab hostility; that, and limiting settlement to those fitted to be the beacons of a Jewish cultural renaissance.

In 1893, he paid a second visit to Palestine, and wrote another essay, with the same title and equally sombre conclusions. He added some negative recommendations: that viniculture be suspended pending greater experience; that the practice of doling out subventions to the settlers be abandoned, since it sapped their independence; and that the educational system in the Jewish schools be overhauled. His exposés provoked a storm of protest among Chibbat Zion followers, and he was on his way to becoming the most-hated figure in Zionist circles, 'a man of strife and contention', as he remarked smugly in his reminiscences. Whether he wanted it or not, and despite protestations of preferring anonymity, he had entered the public domain, a writer whose distinct-ive Hebrew prose and controversial views on Jewish culture and nationalism guaranteed instant recognition. By 1894 he had published enough articles for a volume, *Al Parashat D'rachim* (At the Parting of the Ways), illustrating his conviction that the Jewish people had reached crisis point. Either it could continue along the path of assimilation and dispersal, or it could concentrate on national and cultural renascence. He has no doubt which is the right choice. In one of the volume's best-known essays, 'Slavery in Freedom', he inveighs against those academ-ics, generals and statesmen in emancipated Europe who had bartered their Jewish souls for civil rights and universal ideals. Theirs was a moral and intellectual degradation far more terrible than the backwardness and poverty of Russian Jewry, which could express itself without self-justification, and no more needed to ask why it remained Jewish than he needed to ask why he remained his father's son.

The inherent suspicion with which Achad Ha-Am viewed Herzl and other west European Jews stemmed from this combination of personal prejudice and intellectual conviction. He disliked assimilated Jews for their easy airs and graces and perhaps secretly envied them, but he couched his hostility in lofty arguments about the meaning of Jewish survival. In his preface to the volume, Achad Ha-Am, with weary impatience at the public's inability to comprehend his message, tries to summarize his philosophy of Zionism – and leaves his readers still more perplexed. He rejects the two prevalent, antithetical views about how to build up Jewish settlement in Palestine – by glossy propaganda, which hopes to induce pioneers to emigrate in their tens of thousands, or by its opposite, psychological and spiritual emancipation of Jewry before practical colonization begins.

Both views, he says, are wrong. Propaganda has failed to attract settlers, and education at the expense of physical effort will not prepare the people for their future redemption. What must be imbued is the *essence* of Chibbat Zion, Love of Zion itself, as an attitude of mind and state of feeling, shared by every Jew irrespective of rank, class or party, and impelling all of them to bend every effort to regaining the possibility of a normal and natural life which will permit the full expression of the Jewish spirit. Before the Jews can be concentrated physically in Zion, their hearts and minds must be concentrated spiritually on the love of Zion. That does not require extensive colonization in Palestine, but a few things well done. 'A single model colony, which might win the hearts of the Jews in Palestine, would be worth more than ten tumble-down colonies which depend on our loyalty to Palestine.' Such opacity of thought, directed at those who sought in Zionism a quick release from persecution and poverty, had not endeared Achad Ha-Am to his readership, as he conceded. 'Perhaps in their collected form these articles of mine may meet with more success . . . In any case, they will provide material for the future student of the views and policies which developed out of Chibbat Zion in our generation.'

For a while, Achad Ha-Am retired from literature, but in 1896 the failure of his business (about which he was characteristically reticent) compelled him to take up his pen to make a living. Through the good offices of Kalonymos Wissotsky, a wealthy tea merchant and philanthropic Zionist, he was appointed editor of a new Hebrew monthly, to which he gave the name of *Ha-Shiloah*, after Isaiah 8:6: 'Forasmuch as this people has refused the waters of Shiloah that go softly . . .'. The people might prefer dramatic gestures to going softly, but Achad Ha-Am planned to teach them the value of gradual evolution. He wanted to produce a Hebrew-language journal that would stand comparison with periodicals like the *Nineteenth Century* or the *Revue des Deux Mondes*, despite Hebrew journalism having been in patchy existence for only forty years and the first modern Hebrew novel published as recently as 1853.

The relationship between the prim, exacting pedant and the chaotic world of Hebrew letters was a spectacular mismatch, a tragicomedy of epic proportions. For six years Achad Ha-Am endured the labour of Sisyphus. He was affronted to the core of his being by the sloppy writing, poor taste, unpunctuality and casual failure to acknowledge payment of his contributors. He hacked and rewrote their submissions when not consigning them to the wastepaper basket. 'If I undertook to enter into correspondence about articles that I do not accept, life would be too short . . . I advise you to give up writing, as your attempts show no sign of promise' was a typical response. In meticulous business dealings with his Warsaw publishers, and in the Olympian standards of editorial rectitude he set — not even for a contribution from his idol Herbert Spencer would he compromise, he once told a petitioner — Achad Ha-Am grew steadily more autocratic, demanding and insufferable on behalf of a magazine that never had more than 1200 subscribers in Russia and abroad. The influence of *Ha-Shiloah*, though, far exceeded its readership. And despite a lofty statement of aims in its first number, which made no reference to Chibbat Zion or Palestine but addressed the wider issues of Jewish culture, Achad Ha-Am soon used his position to mount a sustained attack on Herzlian Zionism. The publication of *Der Judenstaat* a few months before the monthly's first appearance in October 1896, and the First Zionist Congress of August 1897, were the goads.

Herzl had tried unsuccessfully to woo Achad Ha-Am into attending at Basel as a delegate. In the end, he consented to be present as an observer only, to restrain the 'rabble of youngsters, in years as in understanding', who made up the Russian caucus. Any hopes he might have nurtured of bringing sobriety to bear on proceedings were swept away in the fervour of the moment. He was overlooked, and piqued accordingly. He was also confirmed in his deep personal animus against Herzl. 'I could not avoid the impression of a *feuilletonist* spirit running through his ideas and opinions,' he wrote to a Moscow correspondent. He was scandalized by Herzl's insouciant answer to the question of what would happen if the National Fund he wished to propose failed to reach its target. According to Achad Ha-Am, Herzl replied, 'What does it matter? If the amount is too small we will keep it a secret and tell nobody.' Such a cavalier attitude to money outraged Achad Ha-Am, who was convinced that Herzl tried to avoid him after that conversation, although he contrived a second exchange of icy formality with the leader. (Herzl, who did not confide his impression to his diary, no doubt felt that he was dealing with a puritanical maiden aunt.) Achad Ha-Am concluded, 'All he said convinced me that he really had nothing of importance to communicate.' So Herzl basked in his public triumph and the prospect of audiences with the great and powerful, while Achad Ha-Am made his way back to Odessa, a spurned mourner at the wedding feast. Revenge came a few weeks later, in a dismissive *Ha-Shiloah* article about the Congress.

After restating his familiar moral plea – 'the emancipation of ourselves from the inner slavery and the spiritual degradation which assimilation has produced in us' – he gave full rein to sarcasm at the expense of those who no longer talked of Chibbat Zion, but prefered to call it by the new name of *Zionism*. 'The founders of this movement are "Europeans", and, being expert in the ways of diplomacy and the procedure of latter-day political parties, they bring these ways and procedure with them to the "Jewish State".' Most of the delegates, who represented the down-trodden masses looking for redemption, had been duped by promises and expectations that could not be fulfilled. At risk of being called a traitor, he, Achad Ha-Am, would warn them of the truth, as he had done seven years previously in 'The Truth from the Land of Israel'. Much sport had been made at Basel of previous colonization efforts, as if one had only to sit back and let diplomacy finish its work. The result would be despair and disillusion, because the 'salvation of Israel will be achieved by *prophets*, not by *diplomats*'.

Four months later, in response to the storm of indignation his bitter little article had aroused, he returned to the attack in a longer, wider-ranging, but no less critical essay, 'The Jewish State and the Jewish Problem'. The essay was his natural *métier*, anything longer was beyond his energies, in contrast to prolix wordspinners like Herzl or Nordau. 'The Jewish State and the Jewish Problem' was his Zionist credo, a rebuttal of *Der Judenstaat*. He took aim at his favourite targets: the susceptibility of the masses to messiah figures, especially if they were Jews of the west who were so au courant that they no longer even spoke Hebrew; the contrast between the moral poverty of emancipated Jewry and the material poverty of eastern Jewry; the vanity of imagining that diplomatic overtures to the great powers would bring about an In-gathering of the Exiles in Palestine; and the crucial distinction between Zionism and Chibbat Zion, being the qualitative difference between a state of Germans or Frenchmen of the Jewish race, and a *Jewish* state, radiating the spirit of Judaism to all the communities of the Diaspora.

'The Jewish State and the Jewish Problem' is Achad Ha-Am's most typical Zionist piece. It glitters with sharp insights and shrewd aphorisms, and its characteristic vein of sarcasm is lightened by glimpses of what might be ironic humour. Stylistically, it is a deft blend of modern and classical Hebrew, at once idiomatic yet biblically allusive, as in his mocking description of the Basel Congress, 'The meeting was magnificent, every speaker was a Demosthenes,[1] the resolutions were carried by acclamation, all those present were swept off their feet and shouted with one voice, "We will do and obey!" – in a word, everything was delightful, entrancing, perfect.' He caresses with feline praise, before inserting the sword.

The Congress itself still produces a literature of its own. Pamphlets specially devoted to its achievements appear in several languages . . . and, needless to say, the 'Zionist' organ itself [*Die Welt*] endeavours to maintain the impression which the Congress made, and . . . searches the press of every nation and every land, and wherever it finds a favourable mention, even in some insignificant journal published in the language of one of the smaller European nationalities, it immediately gives a summary of the article, with much jubilation. Only one small nation's language has thus far not been honoured with such attention . . . I mean Hebrew.

1. Demosthenes (383–322 BC). Athenian statesman, generally regarded as the greatest of Greek orators.

Unpopular though it is to swim against the stream, Achad Ha-Am feels the duty to elaborate on the brief criticisms he had voiced in his original article.

He starts with Nordau's opening address, which had surveyed the material and spiritual suffering of European Jewry. In the east it was caused by the daily struggle for a crust of bread; in the west it was the pain of constant rejection by fellow citizens. Nordau's answer, and the impetus of the entire Congress, was to seek an escape from these troubles by establishing a Jewish state. What a fanciful delusion, says Achad Ha-Am. Such a state – allowing, for the sake of argument, that Turkey and the other great powers would consent to its establishment – would never be economically viable. The world was now one great market and no nation on earth, not even the strongest and richest, could create in a new country instant sources of livelihood to sustain its population. Jews flocking to Palestine in the search for liberty would be driven from it by the deadliest of enemies – hunger. Yet how blithely the speeches at Basel had referred to a National Fund of £10 million for agricultural settlement, when the bulk of Jewry expected to contribute subsisted below the poverty-line. And realistically *thousands* of millions would be required for such a venture.

The end result would mean no significant improvement in the material condition of world Jewry, because due to natural population increase the Palestinian state would not be able to welcome more than a handful of new immigrants, and the communities outside Palestine would face the same struggles as before. Bitter though it was to acknowledge, the Ingathering of the Exiles was unattainable by natural means. Since that was so, the material situation of Jews would always depend on the economic condition of the countries in which they lived, not on the establishment or otherwise of a Jewish state. The only valid basis for Zionism was thus not in the material but in the moral sphere.

That leads Achad Ha-Am to his familiar complaint against western Jewry, couched in biting generalities but with one individual – Herzl – as his clear target. The emancipated western Jew, disappointed at his lukewarm reception in wider society, casts about for a purposeful role in the Jewish community, but with no greater success, 'because Jewish culture has played no part in his education from childhood, and is a closed book to him'. In his frustration he becomes enamoured of the idea of re-establishing in the land of his ancestors a Jewish state — 'a state arranged and organized exactly after the pattern of other states'. Mere contemplation of the vision brings him relief. 'He has an opportunity for organized work, for political excitement . . . and he feels that thanks to this ideal he stands once more spiritually erect and has regained human dignity . . . So he devotes himself to the ideal with all the ardour of which he is capable; he gives rein to his fancy, and lets it soar as it will, up above reality and the limitations of human power. For it is not the attainment of the ideal that he needs: its pursuit alone is sufficient to cure him of his moral sickness, which is a consciousness of inferiority . . .' This, and this alone, is the basis of western Zionism. How different had been the origin and development of eastern Chibbat Zion, which was not satisfied with noble sentiments and fine phrases, but had expressed itself in concrete activity to combat material degradation: the establishment of colonies in Palestine.

Scrupulous logician that he is, Achad Ha-Am has now argued himself into a corner. No one had been more dismissive than he of the feeble colonizing efforts of the Chovevei Zion, but his heart lies in the east, not with the assimilated west. He extricates himself by proposing that a moral tragedy affects eastern Jewry quite as profoundly as it does western Jewry, even though its causes are different. 'In the west it is the problem of the Jews, in the east the problem of Judaism. The one weighs on the individual, the other on the nation. The one is felt by Jews who have had a European education, the other by Jews whose education has been Jewish.' In other words, the essence of the problem is religious and cultural. Not only Jews but Judaism are in the process of coming out of the ghetto. This contact with modernity has overturned Judaism's traditional defences. It can no longer survive in isolation, but wants to absorb and utilize elements of general culture. But the conditions of life in exile are not conducive; the spirit of the times requires the individual to merge his identity into the national *Volksgeist*. Thus Judaism in exile must sacrifice its being and national unity to the characteristics and requirements of each country of the dispersion. The will to live which had previously sustained it is no longer enough. Hence the need for Judaism to return to its historic centre, to pursue its natural development and contribute to the common cultural stock of humanity. It requires little for this, certainly not a state; simply the creation in its native land of a good-sized settlement of Jews, working in every branch of culture from agriculture and handicrafts to science and literature.

Then from this centre the spirit of Judaism will go forth to the great circumference, to all the communities of the Diaspora, and will breathe new life into them and preserve their unity; and when our national culture in Palestine has attained that level, we may be confident that it will produce men in the country who will be able, on a favourable opportunity, to establish a state which will be a *Jewish* state, and not merely a state of Jews.

This concern to preserve the spirit of Judaism is, says Achad Ha-Am, the true meaning of Chibbat Zion, so odd and unintelligible to politicized western Zionists – and equally baffling, one might add, to his fellow eastern Zionists. His complicated attempt to accommodate the theories of Hegel, Spencer and Darwin within a definition of Zionism, which also seeks to embrace the aims of the Haskalah without outraging the guardians of traditional Judaism, was typical of an intelligence which could identify every species of nettle but recoiled from grasping any of them.

Achad Ha-Am repeats a lesson he had taught in a previous essay, 'Imitation and Assimilation', published in 1894. The secret of Jewish survival was that the prophets had warned the people to respect only spiritual power and not to worship material power. Any political goal not based on the national culture would seduce Jews from loyalty to spiritual ideals. All the current leaders of Jewry were far removed from Judaism and its values, and would seek to impose on a Jewish state the foreign culture they had imbibed in Germany, France or wherever. Such a state, discarding its heritage for an ersatz culture, would ruin the Jewish people. He also makes a pertinent geopolitical point. Palestine would never be allowed to idle along as an inconsequential, minor country. Its location and its religious significance would keep it constantly under the scrutiny of the great powers.

The essay ends on a note of defiance. Achad Ha-Am apologizes for some of the harsh expressions used in the article written immediately after the Basel Congress. But, as regards the question at issue, he has nothing to retract. On the contrary, subsequent events have convinced him that 'though I wrote in anger, I did not write in error'. Such unwonted candour reveals the depth of Achad Ha-Am's bitterness towards Herzl and his entourage of western Zionists. The sense of inferiority he ascribes to them was what he felt in their self-assured presence. A few weeks after the Basel Congress he had sent Nordau a copy of his published essays with an accompanying letter of startling toadyism from one whose customary correspondence was terse to the point of brusqueness. Perhaps he regretted his gesture. Those who try to douse their personal emotions to elevate reason — 'The Supremacy of Reason' was the title Achad Ha-Am chose for a major essay on Moses Maimonides — generally give vent to the normal run of human frailties, vanities and jealousies by making them issues of principle.

It was 1911 before Achad Ha-Am attended another Zionist Congress. He spent the intervening years sniping from the pages of *Ha-Shiloah* and denigrating Herzl's political Zionism to friend and foe alike, while propagating his own version of cultural Zionism. One of the charges that he found particularly offensive was that his hostility to Herzl was motivated by jealousy. Never, he pointed out, had he permitted attacks of a personal nature against Herzl in the columns of *Ha-Shiloah*, only arguments on the merits of the case. In private correspondence he was less circumspect, angry about 'the haze of legend' that surrounded every activity of the diplomat from Vienna who would 'buy Palestine from the Turk' and whose gullible supporters 'followed him like sheep, without reflection or criticism'. He had more pressing anxieties, but returned obsessively to a contest in which public sympathy was against him. The continuation of *Ha-Shiloah*, his major source of income, was in constant jeopardy, and in 1899 his father died, leaving him with a mother and two sisters to support — 'a father of two families', as he put it.

That same year he paid his third visit to Palestine, on behalf of the Odessa Committee, to report on colonization activities. On his return he wrote two lengthy and critical articles, printed in instalments over several months; the first, 'The Jaffa Schools', was about the educational deficiencies of the two schools which the Chovevei Zion maintained there; the other, 'The Yishuv and Its Patrons', was a detailed exposé of the economic harm caused by the spoon-feeding of Baron de Rothschild's agents. When it was decided to send a delegation to Paris to make representations to the baron, Achad Ha-Am was a member. His colleagues' timorous approach to the autocratic philanthropist outraged Achad Ha-Am, who lambasted donor and supplicants in another acid article, 'Delegates of a Penniless People'.

Early in 1902, to commemorate the tenth anniversary of Leon Pinsker's death, he wrote a piece entitled 'Pinsker and Political Zionism', which, by neat sleight of historical revisionism, appropriated the former president of Chibbat Zion not only as the superior precursor of Herzlian Zionism but as the originator of cultural Zionism. A far cry from his veiled judgements on Pinsker in 'This is Not the Way', but any stick would do to beat Herzl. His essay did help to rehabilitate the reputation of the author of *Auto-Emancipation*, but only by making exaggerated claims for the perspicacity of a pamphlet which 'fifteen years before Herzl, worked out the whole theory of political Zionism from beginning to end, with a logical thoroughness and an elevation of style unequalled in any subsequent work'. Only a fellow writer would appreciate the wound of having one's literary style denigrated – a dig Achad Ha-Am repeats. 'Herzl's pamphlet [*Der Judenstaat*] has the air of being a translation of Pinsker's from the language of the ancient Prophets into that of modern journalism.' Pinsker's pamphlet is the only one worthy of first place in the *literature* of Zionism, compared with the stream of new pamphlets, 'mostly poor and tasteless *rechauffés*' being poured forth daily. Pinsker was the originator of political Zionism, Herzl merely its apostle. How strange that the spreader of the gospel should fail to acknowledge its creator, claiming it as his own, 'in an inferior form, it is true'. The result was that Pinsker's political Zionism had been debased by his successors, who, having impaired its moral foundations, made promises they could neither fulfil nor repudiate.

In September 1902 the Russian Zionists convened their own conference in Minsk. Cultural revival was the main topic on the agenda, and Achad Ha-Am the keynote speaker. He delivered a magnificent lecture; scholarly, wide-ranging, rigorously argued and a persuasive plea for the establishment of a spiritual centre in Palestine which in the long term would prove at least as valuable as material havens for the downtrodden Jewish masses. 'The establishment of a single great school of learning or art in Palestine, or of a single academy of language and literature, would in my opinion be a national achievement of first-rate importance, and would contribute more to the attainment of our aims than a hundred agricultural settlements.' The lecture was enthusiastically received, and the conference resolved to set up a cultural commission with a broad mandate to develop Jewish education. Acclamation was sweet to Achad Ha-Am, which perhaps emboldened him at the expense of judgement;

or perhaps personal and professional problems were coming to a head. Whatever the reason, within a few weeks he was embroiled in a controversy beside which all previous ones paled.

The cause was publication of Herzl's utopian idyll, *Altneuland*, which Achad Ha-Am reviewed for *Ha-Shiloah*. Even by his exacting standards, it was a savage hatchet piece, dismissive of the novel both as literature and as political prophecy. Apart from the absurdity of imagining millions of penniless Jews settled within twenty years in a barren land which could not support its existing Arab population, what, Achad Ha-Am wanted to know, was specifically *Jewish* about such a society? The name Zion did not once appear. There were theatres, where plays could be heard in several European languages; there was an opera house, an academy on the French model, in Jerusalem a temple in the best German style; there were museums, concerts, newspapers in many languages, all the manifestations of a civilized and cosmopolitan way of life. Only one thing was missing in this liberal, bourgeois Arcadia: Hebrew. The language of the proletariat appeared to be Yiddish, of the upper classes a variety of tongues, but principally German. The only Hebrew to be heard was at synagogue services, or in the song of welcome sung by schoolchildren to admiring visitors. There was no trace of Hebrew literature or culture, or of a recognizably Jewish pattern of life and thought, nothing to differentiate Herzl's society from one African negroes would create for themselves, given the opportunity. The absence of anything original or distinctively Jewish was the wish fulfilment of the assimilationist mentality, that bane of emancipated western Jews.

As was his wont, Achad Ha-Am affected surprise at the stir caused by his review: he was a simple-souled truth-teller. Herzl responded with diplomacy. On his behalf, Nordau riposted in the columns of *Die Welt*, mocking Achad Ha-Am's ignorance of the literary convention whereby a novelist makes his characters speak in the language of the story, and suggesting that the reviewer's problem was that he could not, or would not, leave his ghetto. Herzl's Jewish citizens of *Altneuland* were far from aping western culture since they had helped to shape it, and it belonged to them as much as it did to the French, the Germans and the English. The values of that cultural heritage were still alien to the Jews of eastern Europe, but they should be grateful to western Jewry for opening its possibilities to them.

The old animosities threatened to resurface. Martin Buber, Chaim

Weizmann and many other eastern Zionists took Achad Ha-Am's side; Herzl and Nordau were defended equally staunchly. One agitated young Russian Zionist, although a disciple of Achad Ha-Am's, wrote to him, 'Herzl builds and you destroy. Cease from destruction and begin to build!' But other, more urgent concerns soon took precedence. For Herzl and his supporters it was the impending breakdown of negotiations with the Turkish government: for Achad Ha-Am it was the decision finally to leave *Ha-Shiloah*. Relations with his fellow directors, never easy, had steadily deteriorated. Their suggestions for making the journal more popular and therefore financially viable were met by his blanket refusal to turn it into what he called 'bedside reading'. When the Ahiasaf Publishing Company decreed that unless its editor took a cut in his already exiguous salary the paper would have to cease, Achad Ha-Am felt he had no option but to resign. Within a few weeks his old patron, Kalonymos Wissotsky, offered him a post in his tea firm. Achad Ha-Am made the transition from editorial chair to commerce with mingled relief that 'henceforth I shall be just a plain man, and literary amateur, as I used to be', and wounded pride that 'one of the foremost Hebrew writers, after editing the only Hebrew monthly of any literary value for six years, was compelled to give up editing and accept a position in a business house, so as not to have to eat the bread of beggary and humiliation'.

Although now ostensibly free to turn his thoughts to the major work – perhaps on ethics – which he wanted to leave to posterity, he was temperamentally and constitutionally incapable of doing so. Frequent business trips to the Russian outposts of the Wissotsky tea empire exhausted him, and there was always the excuse of pressing public events: the Kishinev massacre of 1903; the fiasco of the Ugandan proposal at the Sixth Zionist Congress, which prompted him to a bitter article, 'Those Who Weep'. 'In Basel, on the first of Ellul 5657 this [political] Zionism was born, and in Basel, on the first of Ellul 5663 its "soul" departed from it, leaving nothing but a name emptied of all meaning and a programme with a new, far-fetched interpretation.' A few weeks later there was a pogrom in Homel; the death of Herzl; the first Russian revolution of 1905. He was drawn into all these upheavals, as observer, commentator or participant.

It was not coincidental that within a year of being free of Herzl's looming shadow he produced what are generally considered his three most enduring essays, 'Moses', 'Flesh and Spirit', and 'The Supremacy of Reason'; none of them deals with the topic of Zionism. Shortly thereafter, in a whimsical piece, 'Words and Ideas', he summarized, yet again, what he meant by 'a spiritual Centre'. His tone towards critics is benign, patient, condescending; he understands their psychological inability to grasp his meaning, so spells it out for them as simply as possible. Such a relaxed, almost playful, tone was inconceivable during the years of anti-Herzl polemic. As Achad Ha-Am was quick to detect, the vacuum left by Herzl's unfulfilled legacy had freed Zionism of its messianic delusions and left it readier to listen to his limited, gradualist message. Bereft of its monarch, the balance of power in the demoralized Zionist organization slowly swung towards its east European majority, prominent among whom were Achad Ha-Am protégés such as Weizmann, Shmaryahu Levin and Menachem Ussishkin. They fought to redress the balance between political and cultural Zionism, promulgating ingenious formulas to synthesize diplomatic manoeuvring with practical colonizing and educational activities. These otiose exercises in manifesto writing were made redundant by the Young Turks revolution of 1908, with its promise of multinational democracy throughout the Ottoman empire. Tactically bowing to prevailing realities, at its 1909 Congress the executive of the Zionist Organization officially disassociated itself from the slogan of a Jewish state in Palestine guaranteed by the great powers. In his customary opening address, Max Nordau declared that the time had come to drop the idea of a charter from Turkey, given its change of government. Thus soon were Herzl's frenzied efforts discarded, and two years later, Achad Ha-Am felt sufficiently vindicated to attend the Tenth Congress as an observer.

In the meantime, he had been transferred to London by his firm. It did not turn out to be a happy move. He was too set in his ways to adjust – an Odessan provincial at heart. At first, the prospect of browsing in the British Museum enticed him, but its opening hours conflicted with his office ones. He hated his daily journey to 'the Babel' of the City. Nor did he find the milieu of Anglo-Jewry congenial. In Russia he was a luminary, in England recognized only by the few cognoscenti. 'A cemetery with ornamental tombstones' was how he described English Judaism to his editorial successor at *Ha-Shiloah*, and to his friend, the historian Simon Dubnow, he wrote, 'Judaism in our sense of the word is in exile here much more than in Russia.'

Deliberately keeping aloof from the Jewish community, refusing social or literary invitations, confined at home with a largely indifferent wife now that his eldest daughter was married and his other two children were at university, melancholia settled over him like a London fog. Occasional stimulus came from crossing swords in an intellectual controversy: against his friend Dubnow's advocacy of Jewish autonomy within Russia, in an essay entitled 'The Negation of the Diaspora'; against Yiddish as the national language, in 'Rival Tongues' and against the liberal attitude towards Christianity of the English scholar (and anti-Zionist) Claude Montefiore, in 'Judaism and the Gospels'.

Respite of another kind came with a visit to Palestine after the 1911 Zionist Congress. His married daughter lived in Haifa, a city of which he was fond; for once he was not complaining of a real or psychosomatic illness, and the respectful welcome at Basel for his prodigal's return had reassured him. All this is reflected in the tone of the essay in *Ha-Shiloah* in the spring of 1912 under the valedictory title 'Summa Summarum'. It is a surprisingly affirmative, almost optimistic piece. The official programme and the old slogans may not have changed, but he detects in Palestine the slow creation of that spiritual centre he had been seeking, and he is no longer distressed by the discrepancy between Zionism's aims and its achievements. 'Now that I have seen the results of the work so far, I have no such fears as to its ultimate fate.' The centre being created in Palestine will surely become 'a home of healing' for the spirit of the Jewish people. With his mind's eye he sees 'this centre growing in size, improving in quality, and exerting an ever-increasing spiritual influence on our people, until at last it shall reach the goal set before it by the instinct of self-preservation: to restore our national unity the world over, through the restoration of our national culture in its historic home'.

His peroration is positively – well – Herzlian. To those who worry about the future, he replies, Ask no questions! What needs to be done by generations to come will be done. 'For us, we are not concerned with the hidden things of the future. Enough for us to know the things revealed, the things that are to be done by us and our children in a future that is near.' Such spiritedness was unusual for Achad Ha-Am, and unique in his London years.

Two blows shortly devastated the moral structure he had built up, with such care and seeming detachment, to protect himself. In 1912, his second and favourite daughter, Rachel, married a non-Jewish Russian. Such an act of treason (for so he deemed it) compelled him to break off contact with her. And two years later, the civilized nations of Europe went to war. Achad Ha-Am's philosophy of human evolution and moral progress could not survive the slaughter of the trenches. The alliance of despotic Russia with liberal Great Britain and France, in the cause of alleged justice, offended his notion of truth, and he could not stomach the hypocrisy of war propaganda, which Jews peddled as enthusiastically as everyone else. He also felt guilty about being safe in England while the Jews of his native Ukraine were enduring harsh suffering.

An anguished misanthropy enveloped him. In May 1915 he wrote, 'The man I envy more than anybody else is Shackleton,[1] who managed to get away in time to the South Pole – the only place to which the stench of "humanity" certainly cannot reach.' A year later he told another correspondent, 'now that the moral world has reeled back into chaos, and humanity has become utterly vile, I am filled with loathing . . .' The First World War effectively terminated his literary career. Early in 1918, he wrote to a Russian friend, 'In these terrible years I have aged (not so much physically as mentally) at least ten years. I feel completely broken and shattered, though outwardly I go on living as before, and the only difference is that I spend my free time reading papers of all kinds and in all languages. It is a long time since I read a book, and of course I don't write a line.'

Ironically, he was to play a relevant role in the behind-the-scenes diplomatic manoeuvring he so despised which preceded the publication by the British government of the so-called Balfour Declaration, a document of crucial significance to the future of Zionism. Chaim Weizmann, by now a prominent name in the Zionist movement but with no official position, was a lecturer in chemistry at the University of Manchester. His important war work brought him into contact with leading politicians and Whitehall mandarins, and he exploited the opportunity to gain a sympathetic hearing for Zionist aspirations in Palestine after an Allied victory. So shrewd was Weizmann's bridge-building that he became the de facto senior negotiator

1. Sir Ernest Henry Shackleton (1874–1922). British explorer. Leader of the unsuccessful Trans-Antarctic expedition 1914–17.

for the defunct (due to the war) Zionist Congress. Whenever he was in London, he sought Achad Ha-Am's advice deferentially, and kept his former mentor informed of developments. But their friendship nearly foundered on the rock of Achad Ha-Am's fastidious adherence to procedural niceties. He agreed to serve on an ad hoc advisory committee only after receiving formal written assurances about its scope and function; he then chose to be offended by what he deemed to be a lack of consultation on whether, in the speculative event of its ever being formed, a Jewish Legion should serve only on the Palestine front or in other theatres of war. When this goaded an exasperated Weizmann to tender *his* resignation, Achad Ha-Am sent him a letter famous in the annals of Zionist correspondence.

He reminded the younger man that he had still been in school when Achad Ha-Am had been in the line of battle. Due to his personal qualities and to favourable external circumstances, Weizmann had become 'almost the symbol' – the adverb such a characteristic qualification! – of Zionism for many people of influence. His resignation now would do grave disservice to the Zionist cause. Not because he was irreplaceable – nobody was; but who would he resign to, never having been elected in the first place? Exceptional circumstances had chosen Weizmann and would release him in due course, when his task was completed. He could not be kept against his will, but he would surely understand – as someone on whom Achad Ha-Am had perhaps had some influence – that his contemplated action would be construed as 'an act of treason' and 'moral suicide'. None of which would affect his warm feelings of friendship for Weizmann.

It worked. Weizmann stayed on for his rendezvous with history and, when the Balfour Declaration was issued, showed an appropriate sense of occasion by taking it to Achad Ha-Am to inspect. Achad Ha-Am analysed the document at its face value, neither hoping for more nor settling for less than Balfour's letter offered, and took more lasting satisfaction from the laying of twelve foundation stones for the future Hebrew University on Mount Scopus the following year. Now a valued adviser, Achad Ha-Am was also consulted by the Zionist delegation to the Versailles Peace Conference. If the transition from rejected outsider to inner circle confidant playing Herzl's game tickled his sense of irony, he did not say. Frail and elderly, querulously irresolute, he was steeling himself for a major decision: to settle, after so many years, in Palestine.

He arrived with his wife early in 1922. They chose to live not in Jerusalem but in Tel-Aviv, on the street named after him a few years previously, so that, as he wryly observed, the Yishuv Jews who reviled his name with their lips could now tread him underfoot. It was a triumphant homecoming. He was fêted and gawped at, the embodiment of Zionist legend, one of the dwindling band who had seen Herzl plain, now the undisputed moral philosopher of the movement. He derived no pleasure from his new status. The climate was insufferable and, although his street was barred to traffic during his afternoon siesta, he found the noise of Tel-Aviv overwhelming. Too feverish to sleep, too exhausted to work, apart from preparing four slim volumes of his essays and some judiciously sifted letters for publication in Hebrew, he succumbed to despair. 'I am broken, shattered, utterly and incurably depressed,' he wrote to Dubnow. '. . . And all this in Palestine, which has been my dream for years and years. And in the midst of all these blessings, I long for — London! This longing is doubly painful because I regard it as a sure sign that I am suffering from some malady of the spirit . . .'

Achad Ha-Am was one of those people whose lines of character and cast of mind do not change or soften as they grow older, but become more so. In the preface written for his *Collected Essays*, he cautions against misinterpreting the Balfour Declaration and disregarding the rights of the indigenous Palestinian Arabs with the same warnings he used after his first visit in 1891. He urges step-by-step colonization with identical animadversions to those against Herzlian delusions twenty years before, 'Do not press on too quickly to the goal, so long as the actual conditions without which it cannot be reached have not been created; and do not disparage the work which is possible at any given time . . . even if it will not bring the Messiah today or tomorrow.'

To what, then, does this prim, melancholy pedagogue owe his enduring position in the Zionist pantheon? Because people who answer a consistent moral imperative are rare in any walk of life. Most of us trim, adapt, are guided by expedient pragmatism. Those who hammer out an unwavering message of principle are scoffed at for their naivety, accused of living in an ideal world; then, slowly, the public perception of them alters. Their repetition of beliefs impervious to changing fortune, their seeming indifference to easy popularity, evokes grudging acknowledgement and belated respect, then, finally, genuine admiration. So it was with Achad Ha-Am. He no longer cared. His public image of principled morality in the cause of the Jewish people had been bought at the cost of his inner wellbeing; the spiritual centre he craved for Judaism eluded his unsatisfied soul. Death came as a release, on 2 January 1927. In a neat tying of loose ends which the writer in him would have savoured, he was laid to rest beside Max Nordau, his arch-opponent in the ideological battles between political and cultural Zionism.

8

Nachman Syrkin and Ber Borochov – the Marxist Zionists

If Herzl's goal of political recognition and Achad Ha-Am's vision of a cultural centre were the two poles of the ideological debate in the formative years of the Zionist movement, a host of lesser personalities contributed to the controversy. A plethora of essays and pamphlets were churned out in any Jewish journal that would print them. Most of them, and their authors, enjoyed the brief light of publication before obscurity reclaimed them.

The striking point about these mounds of documentation mouldering in obscure archives is how irrelevant they were. Such passion, such vigorous disputation, such scornful rejection of opposing arguments! The manifestos and denunciations rang out from Berlin, Odessa, Vienna and Warsaw, while in eastern Europe the Jewish masses for whom they were intended sank into greater wretchedness, and in Palestine the colonists eked out what living they could. Scribblers who had escaped from the ghetto through education or assimilation, who had neither visited the Yishuv nor intended settling there, peddled their nostrums for alleviating the plight of the Jewish people. Among them, Jacob Klatzkin (1882–1948), a scholar of some eminence and for a time editor of *Die Welt*, was the most radical advocate of secular nationalism and the liquidation of an ossified and unworthy Diaspora. He reserved his harshest scorn for those like Achad Ha-Am who dreamed of a cultural centre, or who, like Simon Dubnow, advocated Jewish autonomy within the boundaries of Russia; the sooner the Diaspora was transcended and a petrified Judaism discarded, the sooner a national renaissance within a Jewish state would occur. Klatzkin fired off his broadsides from Murnau, an idyllic Bavarian retreat; even after the Nazis came to power, he chose to live (and die) in Switzerland.

Jewish Marxists, religious nationalists, utopian socialists, Tolstoyan agrarians, Nietzschean romantics – all had their say on the Jewish problem and how to solve it. As Karl Kraus remarked of Freud's theories, it was the disease that presumed itself the cure. Nevertheless, one or two of these theoreticians had a practical influence on the attitudes and social philosophy of future generations of Zionists.

Micah Berdichevsky (1865–1921), born nine years after Achad Ha-Am, into a similar background, was one such intellectual gadfly. But if Achad Ha-Am came from ghetto aristocracy, Berdichevsky could have claimed that he was from the ghetto approximation to royalty, born into a family of notable rabbinic lineage in the Russian town of Miedzyborz, a hothouse of Chasidism since the middle of the eighteenth century. Like Achad Ha-Am, whose views he later repudiated, he received a traditional education. By the age of seventeen, when a suitable match with a wealthy girl was arranged, he was known as a Talmudic prodigy and a master of the mystical texts of Kabbalah and Chasidism. Berdichevsky, too, secretly devoured the forbidden literature of the Enlightenment. When caught by his scandalized father-in-law, he was thrown out of the house and the marriage annulled. Publicly shamed, cut adrift from his moorings, for a time he tried to rehabilitate himself by studying at a traditional Talmudic academy, the famous *yeshivah* of Volozhin. But the siren call of the outside world was too strong, and in 1890 he left to study at the University of Breslau. Rejecting his pious background with a vengeance, he even enrolled in an art school.

The writer who emerged from these years of secular education would have no truck with vague formulas for a compromise between Jewish tradition and modernity. Nietzsche was in vogue, and Berdichevsky became his Jewish disciple. The doctrine of the Superman was transplanted to a Jewish context; the timid and persecuted Jew would be re-moulded as an *Übermensch*. Another key Nietzschean concept, 'the transvaluation of all values', was adapted by Berdichevsky for his attack on the subordination of Jews to Judaism in one of his earliest essays, 'Wrecking and Building'. 'It is not reforms but transvaluations that we need – fundamental transvaluations in the whole course of our life, in our thoughts, in our very souls.' A clear choice faced the people: to be the last Jews or the first Hebrews. Since the destruction of the Temple and the loss of political independence, the creativity of the Jews had been turned to preserving the past. Dried up spiritually, in a relationship with life and the world that was no longer normal, the Jews had reached a stage of almost total decay. As a consequence, 'some leave the House of Israel to venture among foreign peoples, devoting to them the service of their hearts and spirits and offering their strength to strangers; while, at the other extreme, the pious sit in their gloomy caverns, obeying and preserving what God had commanded them.' The answer was to 'cease to be Jews by virtue of an abstract Judaism and become Jews in our own right, as a living and developing nationality'. Transvaluation would be the elixir of Jewish revival, filling its institutions with life-giving content. A great responsibility rests upon the people – 'We are the last Jews – or we are the first of a new nation.'

At other times, Berdichevsky extols nationality, not culture, as the guardian of human individuality, rejects claims for a special Jewish 'mission' while brooding over Judaism's power to enrich even as it oppresses, and pens paeans of praise to the God of nature which sound like the outpourings of an inebriated pantheist. Erratic in thought and deed, capable, according to his biography in the *Encyclopaedia Judaica*, 'of simultaneously embracing logically contradictory positions and emotions', he married a second time, supported himself as a dentist, lived in deliberate seclusion in Berlin, and wrote in a mixture of styles, using German for serious dissertations, Hebrew for polemics and Yiddish for short stories and homespun philosophy. In the later years of his life he worked concurrently on a compilation of Talmudic and Midrashic legends for popular consumption, and a scholarly study of the faith of ancient Israel, in which he claimed that nature worship and idolatry, not biblical monotheism, had been the folk religion.

Too reclusive and self-absorbed to seek or encourage followers, his death in 1921 scarcely noticed, Berdichevsky's cult of the remade titan struck a chord with later Labour Zionists, particularly in the kibbutz movement, as they sought to refashion the Diaspora stereotype of a Jewish pedlar into the model of sturdy farmer. Like Moses Hess, Berdichevsky was an amiably mixed-up fringe figure whose modest recognition came posthumously.

Nachman Syrkin (1867–1924) was a more consistent and influential thinker. Born in Mohilev, the son of a traditionally pious family, he was stocky, combative, rebellious by nature. He got his own way of wanting a secular education, but was soon expelled from the local school for objecting to anti-Semitic remarks by a teacher. When his family moved to Minsk in 1884, he completed his education at a Russian high school, joined a branch of Chibbat Zion and flirted with the revolutionary underground. This brought him to the attention of the authorities, and he was briefly gaoled – a scandal that sealed the breach with his family.

He wandered to London, where he found work as an actor in the Yiddish theatre for a few months, but then, like many intellectually ambitious young students of his generation, turned up in Berlin, at the age of twenty-one. German universities were a haven for Russian Jews, who were barred from higher education in their own country.

Syrkin enrolled in the philosophy department and threw himself with relish into student politics. He was a founder member of the Russian-Jewish Scientific Society, from whose ranks a number of prominent Zionist figures emerged, Chaim Weizmann among them. Syrkin's first foray into pamphleteering was in 1896, under the gaudy title *Reflections on the Philosophy of History*. In it, he took aim at Marx's concept of economic determinism and offered instead, as befitted a self-confident young man, the element of free will in the historical process.

Socialism, in its various manifestations, was the political creed sweeping Europe, its key concepts embraced by middle-class intellectuals on behalf of the proletariat, its core policies viewed with alarm by a threatened bourgeoisie. The class stratifications of the Jewish world were under as much pressure as those of wider society. In Russia, dozens of politically conscious union cells – the *kassy* – had been formed by Jewish workers, with no overall organization or leadership but spontaneously responding to socialism's promise of a more equitable future. Within a few years, these *kassy* had grouped themselves within a clandestine trade union movement, leading strikes and labour agitation, either on their own or in concert with Russian socialist comrades. The question of whether Jewish workers should form independent unions or throw in their lot with the universal struggle became as thorny an issue for Jewish socialists as the political/cultural controversy was for Zionists.

It was an exhilarating time to be Jewish but emancipated from the small-town confines of the *shtetl*: Russian but safely ensconced in a university atmosphere elsewhere. For an educated young Jew there was only one problem: whether to opt for socialism, which promised power for the masses but usually dismissed as marginal the situation of European Jewry and discounted anti-Semitism as a product of class conflict; or to rally behind the futuristic vision of Zionism, which would eliminate anti-Semitism by transporting the Jewish masses out of Europe but offered little to alleviate their present suffering. Syrkin's ideology developed in the hothouse ambience of student debating societies. In his reminiscences of those years, he said that it had taken all his argumentative skills to stand alone and defend his new synthesis of Socialist-Zionism. The assertiveness acquired at university later made him a prickly presence at Zionist Congresses, frequently interrupting and needling the executive with charges of 'bourgeois leadership' and truckling to 'reactionary tyrants' like Kaiser Wilhelm and Tsar Nicholas. Yet Herzl had a soft spot for Syrkin, impressed perhaps by his stocky vigour and irreverent frankness, and in his diaries ironically called him 'that *exaltado*'.

If Hegel was right, and any great revolution is preceded by innumerable quiet revolutions in the spirit of the age, undetected by contemporaries, a sequence of seemingly disconnected events was about to propel Jewish nationalism into new channels. In February 1896, Herzl published *Der Judenstaat*. Eighteen months later, he convened the First Zionist Congress. In September 1897, one month after the Basel convention, the first Jewish trade union organization, the Bund (a Yiddish abbreviation of General Federation of Jewish Workers in Lithuania, Poland and Russia), was officially established in Vilna. Within another year, Syrkin had published a pamphlet entitled *The Jewish Problem and the Socialist–Jewish State*. Whether Zionism and socialism cared for the relationship or not, they had now to come to terms with each other.

What is instantly attractive about Syrkin's pamphlet – apart from the pugnacious verve of its writing – is that its author, unlike so many of his contemporaries, appears to be at ease with his Jewish heritage. He is a socialist, so naturally he has no patience for what he describes in *Call to Jewish Youth* (published in 1901) as 'Orthodox obscurantism and Talmudic idolatry', which had stultified the Jewish masses, and he repeats with relish Heine's aphorism about Orthodoxy being not so much a religion as a misfortune. What shines from the pages of *The Socialist–Jewish State* is his *pride* in the role of the Jew in world history, a uniquely 'chosen' role, which has incurred exile and persecution in the past, but in the future, through the agency of Zionism, will usher in the socialist millennium. This daring attempt to justify picayune Jewish nationalism within the framework of international socialism begs as many questions as it answers, but was plausible enough to attract a second generation of idealistic young Russians into the Zionist fold. In a few bold strokes, Syrkin paints his picture of the factors which have caused the age-old tension between the Jews and the world around them. After the destruction of the Temple and the beginning of their strange, unparalleled role in history – that of a landless nation – the Jews came into contact with an inimical culture, 'a blend of the disintegrating Greco-Roman civilization and of the spirit of Christianity which had originated in Palestine'. The uncompromising monotheism of the Jews and their moral code were bound to conflict with the spiritual and intellectual constructions of the Greco-Roman world. The naked oppression and barbarity which characterized declining Rome and the Christian Middle Ages offended the prophetic ideals of the Jews, and the power compromise under Constantine, which gave the state control over the Church, was unacceptable to a people faithful to the message of the Torah. Although Syrkin does not spell out that message, it is clear that he has in mind the biblical insistence on strict social justice, irrespective of wealth, power or privilege.

This affords him the opportunity for a few side-swipes at Christianity, on behalf of his own religion. The Church, with 'unmeasured arrogance', had falsified the image of 'the Rabbi of Nazareth', depicting him as the Son of God, whereas to monotheistic Judaism he was merely 'an errant son'. All the panoply of Christian worship were idolatrous superstitions which so repelled Jewry that it could not even acknowledge the ethical content of the proximate new religion. This sense of their 'higher religious estate' sustained Jewish morale in their war against the world. But the world was full of hatred and contempt for the weak yet stubborn exile in its midst. The perennial antagonism between the strong and the subjugated, based on the unequal distribution of power and sharpened by the submissive façade which the weak use to hide their anger, was the source of anti-Jewish hostility.

Syrkin does not merely use the Jews as an obvious socialist metaphor for the oppressed proletariat. In a moving passage he expatiates on Jewish survival in the Middle Ages. Huddled together in the ghetto, gritting their teeth against the hatred of the outside world, the Jews could easily have turned into 'a worthless gypsy community'. But the soul of Israel contained loftier, more humane ideas which, even in degradation, preserved the people. Elevated by their martyr's career to the role of Suffering Servant, the Jews still prayed to God on behalf of those who had cast them out. The Jew of the Middle Ages had two differing characters – the weekday and the sabbath one; if the first moved him to hate the rest of the world, the second raised him above it. Shylock was only a partial representation of the medieval Jew; Lessing's noble Nathan the Wise[1] symbolized his sabbath soul, in which flourished the hope of redemption – 'the hope for the liberation of Israel in the near future and for its national rebirth'. This yearning found tangible expression in the Messiah, who would come to redeem his people; the messianic hope protected the medieval Jew against life's tempests.

That changed with the French Revolution's proclamation of human rights, identified with the victory of the bourgeoisie over the nobility, of which the Jews were incidental beneficiaries. Syrkin is now on the favourite ground of late-nineteenth-century socialists, sociologists, anthropologists and moral philosophers: sweeping, enviably self-assured overviews of the structure of European society, and he goes to the task with gusto. Had anyone presumed to detect flaws in his diagnosis, he – together with Marx, Nordau, Henri Bergson, Eugene Düring and Houston Chamberlain, to mention but a few ploughers of the same furrow – might have retorted with Walt Whitman's sublime certainty, 'Do I contradict myself? Very well then, I contradict myself. I am vast, I contain multitudes.'

According to Syrkin, the basic bourgeois class interest was freedom: freedom of religion and conscience, unlimited rights of property and unfettered social mobility. The Jews, with no effort, power or organization of their own, almost despite themselves, were liberated from the ghetto by the triumph of the principle of equality; 'the wound that had been festering within Jewry since the fall of Jerusalem began to heal with the fall of the Bastille.' Despite the germ of progress, Freedom, Equality and Fraternity was an illusory banner, because the inherent contradictions of bourgeois society would cause its breakdown. Bourgeois society's sole aim was the accumulation of wealth through competition, whereas the traditional values of ghetto Judaism had been discarded to adapt to, and be accommodated within, this new order of society. 'Jewry, which but recently prayed thrice daily for its return to Jerusalem, became intoxicated with patriotic sentiments for the land in which it lived.' It might have seemed that bourgeois freedom and

---

1. Eponymous Jewish hero of play written by Gotthold Lessing (1729–81), in which Nathan, modelled on the personality of Moses Mendelssohn, represents the Enlightenment ideal of universal brotherhood.

assimilation had finally solved the Jewish problem. Not so: the more the bourgeoisie, as the ruling class, betrayed its commitment to liberalism in the pressing struggle for economic power, the shakier became the principles behind emancipation. Emancipation of the Jews could not be harmonized with the basic egotism endemic in bourgeois society.

Now that religion is passé, what, asks Syrkin, is the basis for modern anti-Semitism? Overtly it is racial, but its true origin is in psychology and class dynamics. The critic of the Jews will claim that they are a self-seeking, alien people, the torch-bearers of capitalism, exploitation, usury and the rest, while at the same time accusing them of being the 'yeast of history', fomenting trouble and upsetting the stable order. What lies behind that outcry of bourgeois society? Syrkin answers: It is recognition of the emancipated Jew as a more effective alter ego, a more able mirror image. Bourgeois society and the Jew reflect each other. Both are ready, twenty-four hours a day, to betray their state for their class interests, and their class interests for private gain – with the minor difference that the Jewish bourgeoisie looks after its own oppressed somewhat better.

Syrkin offers half-a-dozen paragraphs on the demography of anti-Semitism in capitalist society which are more perceptive and trenchant than all of Hess, Pinsker and Herzl combined. He identifies the declining middle class (being destroyed by capitalism) and the decaying peasant class (being strangled by the landowners) as the most fertile breeding grounds of anti-Semitism. Both are fighting a losing battle to maintain their former status, and see the Jew as their sharpest competitor; anti-Semitism has thus become the mainstay of the socio-political programme of these classes.

He is magnificently contemptuous of the demagogues who lead the anti-Semitic parties, 'dregs of bourgeois and proletarian society, who have lost every vestige of truth and self-respect, and creatures of the semi-underworld who can be moved only by the lowest of passions'. Petty criminals and moral degenerates, they had engendered the comment of Ludwig Börne, the early German champion of civil liberties, that anti-Semites of the future would be candidates for either the workhouse or the insane asylum. In spite of the moral degradation of its leaders and the disgust of intelligent people, anti-Semitism was on the increase, because the beleaguered classes would unite against the Jew as their common enemy. The reactionary elements in capitalist society — that is, men of great wealth, the monarchy, the Church — would utilize religion and race as a diversion from the class struggle. As a prescription for the eventual rise of fascism, which neither orthodox Marxism nor bourgeois liberalism anticipated or adequately explained, Syrkin's socioeconomic forecast is chillingly prophetic.

Unfortunately, his argument begins to unravel. He tries to juggle several ideas at once, and his propensity for factiousness leads him into obscure vendettas against Jewish fellow-travellers and bourgeois assimilationists. He suddenly declares that a classless society and national sovereignty are the only means of solving the Jewish problem and normalizing the relationship of the Jew and his environment. He does not explain why or how. Instead, he launches an attack on Jewish socialists who have abandoned their Judaism for a spurious internationalism: 'the socialists have inherited assimilation from the bourgeoisie and made it their spiritual heritage.' Internationalism is the ideal towards which history is striving. Beside it, nationalism is a pale creation, a category of history, not an absolute; anyway, socialism has resolved the tension between the socialist ethic, self-determination, and pure internationalism. Whatever that socialist synthesis might be, it is so vague that Syrkin once more has recourse to attacking assimilated Jewish socialists for their 'lack of seriousness' — a heinous crime in the proto-Marxist lexicon. 'The socialism of the Jew must become a truly *Jewish* socialism,' he avers in conscious echo of Herzl and every other Zionist with a fondness for phrase-making.

By describing ideologically correct Jewish socialism (his version) in the reverential tones reserved by Marxists for the proletariat, Syrkin places it, like Caesar's wife, above suspicion. Who would query its validity? It is now but a small step to incorporate Zionism within his international-socialist praxis. His justification for Zionism is provocative: *Socialism is not yet capable of solving the Jewish problem*, because none of the socialist norms apply to the Jews. Theirs is a singular situation, economically, politically, socially. The class struggle exacerbates anti-Semitism, worsens the condition of the Jewish middle classes, demoralizes the intelligentsia, and fails to galvanize the *lumpenproletariat*. Whenever socialist principles and tactical opportunism collide, it is to the detriment of the Jews. The issue is not socialism, but the form it takes in a Jewish context. Syrkin's sad conclusion with regard to the Jew is that, unlike all the other oppressed, 'he has no real, immediate weapon with which to win an easing of his lot. His only alternative, as it was centuries ago, is emigration to other countries.'

He makes claims for Zionism equal to the most starry-eyed visions of its previous exponents. The function of Zionism, a movement 'which has encompassed all segments of Jewry', is 'to give a rational purpose to all those who feel the pain of Exile; and to raise their individual protest to the level of a general moral resistance aimed at the rebuilding of Jewish life – that is the purpose of Zionism . . . It has its roots in the economic and social position of the Jews, in their moral protest, in the idealistic striving to give a better content to their miserable life.' Zionism transcends the class struggle, and can be accepted by each and every class of Jew, because a Jewish state 'can greatly erase the Jewish problems'. The Jewish masses will not accept a capitalist Jewish state; the strong arms of their workers will build the new state, assisted by the middle class and intelligentsia. The fusion of Zionism with socialism will be in harmony with the aspirations of the Jewish masses, and the proletarian revolution will be consummated.

He was sanguine about possible opposition. Other oppressed peoples within the Ottoman empire would welcome the settlers' socialist endeavours. The Jews would form a majority in Palestine, building the land on principles of fraternal socialism, and where there were mixed communities friendly transfers of population would ensue. Macedonians, Armenians, Greeks, all other non-Muslim peoples under Turkish yoke would regain their independence wherever they formed a national majority, supported by Zionist funds. Only the Palestinian Arabs are not mentioned, either because Syrkin assumed they were all Muslims and happy under Ottoman control, or because the peasantry had yet to achieve that stage of proletarian consciousness to applaud the efforts of socialist Zionism. Because of their unique situation, the Jews have a unique opportunity to realize the socialist vision and become standard-bearers of the revolution: 'From the humblest and most oppressed of all peoples it will be transformed to the proudest and greatest.' The Jews will now regain their moral stature and true nature, like 'a sleeping giant arising from the slough of despair and darkness, and straightening up to his infinite height'. Having fused Zionism and socialism to his satisfaction, Syrkin reconciles Judaism with Christianity's most potent symbol. The Jew's tragic history has resulted in a high mission: 'He will redeem the world which crucified him. Israel will once again become the chosen of the peoples!' The pamphlet ends on this exultant note of biblical prophecy.

What critical attention it received was mainly negative, its content too subversive for liberal Zionists, too romantic for dyed-in-the-wool Marxists. But it struck a chord with young Jews, who were imbued with socialist idealism but made to feel uncomfortable about harbouring bourgeois notions of Jewish nationalism. Syrkin had given legitimacy to their need to combine progressive thinking with their yearning for self-determination. Indeed, he had demonstrated that one was a logical corollary of the other; henceforth, becoming a Zionist would be as intellectually respectable as joining the Bund.

Did Syrkin emigrate to Palestine, to put his theories into practice? Of course not. He was a gadfly, snapping away at the fringes of Zionism and socialism. For a time, he worked to establish socialist Zionist groups in Germany, Austria and Switzerland, with mixed success. One such conventicle was Hessiona, founded in 1901, and named for his precursor who 'recognized the eternal striving of man toward perfection, toward historical change and creation'. He produced two short-lived journals in Yiddish and Hebrew, and numerous pamphlets which were smuggled illegally into tsarist Russia. In 1904 he was expelled from Germany and spent some time in Paris and then, after the 1905 revolution, in Russia. He maintained his disruptive participation in Zionist Congresses, giving minority support to Herzl's Uganda scheme in 1903 and two years later joining forces with the territorialist faction to pursue the East African offer.

At times a garrulous orator claiming to speak on behalf of phantom ranks of socialist Zionists, at others a prescient writer, Syrkin always retained a deep emotional attachment to the Jewish masses; this 'proletariat of the proletariat', comprising miserable storekeepers, pedlars, tailors and cobblers, was destined to perish physically and spiritually unless it found redemption in Zionism. He warned as early as 1903 that emigration, even to the United States, would soon become subject to restrictive quotas and that the Jewish masses would benefit only temporarily from equal rights in Russia. Zionism had to be 'more than the colonization projects of Chibbat Zion with its bourgeois limitations; more than the longings for a spiritual centre of the *maskil* (supporter of the Enlightenment); more than the philanthropic Zionism of the west Europeans.' The new society of America beckoned him, and he emigrated there in 1907. New York provided a rich population mix for socialist agitation, and Syrkin joined a branch of the nascent and radically left-wing Po'alei Zion (Workers of Zion) movement, which had originated in Europe under the influence of Syrkin's pamphleteering, but its isolated and geographically widespread cells required more disciplined natures than his to organize them. That task was undertaken by Ber Borochov (1881–1917), whose career, as we shall see, resembled and overshadowed that of Syrkin.

Syrkin was an eminent personality among the groups of émigrés who plotted world revolution from their seedy rooming-houses and dingy cafés of the Lower East Side. He was busy, writing and lecturing ceaselessly in Hebrew, Yiddish, Russian, German and English, and enjoying titular leadership of American Po'alei Zion, supporting the formation of a Jewish Legion in the First World War, taking his place as an American Jewish delegate at the Versailles Peace Conference, and fighting a losing battle to persuade Po'alei Zion to join Lenin's Third International. At a conference of Po'alei Zion in Stockholm in 1919, he was elected leader of a study commission to visit Palestine and draw up plans for mass settlement on a co-operative basis. At last, he would see the Promised Land.

Arab disturbances in Jerusalem did not mar a moving experience. He saw much to please him in the direction of Yishuv society, from the growing collective farm movement to Ha-mashbir, a wholesale co-operative for consumer goods, and the Histadrut, the trade union federation. Its officials welcomed him as one of their mentors, and Syrkin enjoyed his tour of the country as a socialist Zionist celebrity. He had thoughts of settling in Palestine, that retirement home for so many of his generation of Diaspora Zionists, but it was not to be. Successive heart attacks killed him, but, unpredictable to the end, on his death-bed the rational socialist composed a Hebrew prayer and called in a friend to recite with him the 'Viddui', the traditional confession before death of Orthodox Jews.

His championing of free will despite the impersonal forces of history, both in his ideology and his private life, makes Syrkin more appealing than many of his doctrinaire Marxist contemporaries. For all his rigid analytical formulations, he was at heart a romantic in the tradition of Moses Hess, a proud Jew who never rejected his heritage for the lure of international socialism. In 1951 his remains were taken to Israel and buried at the collective settlement of Kinneret, alongside the graves of other founding fathers of Labour Zionism.

Twelve years later, shadowed in death as in life, he was joined by Ber Borochov. Borochov had the added fillip to his reputation of dying young, while actively engaged in the drama of the 1917 Russian Revolution. If Syrkin was the prophet Elijah of socialist Zionism, Borochov was its revered patron saint. At this distance of time, it is hard to understand why. But nowadays, with Marxism having been re-evaluated and found wanting long before the disintegration of Soviet communism, one cannot conceive how, at the turn of the century, Marxist dogma was pored over with the pious, uncritical attention which religious fundamentalists accord their holy scriptures. For Zionist socialists of eastern Europe and the Yishuv, Borochov had written the new Five Books of Moses.[1] Even today, in modern Israel, his stature and his essential *rectitude* are queried with diffidence.

He was born in the Ukraine and brought up in the small city of Poltava, a favoured place of exile with tsarist governments for would-be revolutionaries. Poltava also had one of the earliest Chibbat Zion branches, and Borochov's father was a member, so young Ber imbibed socialism and Zionism with his formal high-school education. Studious by nature, extremely clever, single-minded, somewhat priggish, he embarked on a rigorous regime of self-taught further education, having decided that he would not feel at ease in a Russian university, even had policy been reversed to admit a Jewish student. He read widely in history, philosophy, economics, philology and politics, and emerged with a clear notion of his intended career. He had supreme confidence in his mastery of doctrinal socialism; when a Russian socialist complained to Georgi Plekhanov, the leading Marxist theoretician, that Jewish youth decamped from the Pale of Settlement with a world outlook acquired from a few books, he might have been thinking of Borochov. Borochov joined the Russian Social Democratic Party, but not for long. His concern for specifically Jewish issues, in particular workers' rights and self-defence, clashed with party policy, which placed proletarian solidarity above sectional interests. He was branded a Zionist deviationist. Putting

1. Genesis, Exodus, Leviticus, Numbers and Deuteronomy; the first five books of the Bible, traditionally believed to have been written by Moses under divine guidance, and therefore particularly sacred to Jews.

into practice Socialism's first axiom – the unity of theory and action – Borochov left, to establish the Zionist Socialist Workers Union in 1901, the year when Lenin rejected the concept of Jewish autonomy as incompatible with Marxism.

A year later, at the tender age of twenty-one, his first article, 'On the Nature of the Jewish Mind', was published in a Zionist magazine. It was the start of an intense period of travel, political activism, organizational work with newly formed Jewish socialist cadres and a crystallizing neo-Marxist dialectic incorporating Jewish nationalism within the framework of the international class struggle. But before nationalism, Herzl's weakness for territorialism – *any* territory – had to be dealt with. Borochov allied with Ussishkin and the other 'Zion Zionists' in opposition to the Uganda scheme. He toured Russia to warn embryonic Po'alei Zion groups against the pernicious territorialist tendency, and at the 1905 Congress, when Syrkin claimed to speak on behalf of socialist Zionism in favour of exploring the Ugandan option further, Borochov had outmanoeuvred him by producing a pamphlet, *On the Question of Zion and Territory*, which demonstrated, in a turgid materialist–historical analysis of the Jewish problem, that Palestine was the destined location for Jewish national revival. Later that year, he wrote his first critically acclaimed pamphlet of the socialist Zionist library. *The National Question and the Class Struggle* is a classic piece of Marxist analysis – 'objective', 'scientific', jargon-ridden, lumberingly constructed and deadly earnest. The Marxists admired seriousness, and Borochov was certainly *serious*, in the manner of a schoolmaster having to explain, yet again, a blindingly obvious proposition.

The tone is set in the opening paragraph: 'In order to live, men must produce. In order to produce, they must combine their efforts in a certain way. Man does not as an individual struggle with nature for existence. History knows man only as a unit of a social group. Since men do live socially, it follows that between them certain *relations* are developed. These relations arise because of the production. Indeed, Marx terms them: *relations of production*.' Given that man is a social being, Borochov asks why humanity is divided into several societies. What is the materialist explanation for this, given that the basic cause of every social phenomenon is to be found in economic conditions?

Now comes the first subtly nuanced gloss on holy writ. Borochov points out a difference between relations of production, which are constant, and conditions of production, which vary considerably. He is not questioning the faith. After all, Engels recognized the same distinction in his second letter to the *Socialist Academician*, where he says that among the many factors which make for different economies are geography, environment, race and even human type. Marx too, in the third volume of *Das Kapital*, said that one and the same economic base can develop in different ways because of environment, race and external historic influences. 'Therefore we see, according to the teachers of historic materialism, that one and the same process of development of productive forces can assume various forms according to the differences in the conditions of production.' Having established, in conformity with the orthodox norms of dialectic materialism, that conditions of production are subject to geographic, anthropological and historic factors, Borochov suggests that a sound basis now exists on which to study the *national* question. He posits two sorts of human groupings: the first groups are those into which humanity is divided according to the differences in the conditions of production and are called *societies*, comprising tribes, families, peoples, nations; the second groups, called *classes*, are those into which the society is divided according to relation to the means of production. By extension, just as the class struggle is waged for the material means of production, so the national struggle is waged for the material possessions of social organisms. These may be 'spiritual' – language, customs, mores, etc. – or they may be material, and the '*most vital of the material conditions of production is the territory. The territory is, furthermore, the foundation on which rise all other conditions of production.*' In order to preserve this territorial resource, every nationality has fashioned instruments such as political unity and institutions, language, education and nationalism.

It is a flippant and dangerous fallacy to assume that the proletariat, having no relation to the national wealth, has no national feelings and interests. 'If the general base and reservoir of the conditions of production – the territory – is valuable to the landowning class for its land resources and as a base for its political power; if this territory serves the bourgeoisie as a base for the capture of the world market, and serves the middle classes of society as the consumers' market; and if the organs of preservation of the national wealth have for each of the above-mentioned classes their respective worth, then *the territory also has its value for the proletariat, i.e., as a place in which to work.*'

Borochov has made the national struggle respectable by integrating the class struggle within it. His ingenuity owes a debt to thinkers of the Austro-Marxist school like Otto Bauer, Max Adler and Karl Renner, who, coming from the multi-ethnic Austro-Hungarian empire, had to develop a more sophisticated approach to the nexus of class and nationality. They were willing to grant legitimacy to identifiable national and cultural structures and to proletarian groups possessing distinctive ethnic-linguistic traits, since in the heterogeneous Hapsburg empire ethnic distinctions and class differentiations were often synonymous; so many of the socially oppressed were oppressed because of their nationality. Borochov uses a similar approach to introduce the covert question of Jewish nationalism. Where one nationality has been conquered by another and deprived of its territory and instruments of national preservation, an artificial harmony occurs between the normally antagonistic classes of the subjugated nation. Indicators of nationality, such as the mother tongue, take on a disproportionate significance, and the national question of an oppressed people becomes sharply detached from the material conditions of production. In the distorted social structure, 'all the members of the nation become interested in national *self-determination*'.

This is when class structure and class psychology manifest themselves. Reactionary groups such as the petite bourgeoisie, clerical circles, the landowners, identify their nationalism with traditional values. Historically, it is progressive elements in the proletariat and the intelligentsia of subjugated nations who are the true exponents of national emancipation; their nationalism assumes a purer character. It is a nationalism 'which does not aspire to the preservation of traditions, which will not exaggerate them, which has no illusions about the ostensible oneness of the nation, which comprehends clearly the class structure of society, and which does not seek to confuse anyone's real class interests'. Thus, with the neatness of a geometrical theorem, do national struggle and class struggle converge. National liberation is the necessary prelude to achieving normal conditions of production and assuring the proletariat of the proper base for its class struggle. 'There now appears, in a new and clear form, a healthy class structure, and a sound class struggle.' Viewed in this light, those who belittle nationalism as a reactionary manifestation are 'shallow and ignorant'. Nationalism is a product of bourgeois society, and deserves the same attention as any other societal phenomenon subject to the Marxist critique.

It must be conceded that Borochov achieved a tour de force, an oblique justification of Zionism without emotion or special pleading, according to the criteria of Marxian analysis. Unlike Syrkin or others who claim a unique status for the Jewish condition, he has not strayed from the path of orthodox virtue.

The following year, 1906, at a conference in Poltava, the fragmented Po'alei Zion groups came together and re-named themselves – with more concern for semantic accuracy than catchy brevity – the Jewish Workers' Social Democratic Party: Po'alei Zion. Borochov, with the help of another young theoretician, Isaac Ben-Zvi (later the second president of Israel), wrote the party manifesto. *Our Platform* is his second major contribution to socialist Zionist ideology. Like *The National Question and the Class Struggle*, it makes no concession to eloquence, style or accessibility; unlike the first essay, it is a flawed and only partially convincing piece of analysis.

It begins with a restatement of the relationship between nationalism and the class struggle. 'National movements do not transcend class divisions; they merely represent the interests of one of several classes within the nation. A national conflict develops not because the development of the forces of production of the whole nation conflicts with the conditions of production, but rather because the developing needs of one or more classes clash with the conditions of production of its national group.' Since the Jewish nation – its 'nationhood' is taken for granted – has no peasantry, Borochov's analysis will deal with distinct urban classes: the upper, middle and petite bourgeoisie; the masses who are being proletarized; and the proletariat.

The upper bourgeoisie, cosmopolitan by nature, tends towards assimilation. Were it not for the continuous stream of immigrating 'poor *Ostjuden*', the comfortable Jews of western Europe would not be disturbed by the Jewish problem. Wanting to lose their individuality by assimilating, they are disturbed only by the prevalence of anti-Semitism. His definition of anti-Semitism is the traditional, and incomplete, Marxist one of economic rivalry. 'Anti-Semitism flourishes because of the national competition between the Jewish and non-Jewish petite bourgeoisie and between the Jewish and non-Jewish proletarized and unemployed masses.' It transcends class barriers, menacing the all-powerful Rothschilds as much as poor, helpless Jews. This poses a dilemma for the Jewish plutocracy. 'Two souls reside within the breast of the Jewish upper bourgeoisie – the soul of a proud European and the soul of an unwilling guardian of his eastern co-religionists.' Ideally, he would ignore the misery and poverty of these migrants, but self-interest and *noblesse oblige* compel him to turn philanthropist for pogrom-ridden Jewry. 'Everywhere the Jewish upper bourgeoisie is engaged in the search for a Jewish solution to the Jewish problem and a means of being delivered of the Jewish masses' – a cheap dismissal of the deeply ingrained charitable ethic that since biblical times has been a note-worthy feature of Jewish communities.

The Jewish middle classes, says Borochov, feel the sharp edge of anti-Semitism. On the one hand, they benefit from the spread of political democracy and the elimination of discriminatory legislation; on the other, they suffer from the intensification of national competition and, lacking a territory or a market of their own, fall victim to organized boycotts in trade, industry, social life and the press. Keenly feeling their alienation, but being products of their bourgeois environment, they advocate a vague 'cultural' nationalism or parlour-Zionism, because their economic interests are still bound up in the infrastructure of Diaspora existence. This class is of limited use: 'Its energy can be utilized to a certain extent on behalf of the rehabilitation of Jewish life, but the middle class as a whole can never be the base for a movement of Jewish emancipation.'

There is only one grouping that can provide the human material for Jewish rehabilitation. It is, in Borochov's inelegant phraseology, 'the Jewish petite bourgeoisie and the proletarized masses'. Their situation is raw and acute. Poverty forces them to emigrate to new countries, where they can penetrate only the final levels of production, and once again fall prey to national competition. The Jewish problem migrates with them. America is the first choice of would-be east European immigrants, but the New World exacerbates their plight. Their mass concentration in the large cities results in segregation, hinders their process of adaptation, and exports the Jewish problem, with its inherent anomalies and attendant anti-Semitism, to a new locale. They are condemned to repeat their former economic occupations – manufacturing consumer goods. The urgency to develop their own forces of production remains unsatisfied.

There is only one logical answer to the Jewish problem: a territorial solution, 'the need for concentrated immigration into an undeveloped country', where Jews would assume the leading position in the economy. The colonization of this country, unlike haphazard immigration, would be organized by the conscious Jewish proletariat. The spontaneous, elemental forces operating in Jewish Diaspora life, which Borochov described with the Russian word *stychia*, would produce the concentrated emigration of the petite bourgeoisie and the masses. Their transformation into active participants in the class struggle would take place under the tutelage of the sensitized proletariat. National oppression, exploitation by petty Jewish capitalists, high cultural expectations had all generated a revolutionary ardour hampered by lack of a strategic base. The Jewish proletariat was a 'chained Prometheus who in helpless rage tears the feathers of the vulture that preys on him'. To succeed in utilizing both Jewish capital and Jewish labour to effect the transition from an urban to an agricultural economy, and from the manufacturing of consumer goods to more basic forms of production, proletarian Zionism would require a country neither highly industrialized nor predominantly agricultural but 'semi-agricultural', which held no attraction for other than Jewish immigrants. 'This land will be the only one available to the Jews . . . It will be a country of low cultural and political development. Big capital will hardly find use for itself there, while Jewish petty and middle capital will find a market for its products in both this country and its environs. *This land of spontaneously concentrated Jewish immigration will be Palestine . . .*' In Palestine, the Jewish class struggle and the universal struggle of the proletariat, nationalism and internationalism will be integrated. 'Political territorial autonomy in Palestine is the ultimate aim of Zionism. For proletarian Zionists, this is also a step towards socialism.'

Our Platform is a party political manifesto. One can therefore understand the introduction of images of two souls beating in the bourgeois Jewish breast, or of a chained proletariat tearing at its tormentors. Nevertheless, there is something excessively generalized and conventional about Borochov's survey of Diaspora society (Herzl's observations from the opposite end of the political spectrum) just as his planned economy of Palestine is a socialist counterpoint to the liberal-democratic version of *Altneuland*.

Lack of first-hand knowledge could be offered in mitigation of

Borochov's spectacularly mistaken prophecy about Jewish immigrants in America; when facts did not accord with a Marxist paradigm, the facts had to be altered. But his discovery of a historically determined, elemental *stychic* process that would lead to mass migration to Palestine was equally askew. Written primarily for a European audience, the pamphlet had to address the nationalist–socialist debate as it impinged on Palestine. Borochov had already taken note of the Arab issue in his anti-Uganda essay, *On the Question of Zion and Territory*, where he had emphasized the racial affinity between Palestinian Arabs and the Jewish settlers. 'The local population in Palestine is closer to the Jews in racial composition than any other people, even the "Semitic" peoples; it is highly feasible to assume that the *fellahin* in Palestine are the direct descendants of the remnants of the Jewish and Canaanite agricultural community, together with a very slight mixture of Arab blood.' It was impossible to tell a Sephardi Jew and a *fellahin* apart, so the racial difference between a European Diaspora Jew and a Palestinian Arab would be no greater than that between Ashkenazi and Sephardi Jews.

In *Our Platform*, material determinism rather than racial affinity will be the inevitable impetus for Arab integration, since 'the indigenous inhabitants of Palestine do not constitute an independent economic and cultural type . . . are not one nation, nor will they become one for a long time to come.' The productive factors of the stronger Jewish society will exert assimilatory force on the weaker Arab society: 'Jewish immigrants will undertake the development of the productive forces of Palestine and the local Palestinian population will assimilate in due course, both economically and culturally, with the Jews.' He recognizes that this will not be an easy process. The territorial issue, the class struggle, and the proletarization of the workers will all exact their toll. 'So basic and profound an upheaval in the life of the Jews as territorialism cannot be conceived without a bitter struggle, without acts of cruelty and injustice, without suffering for both the innocent and the guilty.' Conditions of production – the social, cultural and geographical factors mentioned by Marx and Engels – would ensure the assimilation of the local population within the Jewish majority that had territorial and economic control of these conditions of production. Should a minority within the native population prefer to maintain its distinctive identity, the democratic Jewish society would consent; cultural autonomy for the Arabs, political territorial autonomy for the

Zionists. Thus would Arabs be integrated, in the cause of international socialism.

Our Platform was eagerly seized upon by Jewish socialists looking to make Jewish nationalism plausible, and Borochov became the ideologue of socialist Zionism. He participated in the founding, during the Eighth Zionist Congress of 1907, of the World Union of Po'alei Zion as a separate movement within the Zionist Organization. He insisted on the withdrawal of Russian Po'alei Zion, to preserve its proletarian independence. Until the outbreak of the First World War, he travelled and lectured in western and central Europe to propagate the cause of Po'alei Zion, which, within a year of its founding, claimed some 19,000 members.

Borochov revealed a different side to his scholarly inclinations when he produced a closely documented sociological analysis of *The Jewish Labour Movement in Figures.* This disclosed, among other riveting facts, that Jewish workers' unions had called 2276 strikes between 1895 and 1904, and that in Minsk in 1895–6 100 per cent of bristle workers, 75 per cent of binders and 40 per cent of locksmiths were unionized. Of more enduring worth were his contributions to the Russian–Jewish encyclopedia, and two essays on Jewish philology which contain a valuable bibliography of 400 years of Yiddish research.

In 1914, he left Vienna for the United States, to organize the American branch of Po'alei Zion and edit a New York Yiddish newspaper. Contact with the disparate communities of Europe and American Jewry did not soften his dogmatism. He was confirmed in his insistence that Jewish history was one long chronicle of the Jewish masses' struggle to survive. His relationship with Syrkin was uneasily formal; both were jealous of their reputations for originality.

The 1917 Russian Revolution was Marxism in the making. Borochov hurried home to participate, stopping en route in Stockholm at a conference of the International Socialist Commission to help draft Po'alei Zion's manifesto for Jewish and working-class rights in the post-war world order. Once in Russia, caught up in the febrile atmosphere of seismic events, he undertook a hectic series of meetings and lectures. He contracted pneumonia and died in Kiev. He had travelled halfway around the world on behalf of socialist Zionism, reiterating his call for mass settlement in Palestine, but had never visited it – a theoretician to the end of his brief life.

Henceforth, Zionist ideology developed in the land for which it was intended, out of the realities of Palestine not the speculative theorizing of intellectuals in Europe.

PART TWO

PALESTINE

9

A. D. Gordon – The Religion of Labour

Marx wrote, 'Men make their own history, but they do not make it just as they please; they do not make it under circumstances chosen by themselves . . .' This was certainly correct regarding Zionism's history in the first two decades of the twentieth century.

Herzl and his presidential successors in the World Zionist Organization, David Wolffsohn and Professor Otto Warburg, might beaver away at establishing diplomatic contacts in the chancelleries of Europe and Turkey while fighting off criticisms of their leadership nearer home; the balance of power on the Zionist executive might veer from western European to Russian domination; the fierce controversy between Herzlian political Zionism and Chibbat Zion practical Zionism might be solved by the Hegelian formula proposed by Weizmann of 'synthetic Zionism', meaning a little bit of both; Congress delegates might argue about the best way to use the limited assets of the Jewish National Fund (about £50,000 in 1907), whether to revive Hebrew as the national language or to retain Yiddish. It was all rhetorical sound and fury, signifying little.

Zionism could achieve little on its own: 127,000 supporters paid the shekel in 1912–13, and Wolffsohn's proud boast was that the finances were on a sound footing after Herzl's cavalier book-keeping. But with no clear foreign policy orientation, acrimonious executive splits and an over-reliance (*faute de mieux*) on Turkish intentions, the Zionist enterprise was highly vulnerable – long on talk, short on results. The failed revolution in Russia in 1905, the Young Turks revolt in 1907, the outbreak of the First World War, the Balfour Declaration and the successful Russian Revolution of 1917 all had far greater practical consequences for Zionism than any amount of debate or theorizing.

A few Zionist spokesmen – Weizmann, David Ben-Gurion and Arthur Ruppin, the Zionist Organization's representative in Palestine since 1907 – were shrewd enough to interpret the likely course of events and turn them to advantage. Their diplomatic, political and organizational skills created the base on which Palestinian Zionism would build. They seized the moment, while their European colleagues fluttered on the edge of national and international upheavals. Between 1905 and 1914, at least 35,000 new immigrants arrived in Palestine in what became known as the Second Aliyah (Ascent). They were part of the vast migratory exodus from Russian lands which, since 1882, had seen almost two million Jews flee from pogrom and persecution. America, not Palestine, was the Promised Land for three-quarters of the refugees; and if not America, then Great Britain, South Africa or Argentina – anywhere that meant a respite from persecution and the opportunity for economic advancement.

Those who chose Palestine were as varied in composition, class and occupation as the westerly migrants. Possibly they had a more highly developed Jewish consciousness, but what was auspicious about the Second Aliyah was that perhaps as many as 10,000 of them were young people imbued with the nationalist socialism of Syrkin and Borochov, or the array of political ideologies rife in Russia. Many were Haskalah or university-educated, already fluent in Hebrew, and had been politically affiliated abroad. They were intelligent, rebellious, impatient with the exploitative colonial approach of the First Aliyah settlements of Barons de Rothschild and Hirsch, and fired with revolutionary enthusiasm. But even they fell victim to the rigours of pioneering life. It is calculated that by 1914 no more than 1200 of them had stayed the course of farm labour in the settlements; an additional few hundred lived in the towns and cities. Those who stayed laid the foundations of the future Jewish state. Among them were several important names in the political and social development of the Yishuv: Ben-Gurion and Berl Katznelson, leaders of the trade union movement; Yitzchak Ben-Zvi, a Po'alei Zion tactician; Yitzchak Tabenkin, a radical kibbutz leader; Joseph Haim Brenner, Zionism's first major writer of fiction; Moshe Sharett and Levi Eshkol, future prime ministers; Joseph Sprinzak, political activist and first speaker of Israel's parliament; and Aaron David Gordon (1856–1922), mystical exponent of the religion of labour and spiritual mentor to the pioneering settlement movement. Of all the diverse personalities moulded by Russian Zionism, Gordon was the strangest and most compelling.

He was born in Troyanov, a village in the province of Podolia. His grandfather was a noted Talmudic scholar, and his father estate manager for a wealthy relative, Baron Joseph Guenzburg, one of Russia's great landowners and business magnates. Gordon was privileged enough to receive a religious education in Talmud, Bible and Hebrew grammar from private tutors, as well as studying Russian and secular subjects on his own. His formative years were spent on the land, a rural existence which he loved. He was the only one of his parents' five children to survive and they were anxious for him to evade compulsory military service, but Gordon insisted on presenting himself for examination. When he was found medically unfit, he went to work as factotum on a large tract of land rented out by the baron for farming, married, fathered seven children – five of whom, marked by genetic inheritance, failed to survive – and spent the next twenty-three years running the estate. In his leisure time he read widely in Russian literature, especially Tolstoy but also Lermontov, Belinsky and Gorky.

Respected by the workers for his concern with their wellbeing, and popular with the young, whose education he encouraged, Gordon was ambivalent about much of the current Haskalah literature, finding it derivative and inauthentic. Traditional Judaism held even less appeal, particularly so when his one son to reach maturity became intolerantly Orthodox and rejected the family environment. He was sympathetic from afar to the colonizing ideals of Chibbat Zion without then – or ever – formally joining it or any other political organization. What weaned him from ambivalent secularism to positive espousal of Jewish cultural values was reading Achad Ha-Am's collection of essays *At the Crossroads*, published in 1895. Thereafter, he became a keen advocate of compulsory Hebrew-language study for girls as well as boys in his town's dwindling Jewish community.

In 1903, the estate on which Gordon worked was sold to a new owner and he lost his job. Forty-seven and unemployed, he agonized over what to do next. His relatives offered suggestions and business possibilities, and there was talk of emigrating to America. After months of wavering, and despite the vehement opposition of his wife's family, he took the decision to leave for Palestine alone, to work the soil as a farm labourer. He gave his wife and daughter what money he had, to tide them over until they could join him in Palestine. Although biographies are reticent, presenting Gordon's decision to become a settler as the heroic realization of his slowly maturing philosophy, and there are few clues in his own writings, it is likely that he was going through a personal and domestic mid-life crisis. Again, the comparison with the young Achad Ha-Am's attempts to escape, and his struggle between freedom and familial duty, is instructive; but even more pertinent was the example of Leo Tolstoy, whom Gordon admired and identified with. In his later, back-to-nature years Tolstoy, too, had disentangled from his family to lead the simple peasant life. Photos of Gordon, with intense evangelist's eyes and bushy beard, dressed in habitual peasant's tunic, are disconcerting: the image they intend to convey is Tolstoyan, but the viewer is more likely to be put in mind of one of Dostoevsky's holy fools.

Middle-aged and frail, Gordon was a curious misfit among the enthusiastic young pioneers as he went looking for work in the Palestinian settlements. Eventually he found manual employment in the vineyards and orange groves of Petach Tikvah and Rishon-le-Zion. After five years, he brought over his daughter and wife, but his wife died almost immediately. From 1912, he worked in various villages in Galilee, enduring the endemic hardships of malaria, unemployment and hunger, until he joined the founders of Deganiah, one of the country's first collective farms.

He began writing, and attracting followers, in 1909. His articles were mainly published in the journal of Ha-Po'el Ha-tza'ir (The Young Worker), established by the Labour party, as was the Palestinian branch of Po'alei Zion, in 1905. Initially, the Syrkin-inspired Ha-Po'el Ha-tza'ir garnered more support among young newcomers than the Borochovian Po'alei Zion. Its programme (and major difference from Po'alei Zion) emphasized Zionism above Marxism and Jewish nationalism above international socialism. Whereas Po'alei Zion regarded itself as the Palestinian outpost of the world class struggle, Ha-Po'el Ha-tza'ir rejected any ties with socialist parties abroad and gave priority to the collective organization of agriculture. The intense rivalry between the two nascent parties, conducted in a series of public debates, was neatly defined a few years later by Ha-Po'el Ha-tza'ir's foremost ideologue, Yosef Aharonovitch: 'One aspired to the renaissance of the Hebrew nation in the full sense of the word, and envisioned Hebrew Labour as the principal means and a necessary condition for this renaissance; and the second aspired to the renaissance of the Hebrew proletariat . . . to enable it to be distinguished within the world proletariat, and conceived of Zionism as a means to this goal. One group became workers because they were Zionists, and the other group became Zionists because they were proletarians.'

The central tenet of Gordon's philosophy was the healing value of physical labour, especially for Jews coming from Diaspora ghettos. He imbued work with an exalted mystique that thrilled the pioneers of Ha-Po'el Ha-tza'ir, who looked to him as their spiritual mentor, lapping up his metaphysical epiphanies. In biblical Hebrew, the word for 'work' also connotes 'religious service', and Gordon regularly drew on the nuances of the twin derivation, confident that its subtlety would not be lost on his readers. 'Work,' he told them, 'is our cure. The ideal of Work must become the pivot of all our aspirations. It is the foundation upon which our national structure is to be erected. Only by making Work, for its own sake, our national ideal shall we be able to cure ourselves of the plague that has affected us for many generations, and mend the rent between ourselves and Nature.' He was no more a systematic thinker than he was a political animal. He wrote in visionary spurts, after a hard day's labour in the fields where, according to an onlooker, he worked with the fervour of pious Jews reciting their concluding prayers on the Day of Atonement. If he had any intellectual antecedents, apart from Tolstoy, they are to be found in the Populist writer Peter Kropotkin, who celebrated labour as a value in itself, and in Rousseau's idealization of *l'homme naturel* before his inherent goodness is corrupted by society. For Gordon, the Jews would, as an early pioneering song put it, 'rebuild themselves in building the land', and by establishing a healthy agricultural foundation wipe away the corruption of ghetto society with its petty speculation and parasitism.

His ecstatic pantheism, uniting man and nature in cosmic harmony, was expressed in soaring imagery. 'And when, O Man, you will return to Nature – on that day your eyes will open, you will gaze straight into the eyes of Nature, and in its mirror you will see your own image. You will know that you have returned to yourself, that when you hid from Nature, you hid from yourself . . . On that day you will know that your former life did not befit you, that you must renew all things: your food and your drink, your dress and your home, your manner of work and your mode of study – everything!' In an essay published in 1911, entitled 'People and Labour', Gordon accuses Diaspora existence of having alienated Jews from the concept of physical work. Just as they had been cut off from nature for two thousand years, so too they had lost the principal ingredient for national life – 'not labour performed out of external compulsion, but labour to which one is attached in a natural and organic way'. There is a triad of people, labour and land, out of which grows its national culture. 'Labour is not only the force which binds man to the soil and by which possession of the soil is acquired; it is also the basic energy for the creation of a national culture.'

Gordon has the Russian Populist distrust of 'culture' expounded by intellectuals, just as he is suspicious of Zionism filtered through the school of Marx and Engels. Debates at the Zionist Congresses (Gordon did not attend one until 1913) had reduced the ideal of culture to abstract formulations about 'the rebirth of the spirit' or political ideologies, whereas 'A vital culture, far from being detached from life, embraces it in all its aspects.' He presents an extraordinary definition of culture. 'Culture is whatever life creates for living purposes. Farming, building and road-making – any work, any craft, any productive activity – is part of culture and is indeed the foundation and the stuff of culture.' The so-called 'higher culture' of science, art, religion and the like is sustained by demotic underpinnings and could not survive without them, any more than butter could be produced without milk. The pioneers in Palestine are seeking not a sterile, academic culture but 'the fresh milk of a healthy people's culture'. This 'culture of life' is bound up with veneration for the dignity of labour on the national soil.

In Palestine we must do with our own hands all the things that make up the sum total of life. We must ourselves do all the work, from the least strenuous, cleanest and most sophisticated to the dirtiest and most difficult. In our own way, we must feel what a worker feels and think what a worker thinks – then, and only then, shall we have a culture of our own, for then we shall have a life of our own.

In another article of the same year, called 'Some Observations', Gordon uses the disjunction between labour and natural life as a metaphor for the fragmented condition of Diaspora Man. There are two paths to choose from in Palestine, he begins, in distant imitation of Achad Ha-Am's *At the Crossroads.* The first is the practical one of the worldly-wise, the exiguous way of the Galut,[1] which will always mean exile, even in

1. Galut is the Hebrew word for 'exile' or 'diaspora', specifically connoting exile from the Land of Israel.

Palestine. The second is the path to true and meaningful life: 'Let each man choose whichever of the two paths he will.' Given their respective descriptions, it is hardly a choice. However, the point Gordon wishes to make is that it is not enough for the Jew to be taken out of the ghetto; the ghetto, with its material values and limiting prospects, has to be taken out of the Jew. Return to the ancestral homeland will not suffice for a national renaissance; there has to be a Return to Self, a self-rehabilitation through labour and oneness with nature. Such a transformation will not be achieved by the dictates of 'historical necessity', that is, by the vision of universal socialist redemption, which would merely replicate in Palestine the economic conditions and restrictive culture of the Diaspora. In contrast to Po'alei Zion's expectation of a mass migration to Palestine to wage the class struggle, Gordon candidly admits that the majority may follow later but only 'the select few' are capable of laying the foundations of national revival. For the sake of these few, 'one must speak the truth, one must proclaim it day in and day out, in every way and in every tongue.'

It is small wonder that the pioneers of Ha-Po'el Ha-tza'ir idolized Gordon. He encouraged their endeavours and approved their exploits, not like some pulp fiction writer fuelling the legend of Buffalo Bill or Wyatt Earp, but as one of them in the harsh terrain of Galilee, their elderly exemplar, the wise camp-fire philosopher. When they wanted to know the unique purpose of their national movement, he articulated it. It was not to preserve the religion of Judaism or to prevent assimilation; it was to restore the cosmic element to Jewish life: 'It is life we want, no more and no less than that, our own life feeding on our own vital sources, in the fields and under the skies of our Homeland, a life based on our own physical and mental labours; we want vital energy and spiritual richness from this living source. We come to our Homeland in order to be planted in our natural soil from which we have been uprooted, to strike our roots deep into its life-giving substances, and to stretch out our branches in the sustaining and creating air and sunlight of the Homeland.' When they worried that preoccupation with national concerns might dilute their contribution to humanity, he reassured them. What they were doing in Palestine was to mould 'a new people, a human people whose attitude toward other peoples is informed with the sense of human brotherhood and whose attitude toward nature and all within it is inspired by noble urges of life-loving creativity'. When they wondered if political involvement was called for, either in supporting workers' strikes at the settlements or in developing fraternal relations with Jewish socialists abroad, Gordon reminded them of their proper vocation. 'We must shun political activity as destructive of our highest ideals; otherwise we become unwitting traitors to the principle of our true self, which we have come here to bring back to life. Nor must we tie ourselves to the world proletariat, to the International, whose activities and whose methods are basically opposed to ours . . . I believe that we should not even combine with Jewish workers in the Diaspora specifically as workers, much as we respect labour; they should be our allies as Jews, just like any other Jews in the Diaspora who share our aspirations, no more and no less.'

The conscience of his generation and incorruptible high priest of the religion of labour, doubts nevertheless obtrude about Gordon the man and the thinker, for all his efforts to unify life and intellect in the worship of purifying nature. The vehemence of his rejection of the Diaspora is strange in one who spent three-quarters of a seemingly contented career there. As significant, perhaps, is the derision he heaps on psychology 'which pretends to probe so deeply into the nature of human behaviour' in an article, 'Some Observations', written not long after his wife's death. The same concern to keep prying at bay permeates his last piece, 'Final Reflections', written in 1921 when he knew he was dying of cancer. He asks to be remembered not as an individual but only for any intrinsic worth his ideas might have in regenerating national life. 'This has been my custom – I have honoured in silence all those who have passed on – and I would wish that custom to be followed in my case. Let those who wish to honour me do so silently.'

A son disowned, a wife unmourned, a discarded previous existence – were these what prompted Gordon to remake himself and stifle memory in the exhaustion of physical labour? And was he revealing more than was prudent for his public image when he writes about the unsatisfied 'madman of the spirit' who looks at the course of his life and is overwhelmed 'with rancour and pain'? 'He is full of doubts as to whether that peculiar, chaotic world called human life and that strange creature called man can be improved.' But if we respect his dying wish and concentrate on his thought, the reservations multiply. 'Natural life', 'organic unity', 'vital culture', 'return to Nature', 'vital energy and spiritual richness', 'human life of cosmic dimensions' – how frequently and meaninglessly the key phrases flow from Gordon's pen. His quest for the holy grail of national revival in union with nature and consummation in labour evoke uneasy recollections not so much of Rousseau and Tolstoy as of communist and fascist proclamations that would appear in the decades after his death.

Gordon's objections to socialist dogma, and his refusal to throw in his lot with any political party, stemmed from his conviction that renewal of the human spirit had to precede any restructuring of the social order. Marxism sought to change society by changing the system; Gordon wanted to change society by transforming the Jewish individual.

On the one pressing issue of which he had first-hand experience and on which his thoughts would have been respectfully heard, he was platitudinous and unconvincing: the Arab question. In 1918, in a detailed essay on Zionism after the Balfour Declaration, *Our Work from Now On: The People and Labour*, Gordon devoted a special chapter to relations with the Arabs. Previously, his concern had been that private Jewish landowners, by exploiting cheap Arab labour, would exacerbate tensions between the two peoples and jeopardize Zionism's aims: 'The workers are natives, the employers are foreigners. If we do not till the soil with our very own hands, the soil will not be ours – not only not ours in a social, or national sense, but not even in a political sense. Here we shall also be aliens . . . who traffic in the fruit of the labour of others.' But he held out a vague humanitarian hope of goodwill on both sides. 'Through the power of truth, we shall find a way for a life of partnership with the Arabs. Co-operative life and work would become a blessing for both peoples.' In the heady aftermath of the Balfour Declaration, whose key words for Zionists were that His Majesty's Government 'views with favour the establishment in Palestine of a national home for the Jewish people . . .', Gordon becomes more bullish. 'Zionism has won the national right to Palestine, as a people of high political standing.' A land once flowing with milk and honey had been left barren and almost empty of life. 'This is a kind of affirmation of our right to the country, as it was a hint that the country awaits us.' But did not the Arabs, greatly in the majority, also have a claim on the land, and could not the Jewish settlers be accused of dispossessing its natural masters? Let us examine the nature of the Arab claim, Gordon replies to his own question. 'If mastery of the land implies political mastery, then the

Arabs have long ago forfeited their title,' since for centuries Palestine had been under Turkish rule and was now governed by the British. If one discounted, for the moment, rights acquired through living on the land and working it, then 'the Arabs, like ourselves, have none other than a historical claim upon the land, although our historical claim is undoubtedly stronger'.

So it all came down to occupancy and cultivation of the land; no difference qualitatively between the claims, only quantitatively, since for the present Arabs outnumbered Jews. In the future, strengthened by immigration from the Diaspora, the Jews would wish to expand their community and their hold on cultivated lands. Could this not be construed as an attempt to deprive the majority of its rights? No, says Gordon, borrowing aspects of Borochov's argument to emphasize his point, because in peaceful competition between two peoples each had the right to expand without harming the other, and the prize would go to that people which displayed greater dedication, skill and capacity for survival. He is so confident of the outcome that he reminds fellow Zionists that they must be considerate and circumspect in all their dealings according to moral principles worthy of the Jewish people, and must strive for maximum collaboration with the Arabs, even when they meet with resistance and intransigence.

That pious hope was badly shaken by the Arab riots of 1920 and 1921. Brutal killings made mockery of the complacent generalities about co-operation, and in a message to the central committee of Ha-Po'el Ha-tza'ir Gordon discarded his previous illusions: 'The Arabs have all the traits and characteristics of a living nation, though they are not free. They live in this country, cultivate their land, speak in their own national tongue, and so on. Hence, their claim to the country has the validity of the claim of a living people . . . even if it is not expressed in an attractive and cultured fashion but through savage vociferousness, riots, etc. While we are debating whether there is such a thing as an Arab national movement, life goes on, and the movement grows . . .'

He warned against the fallacious notion that the riots had been perpetrated by ignorant mobs, incited by the landowning Arabs. 'The truth is that the labouring Arab masses, no less than the *effendis*, were, are, and always will be against us. And even if some day they rise up against the *effendis*, they will still be against us with the *effendis*.'

Gordon was one of a long line of Zionist thinkers who had diagnosed the Jewish problem but contented themselves with soothing placebos for the Arab problem, in the hope of staving off inevitable confrontation. The future filled him with foreboding in his final months: 'More important, he [the 'madman of the spirit'] doubts whether man has, or ever will have, the desire for improvement.'

He bore his fatal illness with fortitude, working as long as his strength lasted, and was buried in the kibbutz he had helped to found. By his own definition, one of those whose eccentric presence and sudden enthusiasms are viewed with suspicion by prosaic, practical men, Gordon's hymns of praise to Nature and to Work had an enduring influence on the philosophy of the kibbutz movement which, more than any other institution, would reflect the future direction of Zionist society in Palestine.

10

Rabbi Abraham Kook – Religious Zionism

Achad Ha-Am expected no more of his spiritual centre in Palestine than that 'the spirit of Judaism will radiate to the great circumference, to all the communities of the Diaspora, to inspire them with new life and to preserve the overall unity of our people'. A. D. Gordon was more ambitious: 'What we seek to establish in Palestine is a new, re-created Jewish people, not a mere colony of Diaspora Jewry . . . It is our aim to make Jewish Palestine the mother country of world Jewry, with Jewish communities in the Diaspora as its colonies, not the reverse.'

At the time Gordon was writing, there were approximately sixteen million Jews in the world. According to the first, disputed census carried out by the British mandate administration in October 1922, there were 84,000 Jews living in Palestine. They had suffered severely during the First World War. Turkish officials harassed the Zionist leadership, and put on trial those suspected of spying for the Allies, closed the Anglo-Palestine Bank, conscripted young Jews to serve in labour battalions and deported hundreds to Egypt. The Turkish currency collapsed in the winter of 1916, and a plague of locusts devastated the growing crops. When Allenby's army entered Jerusalem in December 1917, the Yishuv had decreased by nearly 30,000 souls since 1914, to around 56,000 Jews, representing just 8 per cent of the total population of Palestine. They still formed the majority in Jerusalem and Tiberias; elsewhere there were 6000 in Tel-Aviv, 2500 in Haifa and around 5500 in the largest agricultural villages of Petach Tikvah, Rishon-le-Zion and Rehovot. About 12,000 others were scattered around 57 smaller settlements.

Antonio Gramsci, the Italian Marxist, wrote in his *Prison Notebooks* that 'the supremacy of a social group manifests itself in two ways, as "domination" and as "intellectual and moral leadership".' The social group which predominated in the Zionist Organization from its founding by Herzl until the 1930s, and from which its leadership came, was European-based, bourgeois, politically liberal, culturally humanist and accustomed to pursuing its aims through the conventional channels of diplomacy. The predominant social group in the Yishuv – bolstered by 35,000 new immigrants of the Third Aliyah between 1919 and 1923, many of them veterans of the Bolshevik revolution – was radically left-wing, daringly experimental, dismissive of bourgeois mores and looking to create a socialist blueprint of the ideal society. The people who had helped to pay their fare to Palestine were from the very classes they wished to overthrow.

Among the new intake, for example, were the first cadres of Ha-shomer Ha-tza'ir (The Young Watchman), a Zionist youth group formed in Galicia during the war years. Many of its members, the *shomrim*, were middle-class, well-educated, steeped in the romantic ideas and symbols of the Free German Youth movement, the philosophy of Martin Buber in his patriotic *Blut und Boden* (Blood and Soil) phase, and the theories of Marx and Freud. Family ties, status symbols, the compromises and hypocrisies of adult society, were not for them. The first kibbutz they founded in 1922, Bet Alfa, was far more radical than Deganiah or any other agricultural co-operative established by Gordon and the previous generation of pioneers. The children's education was to be collective, and they were to sleep in the children's house, not with their parents. All meals were to be taken together; that anyone might wish to be alone was deemed asocial and a residue of bourgeois upbringing. Dance, collective decision-taking, communal dining, regular group confessionals – these were their sacred rites. Sexually, they were that prim combination of puritanism and promiscuity which was a feature of Russian morality under communism. The family was to be liquidated as a social unit, decreed the kibbutz, 'recognizing it only as an expression of erotic life', so comrades would coyly announce that they had 'just become one family' as a euphemism for sexual congress, but adolescents were exposed to classical music and art to sublimate their libidinous urges. By 1927, Ha-shomer Ha-tza'ir had established five similar kibbutzim, and would found several more in the next decade. Alone among Labour Zionist parties, it continued to support the Third Communist International and took an increasingly pro-Stalinist line, despite Stalin's purges during the 1930s.

That the socialist Yishuv and the conservative Diaspora could more or less maintain their organizational partnership throughout these years, regardless of such incompatible value systems, was due to two major factors: first, that the goal of establishing a secure Jewish home-land in Palestine remained paramount, and was given added urgency in the aftermath of the First World War and the Russian Revolution, with dislocation and suffering for Jewish communities throughout the Pale of Settlement; and second, that the focus of attention had shifted to Palestine, where building a national infrastructure was the immediate objective, where there was only one British mandate administration to be petitioned and where growing Arab resistance to Zionism was becoming the overriding concern.

It had been agreed by the Allies at the San Remo conference of 1920 that Britain should administer Palestine and be responsible for the implementation of the Balfour Declaration. The reasons why Lloyd George's foreign secretary sent his November 1917 letter to Lord Rothschild expressing British government sympathy for Zionist aspirations have been detailed and exhaustively analysed by, among many others, the chief Zionist negotiator, Chaim Weizmann, in his auto-biography, *Trial and Error.* The 'why' is still not clear, but was probably a combination of sympathy for Jewish suffering, together with Foreign Office pragmatism in expediting American involvement in the war while thwarting President Wilson's interest in a separate peace with Turkey, tempering the course of events in Russia, and countering French influence in the Middle East. Suspicions about Britain's motives lingered on among the powers, and it was not until July 1922 that the Palestine Mandate was approved by the Council of the League of Nations, meeting in London. According to Article II, the mandatory power was responsible for placing the country under such political, administrative and economic conditions as would secure the establish-ment of the Jewish national home and the development of self-governing institutions, while safeguarding the civil and religious rights of *all* Palestinians; Article IV recognized the Zionist Organization as 'an appropriate Jewish agency'[1] to assist in establishing the national home, and Article VI required the administration, in co-operation with the

1. The public body designated by the terms of the mandate to advise and co-operate with the Palestinian administration in 'such . . . matters as may affect the establishment of the Jewish National Home and the interests of the Jewish population in Palestine'. The executive of the Zionist Organization fulfilled the role.

Jewish Agency, to facilitate immigration and 'close settlement by Jews of the land'.

Sir Herbert Samuel, a professing Jew and a member of Lloyd George's cabinet, had been despatched as the civilian high commissioner in June 1920. He remained until 1925, attempting to implement the vague guidelines of the mandate while meeting Zionist demands and allaying Arab fears; he was the first of a line of administrators who grappled with one of the most thankless, complicated postings of British colonial rule. When not addressing complaints to the high commissioner or engaged in debates about the correct socialist path, the Labour hierarchy of the Yishuv was gathering to itself the reins of political power. 'I am for Bolshevism,' declared Ben-Gurion, first secretary-general of the Histadrut, the trade union federation established in 1920, but what most impressed him about Lenin, he noted in his diary, was his capacity to reflect on 'the fundamental facts of reality' and his tactical genius in knowing when to cast aside what had seemed necessary the day before. Sublimating ideological differences for the sake of the greater whole was the most impressive feature of the Yishuv's intellectual and moral leadership during the first decade of the British mandate.

The Histadrut was itself an amalgam of two mutually suspicious Labour parties, Po'alei Zion and Ha-Po'el Ha-tza'ir, brought together by the persuasive arguments of Ben-Gurion and Berl Katznelson. Composed of existing trade union associations organized by occupation, membership of the new Histadrut was open to all workers regardless of political affiliation, provided they did not 'exploit' the labour of others. Within a few years it had its own Workers' Bank, a construction company, schools, a daily newspaper, a public transport system, cultural and recreational facilities, and a sickness fund for members and their families. It was a workers' commonwealth in miniature, a socialist state in the making, all its members belonging as shareholders to the holding company Chevrat ha-Ovdim (The Workers' Society) which oversaw all its enterprises. With less than 5000 members at its inception, the Histadrut had grown to nearly 110,000 by 1939. Kibbutz membership numbered about 700 in 1922, the year of Gordon's death, 4000 five years later, and nearly 25,000 – more than 5 per cent of the Jewish population, on 110 settlements – at the outbreak of the Second World War. By 1928, three separate but co-operating kibbutz federations had been established, to cater for the subtle but passionate doctrinal differences among the pioneers.

Political merger followed early in 1930, when the leaderships of Po'alei Zion and Ha-Po'el Ha-tza'ir presented a joint platform combining nationalist and socialist rhetoric in sufficient proportions for over 80 per cent of the membership of each party to vote for union. The new party became known as Mapai, an acrostic of Mifleget Po'alei Eretz Yisrael, the Palestine Workers' Party, and would dominate politics for the next thirty-five years.

Bourgeois capital – the prerequisite of Marx's paradigm for the proletarian revolution – was cautious about investing in Palestine, especially during the international recession of the late 1920s, so the Labour Zionists had to create their socialist structures from scratch in a country without a developed industrial economy. The compactness of the Jewish community, and the willingness of many new immigrants to try settling on the land rather than drifting into petty urban trade, was a vivid reversal of the sprawling east European experience which had been repeated in the slums of London's East End and the tenements of New York's Lower East Side. A new 'totally Jewish type' had emerged in Palestine, boasted Shmaryahu Levin, the veteran propagandist and educator, a type that had revived Hebrew as the daily language, organized farming and light industry on collectivist principles, and volunteered to serve in the self-defence organization, Ha-shomer, which guarded Jewish settlements on land bought by Arthur Ruppin and the Jewish National Fund.

It was the dawning realization that Jewish collective enterprise was transforming the character of their country – a feudal agrarian society controlled by a few clans in Beirut, Damascus or Jerusalem – that stimulated Arab national consciousness and provoked increasing hostility. It is a moot point who was more offended by the socialist ideology, communal living and ostentatious sexual equality of the settlements: the Arab *fellahin*, or traditional Orthodox Jews.

Since the days of Judah Alkalai and Zvi Hirsch Kalischer, the relationship of Orthodox Judaism to Zionism had been complicated and sensitive. On the one hand, it was impious to try to hurry the divine plan for the Ingathering of the Exiles and ultimate redemption; on the other hand, a few Orthodox rabbis (including Alkalai, Kalischer and their successors) argued that encouraging immigration and settling in the Holy Land was essential preparation for the coming of the Messiah, quoting proof texts from the Talmud, Moses Maimonides and other hallowed authorities. The majority of Orthodox Jews, however, in the Diaspora and in Palestine, stayed aloof from, or actively opposed, Zionism in its formative years, as did the majority of Reform Jews. But a small Orthodox Zionist party was founded in Vilna in 1902, its guiding spirits Rabbi Jacob Raines, won over by Herzl's personality, and Ze'ev Jawitz, who wrote the party's first manifesto (of the making of manifestos there was no end in early Zionism). It took the name Mizrachi, an abbreviation of Merkaz Ruchani (Spiritual Centre), to make clear what it stood for, and against, in the Zionist Organization. The Law of Moses would always be Israel's spiritual beacon, not the values of Achad Ha-Am and other secularists.

The factional splits within Mizrachi were a religious microcosm of divisions among the socialist Zionists whom they opposed. Loosely allied only in adherence to traditional Judaism and suspicion of any modernizing tendencies, Mizrachi members could not decide whether to act solely as a watchdog against freethinkers within the Zionist movement or to adopt a constructive programme of education and settlement in Palestine. They could rarely agree which was their core creed, Orthodoxy or Zionism. Israel without Torah was like a body without a soul, but the Jewish faith without its national homeland was only half a religion. The practical faction eventually won the day, setting up a modern *yeshivah*, a school and a teachers' seminary in Palestine before the First World War. Rabbis still predominated in the movement. Two of them, Meir Berlin and Yehudah Leib Fishman, were successful emissaries in America, where their brand of religious Zionism attracted new supporters and healthy donations from east European Orthodox immigrants.

In 1922, Mizrachi moved its headquarters to Jerusalem. It established a workers' section, Ha-Po'el Ha-Mizrachi, as a religious riposte to the socialist Histadrut, its own bank, and its first kibbutz, and at its congress of 1926 in Antwerp published an admirably succinct statement of aims: 'The Mizrachi is a Zionist, national and religious federation striving to build the national home of the Jewish people in Palestine in accordance with the written and traditional laws.' To gain control of the Zionist institutions for traditional Judaism, and apply Talmudic law to governing the Yishuv, was Mizrachi's programme, seemingly a forlorn one, given the anti-religious, determinist philosophy of most of the pioneers. But Mizrachi gleaned encouragement from the popularity enjoyed by a remarkable rabbi, the religious mystic Abraham Isaac Kook (1865–1935), Orthodoxy's spiritual equivalent of Labour Zionism's Aaron David Gordon.

Kook was born in a small Latvian village, and received a typical Orthodox education in the Talmud and law codes, which he supplemented by his own studies in Bible, the Hebrew language and Jewish philosophy, especially mysticism. At the age of nineteen, he entered the famous *yeshivah* of Volozhin. His evident piety and fervour were unusual in that dry Talmudic atmosphere. At the age of twenty-three he was appointed to his first rabbinic post in the village of Zaumel, and stayed there for seven years, before being promoted to the large town of Bausk, in Lithuania. There, his reputation grew, as did his interest in Palestinian colonization as an expression of *atchalta di-g'ullah* – the birth-pangs of messianic redemption. He published his first essay on Zionism, in which he accepted Jewish nationalism, even at its most secular, as an unwitting expression of divine purpose.

In 1904 he emigrated to Palestine with his wife and only son, despite offers from important Lithuanian communities. He accepted the position of rabbi of Jaffa and the nearby agricultural settlements. There, he worked closely with Mizrachi in expanding its first school, but had a prickly relationship with the religious Zionist movement, as he did with the ultra-Orthodox rabbis of the old Yishuv, who were suspicious of his overtures to the secular pioneers. In 1909, for example, Kook became embroiled in a controversy about the practical consequences for farmers of the biblical commandment that every seventh year the land should lie fallow. He permitted a dispensation on technical grounds, in a densely argued Talmudic *responsum*, to the ire of the rabbinical establishment, for whom there could be no abrogation of religious law.

Kook was a prolific writer, as the urge took him, without attempting to construct a comprehensive philosophy. A constant sense of God's immanence, a rapturous attachment to the Holy Land and an unremitting love for all members of the House of Israel suffuse his essays. The same passionate fervour with which Gordon yearned to restore the union between Jew and nature pours from Kook's pen, save that he yearned to restore the union between Jew and God, to be consummated in the Land of Israel, where 'man's imagination is lucid and clear, clean and pure, capable of receiving the revelation of Divine Truth and of expressing in life the sublime meaning of the ideal of the sovereignty of holiness'. Because he was that rare creature in mundane human affairs, a radiant mystic, and because mysticism follows its own impulses and revelations, it is not possible to assess Kook's writings by the criteria applied to other Zionist thinkers. This is not special pleading; it is simply to recognize that the metaphysical systems of, say, Pascal and Kierkegaard start from different premises than those of Machiavelli and Hume. Kook accepted without question the basic rabbinic doctrine that God had demonstrated Israel's election as His chosen people by giving them the unique gifts of the Torah and the Holy Land. There is nothing original or controversial about his theology. What was unusual for someone of his traditional background was his openness to modern cultural and scientific knowledge, and his readiness to incorporate it into a teleology of divine purpose. 'The spirit of Israel,' he wrote, 'is so closely linked to the spirit of God that a Jewish nationalist, no matter how secularist his intention may be, is, despite himself, imbued with the divine spirit even against his own will.'

Having travelled to Europe to attend an Orthodox conference, Kook was stranded in Switzerland when the First World War broke out. He was maintained there for more than a year by a wealthy supporter before going to London as temporary rabbi of a small congregation. He did not return to Palestine until the summer of 1919, and shortly afterwards he was appointed chief rabbi of the Ashkenazi community in Jerusalem. Two years later, the first civilian British high commissioner, Sir Herbert Samuel, called a conference of Palestinian Jewry to create their own religious law courts and institutions. The British were following the Ottoman model of religious administration, which had granted extensive autonomy to the various faiths in Palestine. Kook was elected president of the new rabbinic appeal court, and therefore, in effect, the first Ashkenazi chief rabbi of Palestine, a post he held until his death. Although many of the routine chores of office irked him, Kook's personal prestige, his commitment to Zionism and his receptivity to dialogue even with the most avowedly atheist accorded him a respect in Yishuv society rarely granted to his fellow custodians of rabbinic law. For their part, they resented his primacy, opposed his schemes to broaden the base of *yeshivah* studies and jealously guarded their traditional privileges. While Kook dreamed that pioneering in Palestine might presage the restoration of the Sanhedrin and the rebuilding of the Temple, they preferred to guard their patronage as legal interpreters and distributors of charity from the Diaspora.

By virtue of his stature, Kook could not avoid involvement in the public issues of the time. Shortly after his appointment as chief rabbi, Arab riots against Zionism broke out in Jaffa; sporadic incidents continued until 1929, when a previous dispute about Jewish and Muslim prayer rights at the Wailing Wall was fanned into widespread violence. Sixty Jews were killed in Hebron, and forty-five killed or wounded in Safed. Neither the British government nor the Zionist leadership had any doubt about Arab culpability, incited by the mufti of Jerusalem, Hajj Amin Al'Hussaini. There were demands for a strong Jewish response but, at meetings of the Jewish Agency executive, Kook expressed willingness to negotiate with the mufti to effect a compromise about the prayer arrangements. His offer was not taken up. If that made him unpopular with right-wing hardliners of the Revisionist movement, he restored the balance four years later by affronting Labour Zionists with his defence of Avraham Stavski, accused of murdering Chaim Arlosoroff, rising star of the Mapai party. To charge a Jew with the killing was, said Kook, a Jewish version of the ancient blood libel.

He was safer away from the murky world of politics, as he recognized in a reflection written during his Swiss exile: 'It is not fitting for [the sons of] Jacob to engage in political life at a time when statehood requires bloody ruthlessness and demands a talent for evil.' His gift was for seeing harmonizing sparks of the divine spirit in all things, sacred or profane, spiritual or scientific. For Kook, Darwin's theory of evolution did not contradict the Genesis account of man's origin, but confirmed the insights of Jewish mysticism, which had always regarded the world as continuously evolving towards the ultimate goal of holiness. This aptitude for seeing all human creativity as 'vessels of the spirit of the Almighty' and as particles of the divine scheme of universal restoration exasperated religious traditionalists, but was oddly reassuring to rebellious young pioneers anathematized for their iconoclasm. 'We lay *t'fillin* [the phylacteries donned by observant Jews before reciting morning prayers], the pioneers lay bricks,' Kook would say. He viewed their rejection of Orthodoxy allied to a passion for social justice not as heresy but as a valuable corrective to any religious faith that 'ignores the need of improving the state of the world . . . and instead hovers in a rarefied atmosphere and boasts of the perfection of the soul'. While he did not consider that theology should provide a programme for social reform, he wrote that 'a consistent application of all the laws of the Torah in social and economic matters' would not tolerate the capitalist system, since the biblical principle of 'Do what is right and good in the sight of the Lord' limited the privileges of the private property owner and imposed obligations upon him.

Some commentators have suggested that Kook's purpose was to woo Labour Zionists back to Orthodoxy, but that is to ascribe motives he was too transparent to harbour, and to misunderstand his mystical eschatology, in which all the builders of the Holy Land, heretics included, were instruments of the coming redemption. Even the most ardent secular nationalists and aggressive disbelievers were blithely corralled within Kook's cosmology: 'An individual can sever the tie that binds him to the source of life, but the House of Israel as a whole cannot. All of its most cherished possessions – its land, language, history and customs – are bathed in the radiant sanctity that comes from above.'

It is hard to feel hostility towards an opponent who compliments you, which may be why several hundred *kibbutzniks* joined the thousands who lined the streets of Jerusalem for Kook's funeral. They were paying their respects to a good human being who transcended the confines of organized Orthodoxy and rose above the low esteem in which rabbis generally were held. Neither a major thinker nor an outstanding scholar, Kook's personal qualities long outlasted his achievements. He was a compelling minor actor on the Zionist stage, an exemplar of what religious Zionism might have contributed to the national revival had it been less hide-bound and more courageous.

The antipathy between Orthodox religiosity and secular pioneering was soon to become an issue for the Yishuv, but it was of little significance compared to the quandary that could be avoided no longer: not the Jewish problem but the Arab problem.

II

Recognizing the 'Arab Problem'

In an article published in *Ha-Shiloah* in 1907, Yitzhak Epstein, a Russian-born teacher who had settled in Palestine in 1886, voiced an anxiety that was brushed aside by his Zionist contemporaries but came back to haunt them like a biblical prophecy. He wrote,

Among the grave questions raised by the concept of our people's renaissance on its own soil there is one which is more weighty than all the others put together. This is the question of our relations with the Arabs. This question, on the correct solution of which our own national aspirations depend, has not been forgotten, but rather has remained completely hidden from the Zionists, and in its true form has found almost no mention in the literature of our movement.

Epstein was exaggerating somewhat, to make his point. After all, Achad Ha-Am's first article in 1891 had drawn pessimistic attention to the nature of Jewish–Arab relations. In *Altneuland* Herzl had devoted seven pages (out of 300) to an optimistic assessment of future co-operation between the two, and Borochov's reputation as a Marxist dialectician rested in part on his analysis of the ethnic and class interests uniting Zionist settlers and Palestinian Arabs. Nevertheless, it is striking that Epstein's 'Hidden Question' came so low on the agenda of Zionist priorities. 'If you look at pre-war Zionist literature,' said Chaim Weizmann in a speech in 1931, 'you will find hardly a word about the Arabs.' It was from the First World War onwards – more precisely from the publication of the Balfour Declaration in 1917 – that Jewish–Arab relations deteriorated drastically.

It is conceivable, though unlikely, given the incompatible claims of two national movements fighting for the same territory, that a more sensitive appraisal by the Zionist newcomers might have averted the clash; but sensitivity would have vitiated the realization of an ultimate political objective prudently alluded to only in circumlocution. The objective was not merely a national home for the Jews, as proffered by the Balfour Declaration, but through massive immigration to transform the demography of Palestine, so that the Jewish minority acquired equal status in the eyes of the mandate authorities and international opinion, and a plausible basis for demanding self-government. This was the tacitly understood goal of Zionist policy during the mandate period. The practical demands of creating an autonomous Jewish society in Palestine ready for eventual statehood took precedence over theoretical ruminations about co-existence with the Arab majority. At the time of the serious riots of 1929, there was no Arab department in the Jewish Agency, nor was any Arab-language newspaper published by the Zionists.

With rare exceptions, Zionist analysis of the Arab problem was reactive – a response to specific outbreaks of Arab hostility – rather than part of any strategy. Since the moral justification for Zionism was never questioned, even by those Jewish thinkers sympathetic to the indigenous population, proposals for an accommodation with the Arabs invariably proceeded from the assumption that in time, given adequate guarantees, they would accept the Zionist entity in their midst; failing that, superior Zionist organization, technology and morale would prevail in any conflict between the two peoples. That a clash *was* inevitable was the unspoken conviction of Ben-Gurion, Weizmann and others in the Zionist leadership of the twenties and thirties, even while they proclaimed pious hopes for friendship and co-operation between the communities. Their pessimism had been foreshadowed a quarter of a century earlier by an Arab source. In 1905, Nagib Azouri, a Jaffa-born, French-educated Christian Arab, had written a book entitled *Le Reveil de la Nation Arabe*. In its introduction, he remarked on two important phenomena evident in his day: the awakening of the Arab nation and the secret efforts of the Jews to restore their ancient kingdom. 'These two movements are destined to fight each other persistently, until one prevails over the other.'

The Young Turks revolt of 1907–8 provided the impetus for the spread of Arab national consciousness, and transformed the nature of the dispute over Palestine. It ceased to be a local confrontation fuelled by unfamiliarity and mutual apprehensions between a suspicious native population and new settlers and became a struggle for hegemony between two peoples responding to the changed balance of power in the Middle East after the First World War.

Zionist imperatives required validation of its aims and thus a wishful misreading of Arab motives. Whereas the Zionists had come to Palestine as the emissaries of culture, and intended to 'expand the moral boundaries of Europe to the Euphrates', in Nordau's grandiose but geographically imprecise phrase, the native population of Palestine was a hapless pawn in the dream of pan-Arab nationalism fomented from Beirut, Damascus and Mecca. 'The Palestinian Arab community is not part of the Arab people or the Syrian people, nor is it a nation in its own right; it is made up of eleven ethnic communities and of numerous smaller sects,' Yitzchak Ben-Zvi still deluded himself in 1921, after the May riots. By the time Zionists could bring themselves to acknowledge the reality of a *Palestinian* Arab nationalism, which owed its emergence and political significance to the pressure of Zionism, any possibility of rapprochement had vanished. The ideological power struggle in Zionist ranks from the Second Aliyah (1904–14) to the Second World War (1939) revolved around the best way of implementing Zionist aims while combating Arab hostility: by integration, binationalism, separatism, or preparing for war while still going through the motions of seeking a diplomatic solution.

Although the vast majority of Zionist pioneers took for granted their role as harbingers of superior western values to the backward orient, there were isolated voices in favour of a more adaptive approach. Seven years before Epstein's article in *Ha-Shiloah*, Jerusalem-born Eliyahu Sapir had drawn attention to anti-Zionist propaganda in the Arab press. In a piece entitled 'Hatred of Israel in Arab Literature', he distinguished between the hostility of the Christian Arab minority and the quiescence of the Muslim majority, arguing that the future of Zionism depended on reaching a rapport with the Muslim Arabs, since they are 'one of those nations – or the sole nation – close to us and to our hearts'. Jewish life had flourished under the medieval Arab caliphates, whereas in Christian Europe, even after the Enlightenment, it had always been plagued by anti-Semitism. The Arabs were basically just, virtuous and kind, and any anti-Jewish sentiment had resulted from political motives: their perception that the Jews were a stumbling-block to Islamic expansion. With the triumph of Islam, that motive no longer existed. The historical lesson to draw was that 'in the land of our fathers and the neighbouring countries we must proclaim our worth, and our very existence and activities must constitute an open protest against all the slander and calumny being directed against us. And the most important thing is to feel entirely at home and not as guests in these countries, in their language and in their culture.'

Like Sapir, Epstein was prone both to idealize Israel's mission as 'a light unto the nations' and to romanticize 'the noble Arab', but there was a harder edge to his analysis of Zionism, which probably accounts for the attention his article received, while Sapir's had barely been noticed. Epstein echoed Achad Ha-Am in criticizing the settlers' attitude towards the *fellahin*, and in castigating the Zionist leadership who played at higher politics 'while the question of the resident people, the [country's] workers and actual owners, has not yet been raised, either in practice or theory'. It was a flagrant error to minimize the loyalty of a 'strong, resolute and zealous' people to Palestine: 'While we harbour fierce sentiments towards the land of our fathers, we forget that the nation now living there is also endowed with a sensitive heart and loving soul. The Arab, like all other men, is strongly attached to his homeland.'

Epstein cautioned Zionism against assuming the guise of a colonial movement, since both morality and political expediency required Arab consent for it to succeed. 'We must on no account cause harm to any people, and in particular to a great people whose hostility would be highly dangerous.' Amicable co-operation would be mutually bene-ficial; one people would regain its homeland, the other would benefit economically, socially and educationally, thus hastening 'the renais-sance of two ancient and gifted Semitic peoples with great potential-ities, who complement each other'. It did seem to be a *de haut en bas* relationship, however. 'We must throw wide open to the residents of this country our public institutions, hospitals, pharmacies, libraries and reading rooms, cheap eating places, savings and loan funds; we shall organize popular lectures, plays and musical performances in accordance with the spirit of the people and in their language; we shall allocate an important place to the Arabic language in our schools and shall will-ingly admit Arab boys; we shall open our kindergartens to their infants, thus helping poor families, bringing them economic, hygienic, and above all, moral and spiritual benefits.' Well-meaning and sincerely motivated though it is by admiration for a people whose 'physical development surpasses that of all the people of Europe', Epstein's zeal has a colonial arrogance: we will integrate into Arab society and receive its blessing on our endeavours; in return we will raise its level to ours.

In the same year, a contemporary of Epstein's went even further. Writing in *Ha-Me'orer*, a short-lived London literary journal, Rabbi Benjamin (the pseudonym of Yehoshua Radler-Feldmann, a Galician settler but not a rabbi) proposed assimilation as the best method of achieving acceptance. The rabbi *manqué* dressed his argument in pseudo-biblical phraseology: 'And you shall give him your sons and take his sons unto you, and the blood of his heroes will be mingled with your blood and you will increase, and like will find like, and they will become one kind.' But the assimilation Rabbi Benjamin so airily advocated was of the Arabs by the Jews. Five years later he took issue with Achad Ha-Am's gloomy prognosis about the unlikelihood of mass Jewish settlement, asserting that Palestine had room for five million newcomers, to whom a few hundred thousand Arabs would present no hindrance if the two peoples united 'for a single objective and for mutual assistance'. The Arabs would be taught 'a civilized and clean way of life' by the example of Jewish experience, ability and energy. Not expediency but altruism dictated his approach. 'The question of relations between Jews and Arabs does not belong to the sphere of politics, of considerations and interests, calculations and cunning; it is a moral and social issue, a matter of relations between fellow men.' He criticized the nascent labour movement for its insistence on employing only Jewish workers. While sympathizing with the young pioneers for whom the 'conquest of labour' was an article of faith, he disapproved of their blanket refusal to hire Arabs in Jewish colonies, because the vitality of the Yishuv depended, among other conditions, on 'the fostering of a benevolent attitude towards the nation residing in this country'.

More soberly analytical was Yosef Luria, a Romanian-born journalist and teacher and another settler of the class of 1907, who concluded, from the antipathy of Turkey's new regime towards Zionism and the failure of Turkish Jewry's representatives to lend support, that 'the Arabs constitute the main force in Palestine'. Their response to Zionism was crucial: they constituted a large block in the Turkish parliament and were prominent in the civil administration. The authorities would bow to their wishes concerning Jewish immigration. Could the Arabs be persuaded to modify their opposition to Zionism? Writing in *Ha-Olam* (*Die Welt* under its new Hebrew name) in 1911, Luria laid the blame squarely on Zionist myopia. 'During all the years of our labour in Palestine we completely forgot that there were Arabs in the country. The Arabs have been "discovered" only during the past few years. We regarded all European nations as opponents of our settlement, but failed to pay heed to one people – the people residing in this country and attached to it.' The Jews of Palestine had made no effort to achieve cultural and social affinity with them; even more dangerous, Zionism had done nothing to counter hostile Christian Arab propaganda and dispel the fear of the Muslim masses that 'the Jews would push them out of the country'. Luria concluded with a stern warning: 'We have been silent all these years and still are. The fate and development of our endeavours are in their hands, and yet we remain silent and wait.'

The most sophisticated advocate of integration was Dr Nissim Malul, a Palestinian-born Sephardi Jew, who was educated and later taught at Cairo University. From his historical perspective as an eastern Jew, he was not cowed by the threat of Arabism. Total immersion in Arab culture was a prerequisite for a revival of Hebrew culture, he wrote in a 1913 article entitled 'Our Position in the Country'. If the heirs of Judah Halevi and Maimonides wished to follow in their footsteps, 'we must consolidate our Semitic nationality and not obfuscate it with European culture. Through Arabic we can create a true Hebrew culture. But if we introduce European elements into our culture, then we shall simply be committing suicide.' Malul was a member of a group of oriental Jews in Jaffa who sought to promote Jewish–Arab understanding by means of a joint teachers' association. More significantly, he had returned from Egypt in 1911 to work for Arthur Ruppin.

In themselves, Sapir, Epstein, Rabbi Benjamin, Luria and Malul were fringe figures, eccentrics who had 'gone native' in their admiration for the Arab national character and culture, and clung to a naive optimism that practical aid to the local population would encourage receptivity to Zionism's ambitions. Their views found little sympathy among Jewish settlers, for whom superiority, not 'Semitic symbiosis', was the characteristic attitude towards Arabs. But in 1925, when Zionist–Arab relations were set inexorably on collision course, these veterans came together under the leadership of Arthur Ruppin to found Brit Shalom (Covenant of Peace), the association which proposed binationalism as the proper solution to the conflict between two peoples claiming the same land. Brit Shalom is usually given short shrift in histories of Zionism. Numbering between 100 and 200 supporters (depending on its detractors or sympathizers), including some of the most illustrious names in the intellectual life of the Yishuv, with no popular base or organizational framework, uncertain whether its role should be study and research or active political involvement, co-operation with the official Zionist leadership or independent work, it was derided as the brainchild of idealistic central European humanists – 'all those Arthurs, Hugos and Hanses' in the sneer of one critic – who did not grasp the realities of the Jewish–Arab conflict.

The significance of Brit Shalom lies in its failure. It correctly foresaw the consequences of Zionist policy, and while there is no proof that its approach would have been any more successful, it can be claimed with the benefit of hindsight that it represented the one brief, genuine attempt to bridge the chasm between Zionism's aims and recognition of the indigenous population's rights. Moreover, it was a noteworthy affirmation of liberal values at a time when these were being discarded in Europe, and where support for totalitarianism – whether of the right or the left – was growing and finding its echo among Zionists. The wan flicker and demise of Brit Shalom is a handy metaphor for the wider fate of political liberalism in the twentieth century.

Brit Shalom's founders set out their credo in their first publication, *Sh'ifoteinu* (Our Aspirations), issued in Jerusalem in 1927. It was not a political manifesto, but a statement of their Zionist authenticity. They claimed descent from Herzl's enlightened attitude towards the Arabs, as expressed in *Altneuland*; from Achad Ha-Am's realism regarding the scope of the Balfour Declaration; from A. D. Gordon's humanitarian ideals; and from Yitzhak Epstein and Rabbi Benjamin's views on integration. Brit Shalom, they wrote, was intent on creating in Palestine 'a binational state, in which the two peoples will enjoy totally equal rights as befits the two elements shaping the country's destiny, irrespective of which of the two is numerically superior at any given time'. Subtly modifying Zionism's basic premise, they sought to establish for the Jews in Palestine 'a firm and healthy community, which will consist of Jews in *as large a number* as possible, regardless of whether thereby the Jews will become *the majority as compared to the other inhabitants of the country*, since the question of the majority in the country should in no way be connected to any advantage in rights'.

Typically, Ben-Gurion pounced upon the opacity of this formula when a delegation of Brit Shalom supporters went to discuss binationalism with him. 'The formula you have proposed does not say anything, it only confuses and therefore damages us without giving anything to the Arabs. Is it not sufficient that we have one formula, "national home", the meaning of which no one knows, without you adding a second formula which says nothing? . . . What does the formula "binational state" mean? Sprinzak [Joseph Sprinzak, of Ha-Po'el Ha-tza'ir] says we do not wish to be a majority, but to be "many". What is many? A hundred thousand? A hundred and fifty thousand? Many in relation to whom, to the Arab population in Palestine or the Jewish population abroad? . . . I have an Arab problem only on a Zionist basis, when I want to solve in Palestine the problem of the Jewish people, that is to say, to concentrate it in Palestine and make it a free people in its own land . . . This expression "many" is just an evasion of the central and principal problem of Zionism – the promotion of large-scale Jewish immigration . . .'

That such a cosmopolitan group of intellectuals, academics, left-wing socialists and visionary humanists could agree on a general statement of principles was an achievement in itself, but it highlighted the central weakness of Brit Shalom. Adopting the moral high ground was all very well, but devoid of meaning if not applied to political action, from which Brit Shalom shrank. Its spokesmen included such respected figures as Robert Weltsch, editor of *Judische Rundschau*, the journal of the German Zionist movement; Jacob Thon from the settlement department of the Jewish Agency; Chaim Kalvarisky, director of the Palestine Jewish Colonization Association in the Galilee; Judah Magnes, chancellor and first president of the Hebrew University; and Hugo Bergmann, Martin Buber, Ernst Simon and Gershom Scholem, faculty members of the university. They were all men for whom Zionism was a moral crusade or it was nothing.

Thus Bergmann, writing in the third issue of *Sh'ifoteinu* in 1929, makes Zionism synonymous with Judaism's ethical teachings: 'We want Palestine to be ours in that the moral and political [*sic*] beliefs of Judaism will leave their stamp on the way of life in this country, and we will carry into execution here that faith which has endured in our hearts for two thousand years.' That faith and 'historical destiny' mean, for Bergmann, 'the task of battling for a change of values in the life of nations ... eradicating the majority spirit in national issues, creating a new moral, national and political order in the world which would guarantee to national minorities those same rights which the majority enjoys, and would render null and void the political value of numerical ratios between peoples.'

Never before had such a quixotic purpose been suggested for Israel's special mission and destiny. But Bergmann chose to discern in Judaism a propensity to binationalism and universalism rather than majority status and sovereignty. 'The historic task of the Jewish people at this time is to rebuild the ruins of Palestine together with the inhabitants of the country, and to be restored to life in all the countries of exile through this endeavour. It is not a state to which we aspire, but a homeland.' Intimations of manifest destiny came easily to the binationalists. Martin Buber, Bergmann's mentor, saw Zionism as the bridge between east and west, in imagery as windy as anything by Max Nordau. 'We shall strive towards this destiny not as servants of a great Europe, doomed to destruction, but as allies of a young Europe, still weak but consecrated to the future, not as a middle man of a degenerating civilization, but as champions of a new civilization whose creation we are party to ...'

Judah Magnes, the most courageous and consistent advocate of binationalism, was more circumspect, as befitted a disciple of Achad Ha-Am. In a pamphlet entitled *Like Unto All the Nations*, written in 1930, when the Yishuv was still reeling from Arab attacks against the defenceless Jewish communities of Tiberias, Safed and Hebron, he asked, 'What is Zionism? What does Palestine mean for us? ... I can answer for myself in almost the same terms that I have been in the habit of using for many years.

'Immigration.

'Settlement of the land.

'Hebrew life and culture.

'If you can guarantee these for me, I should be willing to yield the Jewish state and the Jewish majority ...'

The one principle which united the diverse supporters of Brit Shalom, and aroused the ire of their opponents, was renunciation of Jewish majority rule. In 1925, when 30,000 Jews were streaming into Palestine, Weltsch declared that the majority issue was unimportant, since even if the present rate of immigration were maintained, Jews would constitute 51 per cent of the population only in forty years' time. It was essential to find ways of achieving co-operation based on equality of status between two peoples who would live side by side. 'We want, therefore, not a Jewish state, but a binational state in Palestine. Within the framework of such a state, we see the possibility of creating that which now is lacking – the complete legal basis upon which independent, free and normal national life can be grounded, within the fabric of general society.'

Yosef Luria cited Switzerland and Finland, two countries with multinational and binational constitutions respectively, which granted equal cultural and linguistic status to all national groups regardless of size and guaranteed their rights, as models for Palestine. 'It is the land of two peoples, who live there or should live there by equal national right; any political institution must be based solely on a political arrangement which cannot be changed for the worse by majority vote. Without acceptance of this principle, the parliament will inevitably become the instrument of the majority, which will suppress the national rights of the minority.'

The dangerously ingenuous gadfly Rabbi Benjamin, writing in the second issue of *Sh'ifoteinu*, argued by means of tortuous semantics that the quest for Jewish majority status was a minimalization of the Herzlian dream, whereas the Brit Shalom formula of *as large a number as possible* was maximalist Zionism. 'This point of view speaks of "a large number" (which is unlikely to offend anyone, even if the "large number" is in fact greater than the majority) and not of a "majority" (a term explicitly directed against someone), but it does not entail renunciation on anyone's part of the desire to become the majority . . . I, for example, long to unite all of the Jewish people from all the diasporas *in this country and in the neighbouring countries.* Not half a million Jews but thirty times more! And as for ways of realizing the Herzlian dream, I myself believe it can be achieved through a brotherly alliance with the Arabs.'

Brit Shalom owed its genesis to the humanitarian concerns of its founders, anxious to find a path which recognized the equal rights of the Arabs. Its first president was Arthur Ruppin, whose career, perhaps more than any other single individual, illustrates the moral ambiguity at the heart of Zionism. Ruppin enjoyed the soubriquet 'father of Zionist settlement'. Born in Posen in 1876, his family moved to Magdeburg when he was eleven years old, having suddenly lost their wealth – a factor that preyed constantly on Ruppin thereafter and probably influenced his choice of career as well as his obsession with planning. Forced by poverty to leave school at the age of fifteen, he passed his examinations as an external student while working in the grain trade. He studied law, economics and the natural sciences at the universities of Berlin and Halle. In 1903 he took up a post at the Bureau for Jewish Statistics and Demography in Berlin, received the Haeckel Prize for his doctoral research, and began writing his first and most enduring book, *Die Juden der Gegenwart* (The Jews in the Present Time). He based his analysis of Jewish sociology on statistical and demographic evidence rather than the emotional rhetoric beloved of Herzl and Nordau, but the book brought him to the notice of the Zionist movement, on whose behalf he travelled to Palestine in 1907 to report on the settlement situation. He was appointed head of the Zionist Organization's Palestine office in 1908, at the age of thirty-two. From then until his death in 1943 he was the man chiefly responsible for the purchase of land in Palestine and the systematic expansion of settlement policy.

It was thanks to Ruppin that the pioneers of the Second Aliyah received the crucial financial support that enabled their embryonic smallholdings to survive. It was due to his foresight and canny negotiating that contiguous tracts of land in the Jezreel Valley and other, less promising regions were bought for agricultural development by the Jewish National Fund. He was instrumental in the rapid expansion of Tel-Aviv, and the acquisition of land in Haifa, on Mount Carmel and in the Greek quarter of Jerusalem for what would become prosperous Jewish suburbs. It was his expertise that helped steer the Yishuv economy through the financial and political crises of the twenties and thirties, while it was also absorbing tens of thousands of refugees from Germany and Nazi-occupied Europe. If any one person can be said to have promoted Zionism at the expense of the native Arab population, it was Ruppin. Outwardly, the dry statistician with a flair for planning, organization and administration went about his work of strengthening the Labour movement and socialist kibbutzim while winning the confidence of American Jewish capitalists to invest in the Yishuv. Inwardly, the dichotomy between ideals and achievement increasingly perplexed him.

By inclination, he was a communist. 'I could not imagine a higher aim than to be working in Russia now on the peaceful reorganization of that country . . . I very much respect the magnificent ideas inherent in Bolshevism,' he wrote in his diary of 1921. He was hopeful that in Palestine the same ends could be achieved without the destructive violence of Russia. 'European capitalism has not yet arrived in Palestine; therefore, nothing will have to be destroyed before anything can be built . . . A new and more just social order will issue from Palestine.' That required practical collaboration with the Arabs. 'I think that I shall not be able to continue working for the Zionist movement if Zionism does not acquire a new theoretical foundation. Herzl's conception of the Jewish state was possible only because he ignored the existence of the Arabs and believed that he could manipulate world history by means of the diplomatic methods of the Quai d'Orsay . . . More than ever before, so it seems to me, Zionism can find its justification only in racial affiliation of the Jews to the peoples of the Near East.' The disparity between universal moral values and Jewish nationalism saddened him. 'Over and over again I am troubled by the thought of how Zionism can be blended into a wider framework, related to all the great humanitarian problems.'

It was during the relatively benign early years of the British mandate, between the Arab uprisings of 1921 and 1929, when Weizmann and the Zionist leadership were persuaded that the situation with the Arabs was tolerable, that Ruppin gave vent to these forebodings. 'What continually worries me is the relationship between Jews and Arabs in Palestine. Superficially, it has improved, in that there is no danger of pogroms, but the two peoples have become more estranged in their thinking. Neither has any understanding of the other, and yet I have no doubt that Zionism will end in a catastrophe if we do not succeed in finding a common platform.' So it was that Ruppin initiated discussions with like-minded colleagues that led to the formation of Brit Shalom in 1925. Five years later, when it was disintegrating, Ruppin recalled the impetus for its foundation: 'One of the determining factors was that the Zionist aim has no equal in history. The aim is to bring the Jews as a second nation into a country which already is settled as a nation – and fulfil this through peaceful means. History has seen such penetration by one nation into a strange land only by conquest, but it has never occurred that a nation will fully agree that another nation should come and demand full equality of rights and national autonomy at its side.' In

Ruppin's view, such unique circumstances required the special evaluation and study dear to a sociologist's heart, rather than conventional politico-legal formulas. But because the circumstances *were* unique, politics inevitably obtruded.

It was the question of a Legislative Council that splintered Brit Shalom. Bergmann, Judah Magnes and other supporters were pressing for elections to an Arab–Jewish representative assembly, but Ruppin demurred, predicting that a clash of interests over acquisition of land, the introduction of Jewish-only labour and the wage differential between Jewish and Arab workers would ensure that 'the Arabs will use the rights promised them by the constitution in order to prevent, as a majority, any economic development of the Jewish minority'. Furthermore, he doubted whether 'one can immediately apply to Palestine the principles of democracy . . . as long as the majority of Arabs remain illiterate the crowds will blindly follow a few leaders'. Finally, he saw the association as a study and research forum, not a political party. 'If we enter the political arena, it will lose its good name for ever.' It did so anyway after the Arab riots of August 1929, when it became the scapegoat for Jewish grief and anger. Emotions were compounded when Magnes pressed ahead with the Legislative Council proposal, arguing on behalf of the Arabs that 'the way to train a people in self-government is to place responsibility on it, not to withhold self-government from it,' and answered the question of whether the 'butchers of Hebron and Safed' should be rewarded with the provocative retort 'Are my own hands clean of blood? . . . let at least Israel not be hypocritical and self-righteous.'

This was too much for Ruppin. Irresponsible publicity without adequate preparation of the Jewish public, and the fact that 'the Arabs interpret our conciliatory tone as weakness', obliged him to resign from the presidency of Brit Shalom. It also marked a change in his attitude to Jewish–Arab relations. While not totally abandoning his faith in binationalism (two years later he worked with Magnes on a draft for a binational constitution), he doubted its efficacy. 'What good does it do,' he reflected wanly in his diary, 'that a small circle has reached agreement, when there is no prospect of making the draft acceptable either to the Jews or the Arabs?'

Ruppin persisted in his opposition to the idea of a Legislative Council, explaining why in a letter to Victor Jacobson, a colleague on the

Zionist executive. 'The situation is paradoxical; what we can get [from the Arabs] is of no use to us, and what we need we cannot get from them. At most, the Arabs would agree to grant national rights to the Jews in an Arab state . . .' The large-scale immigration of German Jews between 1933 and 1935, made possible by an arrangement with the Hitler government which Ruppin helped to negotiate, finally convinced him of the futility of trying to reach a binational solution, and he advised the British high commissioner not to proceed with the proposed Legislative Council. By now, his position in the decision-making circles of the Zionist movement was under threat, despite his public prestige, and eventually he was replaced in the settlement department of the Jewish Agency.

The widespread Arab revolt which erupted in 1936 was the final nail in the coffin of his hopes for an agreement between the two communities. Henceforth, he accepted the line of Weizmann and the Zionist leadership, with the dispirited pessimism of one who had given up trying to reconcile his employment with his ideals. A letter to his former supporter Robert Weltsch, written in March 1936, revealed how far Ruppin had moved from his youthful confidence that the economic benefits from Jewish colonization would mollify Arab hostility: 'Not negotiations, but the development of Palestine towards a larger percentage of Jews in the population and a strengthening of our economic position can and will bring about an easing of tension . . . When coming to an understanding with us will no longer mean that the Arabs will have to make concessions to us, but only a question of coming to terms with realities . . . that we are living in a latent state of war with the Arabs which makes loss of life inevitable . . . if we want to continue our work in Palestine, we will have to accept such losses.'

Ruppin, the constructive architect of Zionist expansion, found constant tension between upholding moral principles and pursuing settlement policy in a country whose inhabitants were hostile. As he reflected after one Brit Shalom meeting, 'In general, it has become clear how difficult it is to realize Zionism while constantly adapting it to ethical demands. Has Zionism in fact deteriorated to pointless chauvinism?'

In 1918, Max Weber had published a widely discussed essay, 'Politics as a Vocation'. In it, he argued that there was a fundamental distinction between the ethics dictated by the exigencies of power and the imperatives of individual moral conscience. From a sociological perspective, according to Weber, those responsible for the public weal are often obliged to employ morally dubious means towards ends for the common good. 'He who lets himself in for politics,' Weber wrote, 'that is, for power and force as means, contracts with diabolical powers and for his action it is *not* true that good can only follow from good and evil only from evil, but often the opposite is true. Anyone who fails to see this is, indeed, a political infant.' Weber's thesis was forcefully repudiated by, among others, Martin Buber and Ernst Simon, both professors at the Hebrew University and supporters of Brit Shalom. They were debating in the groves of academe, whereas Ruppin and less pernickety colleagues on the Zionist executive were facing the issue on a daily basis. Brit Shalom could not steer its way between the exigencies of power and the dictates of individual conscience, and petered out. Its ineffectuality and the increasingly forlorn figure cut by its founder were symptomatic of Zionism's ambivalent interest in reaching a peaceful accommodation with the Arabs. Henceforth it was the political realists, of the left or of the right, who dictated the course of Palestine's future.

12

Vladimir Jabotinsky – From Liberalism to Fascism

Between the two world wars and during the years of the mandate administration, Zionists were engaged in a triangular struggle: with the British government, with the Arabs and among themselves. The internecine conflict was the bitterest and most keenly fought, leaving scars not fully healed in the state of Israel to the present day.

Although Chaim Weizmann was titular head of the World Zionist Organization for most of this period, two men came increasingly to dominate Yishuv politics: David Ben-Gurion and Vladimir Jabotinsky. Their antagonisms – ideological, not personal, they had a wary regard for each other – led to the brink of civil war. It was a clash of culture and class, of socialism and right-wing nationalism, of worker and bourgeois. In the end, Ben-Gurion, the pragmatic socialist, prevailed. His courtly opponent, a disciple of nineteenth-century liberalism, went down in Zionist history as a crypto-fascist, 'il Duce' or 'Vladimir Hitler'.

No one since Herzl aroused as much adulation among the Jewish masses as Jabotinsky, or as much loathing. His followers were entranced by his grace, his panache, his fluent oratory in six different languages. His detractors were contemptuous of the flamboyant gestures, the glib slogans, the insistence on style and élan, the fondness for banners, parades and paramilitary uniforms which he shared with groups of the European radical right. Jabotinsky claimed to be Herzl's spiritual heir. The two men had more in common than a burning desire to create a Jewish state by mass immigration to Palestine. Differing in temperament, background and education as they did in appearance (Herzl was not tall but he was commanding, Jabotinsky was short and bespectacled), they laboured under a similar handicap. Both gave the impression to sceptical fellow Zionists that they were too much at ease in the wider, non-Jewish world; that, as Achad Ha-Am remarked sniffily of Herzl, there was something of the literary poseur about him, and as Weizmann, who had more political reason than most to hate Jabotinsky, wrote, not unsympathetically, in his autobiography, 'Jabotinsky, the passionate Zionist, was utterly un-Jewish in manner, approach and deportment. He came from Odessa, Achad Ha-Am's home town, but the inner life of Jewry had left no trace on him . . . he was rather ugly, immensely attractive, well spoken, warm-hearted, generous, always ready to help a comrade in distress; all of those qualities were, however, overlaid with a certain touch of the rather theatrically chivalresque, a certain queer and irrelevant knightliness, which was not at all Jewish.' If Weizmann, more cosmopolitan than any contemporaries in the Zionist movement, felt so bemused by Jabotinsky, it is easy to imagine how the parochial, deadly serious socialists of the Second Aliyah reacted to him. They found him dangerous, unpredictable and irresponsible.

Jabotinsky was born in Odessa in 1880. According to his auto-biography, revealingly entitled *The Story of My Life* – for Jabotinsky, as for Keats, a man's life was a continual allegory – there was no inner contact with Judaism in his home and although he did have a *bar mitzvah*, he never 'breathed the atmosphere of Jewish cultural tradition'. His father died when he was young and his mother was an admirer of all things German. His Odessan childhood left a deep imprint, 'I have never seen such an easygoing city – there is no city like Odessa when it comes to the mellowness of joy or the light scent of intoxication floating about the air.'

After schooling in a Russian *gymnasium*, Jabotinsky went on to study in Berne, where he had his first encounter with Zionism at a lecture given by Nachman Syrkin. A compulsive journalist throughout his life, he sent articles to Odessan newspapers, sometimes using the pen-name 'Altalena', which Jabotinsky mistakenly thought was Italian for a 'crane' – it means 'swing'. (That name assumed ironic significance in June 1948; it was given to an illegal armament ship brought to Israel by Jabotinsky's former followers in the breakaway Irgun group. The ship was shelled and sunk on the orders of Ben-Gurion's provisional government; one of the last people to swim ashore was Menachem Begin.) From Berne Jabotinsky moved to Rome. The three years he spent there were the formative period of his intellectual development. He wrote later:

If I have a spiritual homeland, it is Italy, much more than Russia . . . All my views on nationalism, the state and society were developed during those years under Italian influence; it was there that I learned to love the art of the architect, the sculptor and the painter, as well as the Latin song . . . At the university my teachers were Antonio Labriola and Enrico Perri, and the belief in the justice of the socialist system, which they implanted in my heart, I kept as self-evident until it became utterly destroyed by the Red experience in Russia. The legend of Garibaldi, the writings of Mazzini, the poetry of Leopardi and Giusti have enriched and deepened my superficial Zionism; from an instinctive feeling they made it into a doctrine.

That candid and charming reminiscence is revealing. Art, poetry, a passing interest in socialism, the 'legend' of Garibaldi and no Jewish source whatever: those are the influences which confirmed Jabotinsky in his Zionism. In comparison, Herzl was an encyclopedia of Jewish learning. As a Zionist then, Jabotinsky returned to Russia in 1901 and joined the editorial staff of *Odesskiya Novosti*. The Kishinev pogrom two years later, and the threat of similar violence in Odessa, spurred him to the one conviction that he held throughout his political career: the urgent need for a Jewish defence force. He went as a delegate to the Sixth Zionist Congress, was dazzled by Herzl, but voted against the Uganda proposal.

Having embraced the Zionist creed, Jabotinsky travelled enthusiastically to spread the gospel. He was a valuable propagandist – or agitator, as they were then called – for Zionism, both a compelling orator and a prolific columnist. His literary output was prodigious. He quickly mastered Hebrew, so that by 1910 he had elegantly translated Edgar Alan Poe's *The Raven* and toured the Jewish communities of Russia to advocate Hebrew as the language of future instruction. Two of his verse plays in Russian were staged at the Odessa municipal theatre, and his 1910 Russian translation of Chaim Nachman Bialik's *Songs and Poems*, which went through seven printings in two years, was regarded as a classic in its own right. According to Maxim Gorky, Jabotinsky's absorption in Zionism was a great loss to Russian literature; but the young writer had decided that it was undignified when Jews took a leading part in celebrating the centenary of an anti-Semitic author like Gogol. He regretted having participated in the 1906 Helsingfors meeting which passed a resolution in favour of equal rights for Jews and other nationalities of the Russian empire. From now on, 'I have nothing to learn from pogroms suffered by our people; they can tell me nothing I did not know before . . . I love my people and Palestine: this is my creed, this is the business of my life.'

In a 1910 article, 'Homo homini lupus' (Man is a Wolf to Man), he declared liberalism to be dead. He defined liberalism as 'a broad concept, vague because of its all-encompassing nature; it is a dream about order and justice without violence, a universal dream woven of sympathy, tolerance, a belief in the basic goodness and righteousness of man.' There was no foundation for the classical liberal view that 'anyone who has himself suffered for a long time under the yoke of a stronger one will not oppress those weaker than he'. He cited the Polish people in Austrian-ruled Galicia who oppressed the Ukrainian minority while themselves being subjugated by the Austrians. 'Only the Bible says "thou shalt not oppress a stranger, for ye know the heart of a stranger, seeing ye were strangers in the land of Egypt." Contemporary morality has no place for such childish humanism.' It was a cruel world, and neither political reforms nor culture would change it.

Stupid is the person who believes in his neighbour, good and loving as the neighbour may be; stupid is the person who relies on justice. Justice exists only for those whose fists and stubbornness make it possible for them to realize it . . . Do not believe anyone, be always on guard, carry your stick always with you – this is the only way of surviving in this wolfish battle of all against all.

To justify the abandonment of liberal values (which he would nevertheless claim to espouse for the rest of his life) and to express his growing contempt for international socialism, Jabotinsky summoned up the ghost of one of his Italian heroes, Garibaldi. Imagine, he asks in a 1912 article entitled 'Reactionary', how young radicals in a contemporary world as divided and enslaved as Italy once was, would respond to a modern Garibaldi. Garibaldi was operating in a society of nationalist fervour, rife with patriotic slogans, forgoing all other ideals in the struggle for liberation. 'One's whole strength was consumed solely by national questions and *amor patriae*', but today's socialists would dismiss Garibaldi as divisive, a reactionary chauvinist, an obfuscator of class consciousness, a seducer of youth from universal human ideals. Did Garibaldi remind his compatriots to love the Germans like brothers? On the contrary, his every action was to intensify their hatred of the foreigner; 'he demanded unity of rich and poor in the name of love of the homeland; he demanded that they forget all conflicts and put aside all internal quarrels, until the nationalist ideal is realized.'

Here the basic tenets of Jabotinsky's political philosophy are first intimated: subservience to the overriding concept of the homeland; loyalty to a charismatic leader, and the subordination of class conflict to national goals. It irked Jabotinsky when, over twenty years later, he was accused of imitating Mussolini and Hitler. His irritation was justified; he had anticipated them.

A spell in Constantinople editing four publications for the World Zionist Organization ended in Jabotinsky's resignation after a disagreement with David Wolffsohn, the Zionist president. He was at something of a loose end, an ageing *Wunderkind*, married, with no obvious career prospects. The First World War came at an opportune time. 'What would I have done if the world had not broken out in flames?' Jabotinsky mused in his autobiography. 'I had wasted my youth and early middle age. Perhaps I would have gone to *Eretz Israel*, perhaps I would have escaped to Rome, perhaps I would have founded a political party . . .'

Instead, he was appointed roving correspondent of a Moscow daily, and found himself in Alexandria, where hundreds of young Yishuv Jews had been deported by the Turkish authorities. It was the opportunity to put into practice his dream of a Jewish military force, a 'Jewish Legion', to fight alongside the Allies in liberating Palestine. Five hundred men volunteered. With Joseph Trumpeldor, a socialist pioneer and former officer in the Russian army, Jabotinsky approached General Maxwell, the British commander, with his proposal, but was offered mule transport duties in Gallipoli for his unit. Such a rebuff offended Jabotinsky's sense of honour, unlike Trumpeldor, for whom fighting the Turks, in whatever capacity, was a step on the road to Palestine. 'You may be right,' Jabotinsky told him, as the Zion Mule Corps of 562 men prepared to leave for the Dardanelles, 'but I personally will not join a unit of that sort.'

He travelled instead to Rome, Paris and London, to pursue the idea of a Jewish Legion. The official Zionist leadership, maintaining its stance of neutrality, was unsympathetic, but Weizmann gave discreet encouragement. Eventually, a couple of months before issuing the Balfour Declaration and as part of its wider strategy of gaining Jewish support, the British government agreed to the formation of a volunteer

Jewish regiment. The 38th Battalion of Royal Fusiliers was recruited, to be joined in 1918 by the 39th (American) and 40th (Palestinian) battalions, which were all consolidated into the First Judean Regiment, with a menorah as its insignia, which accompanied Allenby on his Palestine campaign. Jabotinsky enlisted as a lieutenant in the 38th, and was decorated for leading the first company across a ford of the Jordan – the only combat, apart from night patrols, that the battalion saw. Malaria was a sterner enemy than the Turks.

At the beginning of 1919, the Judean Regiment in Palestine numbered 5000 men, one-sixth of the British army of occupation. By the spring, and despite all the arguments brought to bear by Jabotinsky about maintaining the Legion as a bulwark against Arab hostility, only 300–400 remained in uniform; the rest had pressed for their discharge or been demobilized by the military administration. Weizmann and other Zionist leaders acquiesced in a decision that Jabotinsky called 'our most fateful political mistake'. His assertion a few years later that 'half the Balfour Declaration belongs to the Legion' was an old soldier's idle boast, but in keeping with his insistence on the importance of a Jewish standing army for a people who had been unable to defend itself. The charge of 'militarism' did not worry him – 'We ought not to be deterred by a Latin word,' he retorted – any more than the early Zionists had cringed at the nationalist label. There were two kinds of militarism – the one aggressive, out for territorial conquest; the other defensive, to protect a homeless people facing death: 'If this is militarism, we ought to be proud of it.'

His logic appeared to have been vindicated in the spring of 1920, when Arab mobs in Jerusalem attacked Jews during the Passover festival. Jabotinsky was head of Haganah, the clandestine defence force in the city, and led it against the rioters. He was arrested, together with Arab ring-leaders, and sentenced to fifteen years' penal servitude, a scandalously harsh punishment which sent ripples of indignation through the Yishuv. One of the first acts of Sir Herbert Samuel when he arrived as high commissioner later in the year was to grant an amnesty to Jabotinsky and the other Jewish prisoners. They emerged from Acre gaol to a heroes' welcome, although bitter that the Arab rioters had also been pardoned. Jabotinsky, who had enjoyed preferential treatment as a political prisoner during his brief incarceration, issued a statement saying that he remained 'a true and devoted friend of England and a staunch admirer of British justice'.

In truth, it had been the kind of incident to gladden Jabotinsky's heart, delight his sense of the theatrical, and yield an unexpected political bonus; heroic military posturing leading to a martyrdom elegantly endured and a vindication graciously acknowledged. At about the same time, it is worth noting, Gabriele D'Annunzio, the Italian poet, novelist, soldier-romantic and early supporter of fascism (and for Jabotinsky an envied role model), was mounting a gallant and futile defence of the mini-state of Fiume. D'Annunzio was forgiven and allowed to go and live on Lake Garda, where he polished his thoughts on patriotism and entertained Mussolini. Jabotinsky pressed for and received a full military pardon from the British commander-in-chief in Egypt, reiterated his conviction that the Yishuv needed its own army, and in March 1921 joined the Zionist executive as probably the most popular Jew in Palestine.

Within two years he had dissipated the goodwill. Appointed head of the political department – a strange choice, given Weizmann's judgement that he had no aptitude for practical politics – and director of propaganda, for which he was eminently suited, Jabotinsky demonstrated that he was incapable of being a team player. Surprisingly, he endorsed the executive's decision to accept the 1922 White Paper which detached Transjordan from the area of the Balfour Declaration, justifying his quiescence as a gesture of solidarity – 'I felt it my moral duty to share with my colleagues in the shame of defeat' – but his penchant for criticizing collective policy had already led to an open rupture.

The breaking-point came during the Twelfth Zionist Congress at Carlsbad in 1921. Jabotinsky held talks with Maxim Slavinsky, the representative of Atman Petliura's Ukrainian government-in-exile. Petliura was a fervent anti-communist and a rabid anti-Semite. After the 1917 Revolution, his gangs had roamed the countryside, wreaking pogroms and destruction on hundreds of Jewish communities; nearly 17,000 Jews had been killed. He was now trying to raise an army to invade the Bolshevik-held Ukraine, and Jabotinsky, fixated with self-defence, proposed that a Jewish gendarmerie should follow Petliura's army, to protect the Jewish population. He defended his scheme for co-operating with the most brutal Cossack since Bogdan Chmielnicki[1]

1. Bogdan Chmielnicki (1593–1657), Ukrainian Cossack leader whose 1648 uprising against Polish sovereignty led to nearly twenty years of warfare, the murder of some 50,000 Jews and the destruction of nearly 750 communities.

in the seventeenth century by paraphrasing Mazzini: he would make a pact with the devil on behalf of Palestine and the Jews. The Congress, and wider Jewish world, was shocked. Demands for Jabotinsky's resignation flooded in. In the event, the planned invasion never occurred, because the west lost its enthusiasm for financing interventionist adventures and ditched Petliura, who was shot dead by a Jewish student in Paris in 1926.

Lasting damage had been done to Jabotinsky's political reputation, however, and his decision to leave the executive was accepted without regret. Hereafter and more in keeping with his autocratic personality, he operated not as a loyal opposition within the Zionist Organization but as an alternative to it, untrammelled by the responsibility of decision-making and free to publicize his views on nationalism, the Arabs, and British–Zionist relations, assured of their mass appeal to an increasingly perplexed and disaffected Jewish audience in the Yishuv and Europe.

Given that for Jabotinsky, echoing Garibaldi, 'there is no value in the world higher than the nation and the fatherland', it is not altogether surprising that he should have recommended an alliance with an anti-Semitic Ukrainian nationalist. In 1911, in an essay entitled 'Schevenko's Jubilee', he had praised the xenophobic Ukrainian poet for his nationalist spirit, despite 'explosions of wild fury against the Poles, the Jews and other neighbours', and for proving that the Ukrainian soul had a 'talent for independent cultural creativity, reaching unto the highest and most sublime spheres'. Whereas 'Greater Russia' supporters derided Ukrainian culture as provincial, Jabotinsky discovered in it vitality, originality and authenticity – characteristics essential to his definition of a national movement aspiring to statehood.

His frequent writings on nationalism and race derived from theories about 'superior' Aryan peoples and 'inferior' Semitic ones put out by disreputable anthropologists at the turn of the century. Jabotinsky could spout pseudo-scientific jargon with the best of them. National supremacy and racial superiority are reciprocal, 'they show a psycho-physical parallelism'. When national and racial identity correspond, one has the criterion for judging the model nation: 'Let us draw for ourself the ideal type of an "absolute nation". It would have to possess a racial appearance of marked unique character, an appearance different from the racial nature of that nation's neighbours. It would have to occupy from time immemorial a continuous and clearly defined piece of land; it would be highly desirable if in that area there would be no alien minorities, who would weaken national unity. It would have to maintain an original national language, which is not derived from another nation.'

Such vapourings, unpleasant enough in 1913, had taken on sinister connotations by the 1930s, but Jabotinsky, in a Yiddish pamphlet entitled *A Lecture on Jewish History*, published in Warsaw in 1933, had not altered his views.

Every race has a different spiritual mechanism. This has nothing to do with the fact whether there exist 'pure' races or not; of course, all races are 'mixed', and this includes us, the Jews. But the mixture is different from case to case . . . The nature of the spiritual mechanism depends on race; the degree of intelligence, a stronger or weaker tendency to look for novel experiences, the readiness to acquiesce in the existing situation or the courage to make new discoveries, the stubbornness or, conversely, the kind of character which gives up after the first unsuccessful attempt: all these modes are themselves a product of race . . .

Jabotinsky's score card neatly demonstrated, of course, that the Jews were a 'superior' race, ready for statehood, while the Arabs were not. But to detach the Jews from their Semitic roots and anchor them in the mainstream of European culture required a certain legerdemain with history that Jabotinsky was brazen enough to make:

We Jews have nothing in common with what is denoted 'the East', and thank God for that. It cannot be argued that we belong to the Orient because we came originally from Asia. All Central Europe is full of races who also came from Asia – and at a much later period than we. All the Ashkenazi Jews, and certainly half of the Sephardi ones, have been resident in Europe for two thousand years. This is a sufficient long time for spiritual integration. Moreover, not only have we been resident in Europe for many generations . . . we are also one of the peoples who have created European culture . . . The spiritual atmosphere of Europe is ours, we have the same rights in it just like the Germans and the English and the Italians and the French.

For Jabotinsky, the confrontation between east and west was one of passivity against activism, submission to oppression against love of liberty, social and sexual discrimination against equality and justice. In so far as uneducated Jews had 'traditions and spiritual prejudices which are reminiscent of the east, they must be weaned away from them . . .' Why, then, should the Jews want to go back to the primitive east? Because they were shouldering the white man's burden, 'As Nordau has put it so well, we come to the Land of Israel in order to push the moral frontiers of Europe to the Euphrates.' What the Arabs of Palestine decided to do was their own affair, but the Jews would offer them one favour, 'to help them to free themselves of the east'.

In a 1925 article entitled 'On Islam', Jabotinsky cited the Italian victory at Tripoli in 1911 and the success of a French expeditionary force over Faisal in Damascus in 1920 as instances where a handful of European soldiers had defeated overwhelmingly larger but ill-equipped Muslim forces; and in another article two years later, 'The Pedlars of Culture', he argued that all the great names of medieval Islamic history were not Arabian or even Muslim but of Syrian, Jewish, Persian or Afghan origin. He wrote in this vein, he insisted, not 'to humiliate the Arabs or make fun of them' but to query the illusion of a unified Arab world: 'Today just as a hundred years ago, one can clash with every and any Muslim nation without getting entangled in a confrontation with Pan-Islamism.'

Jabotinsky categorized his attitude to Arab national aspirations as one of 'polite indifference', but it was more ruthless than that. His monistic pursuit of Jewish nationhood left no room for a competing nationalism in territorial proximity. Writing in 1916 about Turkey's role in the war, he had forcefully rejected the notion of a united Arab nation in such a culturally diverse region as the Middle East, but had conceded that in Egypt and Syria the rudiments of a national movement existed. This posed the question that if Arab nationalism had emerged on a territorial basis elsewhere, might it not do so in Palestine? It was to address that problem that in 1923 he wrote two important and tendentious articles under the title 'The Iron Wall', a phrase which was to become a fighting slogan of the Zionist–Arab struggle.

Jabotinsky set the problem in the context of moral philosophy: 'Can one always achieve peaceful aims by peaceful means?' The answer lay with the Arabs, since the crux of the problem was the Arab attitude to Zionism, rather than the reverse. He analysed the Arab stance from the basic premise that 'a voluntary agreement between us and the Arabs of Palestine is inconceivable, now or in the foreseeable future'. He understood the Arab position full well; no indigenous population in history had willingly accepted foreign settlers, no matter how large the living-space. It was an insulting evaluation of the Arab character to imagine that they could be fooled by a watered-down version of Zionist object-ives or by the bribe of cultural and economic advantages. Arab antagon-ism stemmed not from an imperfect understanding of Zionism's aims, as 'Arab-lovers' and 'peace-lovers' claimed, but from understanding those aims only too well. Jabotinsky could sympathize with Arab objec-tions, but he would fight to the bitter end for the compelling logic of Jewish national aspirations. Therefore,

we cannot promise any reward either to the Arabs of Palestine or to Arabs abroad. A voluntary agreement is unattainable, and thus, those who regard an accord with the Arabs as a *conditio sine qua non* of Zionism must admit to them-selves today that this condition cannot be attained and hence we must eschew Zionism. We must either suspend our settlement efforts or continue them without paying attention to the mood of the natives. Settlement can develop under the protection of a force which is not dependent on the local population, behind an iron wall which they will be powerless to break down.

That 'iron wall' was an official Jewish military force for keeping order, rather than having to rely on British bayonets. Building settlements under military protection did not imply that Jews and Arabs would be condemned to a perpetual struggle. Quite the reverse; 'as long as there lingers in the heart of the Arabs even the faintest hope that they may succeed in ridding themselves of us, there are no blandishments or promises in the world which have the power to persuade them to renounce their hope — precisely because they are not a mob, but' (Jabotinsky is forced to concede) 'a living nation'. Only when the wave of Arab opposition had been broken against the 'iron wall' would moderate elements with more measured responses come forward to negotiate with the Jews. Then, talks could take place about mutual concessions, respect for the rights of the local population and its pro-tection from discrimination and dispossession. His policy of speaking softly and carrying a big stick would reap dividends. Offering satisfact-ory guarantees to the Arabs would mean that both peoples could live in peace as neighbours. 'But the sole way to this agreement is through the iron wall, the establishment in Palestine of a force which will in no way be influenced by Arab pressure. In other words, the only way to achieve a settlement in the future is total avoidance of attempts to arrive at a settlement in the present.'

There was a persuasive realism to Jabotinsky's article, allied with courtly respect for adversaries far removed from his refusal, at his trial three years earlier, to respond to questions put by an Arab court secretary: 'I refuse to answer a court secretary who belongs to the tribe of murderers whose attacks on innocent people, coupled with pillage and raping, are still going on beyond these walls.'

Jewish public response was positive, but critics queried the moral implications of basing order on military might. Jabotinsky returned to the subject in a second article, 'The Morality of the Iron Wall'. He did not try to argue that armed force was moral, but invoked a higher sanction: 'Zionism is a positive force, morally speaking – a moral movement with justice on its side.' Consequently, 'if the cause is just, then justice must triumph, without regard for the assent or dissent of anyone else.' The Arabs could not counterclaim with their right to self-determination, because the enlightened world saw the national right of the Jews as more just and valid in every respect. Jabotinsky now turned his critics' argument against themselves. The moral problem did not lie in the need for an 'iron wall' but in the very concept of Zionist settlement in Palestine: those who wished to retain their moral purity should, logically speaking, renounce the Zionist dream. But not even the most altruistic 'seekers after peace' would abandon their hope of a national territory, because the world 'does not belong only to those who have too much land, but also to those who have none. Requisition of an area of land from a nation with large stretches of territory in order to make a home for a wandering people, is an act of justice, and if the land-owning nation does not wish to cede it (and this is completely natural) it must be compelled. A sacred truth, for whose realization the use of force is essential, does not cease thereby to be a sacred truth.'

The two 'iron wall' articles provided the intellectual rationale not only for Jabotinsky's followers but for sections of the Labour movement in their subsequent dealings with the Palestinians, and they are often quoted for their baneful influence on the future course of Jewish–Arab relations. Yet they rank among his more sympathetic pieces of journalism. Despite the overblown clichés of statehood – Justice, Truth, Morality laid on the altar and made subservient to the state's sacrosanct needs – they do have the merit of honesty, a quality not always apparent in his other writings or in the sanctimonious pieties with which the Zionist leadership cloaked its indecision over the Arab problem. At least Jabotinsky makes no bones about Arab hostility or its validity, and proposes a solution in accord with those Roman virtues he admired: military strength, resolution, magnanimity to the vanquished.

Jabotinsky had resigned from the Zionist executive over the issue of a Legislative Council. In theory, he was willing to recognize the civil and national rights of Palestinian Arabs, as (in a convenient change of mind) a proud member of the group which had drawn up the 1906 Helsing-fors programme. But until the fundamental goal of a Jewish majority in Palestine had been achieved, negotiating from minority status would be tantamount to committing national suicide. He scornfully rejected those who would turn Zionism into 'a clandestine smugglers' organiza-tion' with their cautious approach of building in silence, adding dunam to dunam, cow to cow. That would not galvanize popular support: 'The Jewish national movement has no coercive power, and in saying this we have said everything. When we require people or funds, we can recruit them by rousing the enthusiasm of the masses or of individuals. The act of rousing enthusiasm is known as propaganda, and propaganda cannot be silent, least of all in a nation which is widely scattered.'

Jabotinsky was outlining the future course of his career.

13

Jabotinsky – Demagogue of the Right

Jabotinsky became the great propagandist, a demagogue pained by the lack of breeding and crude excesses of some of his followers but compelled by his code of chivalry to defend their actions. His greatest appeal in Europe and Palestine was among a social group he disdained: small businessmen, traders, white-collar workers and self-employed artisans who had been pushed to the fringes of a changing society and resented their loss of status. He manipulated all the paraphernalia of cultural myth and patriotic symbol to enhance their national pride, stiffen group loyalty and direct their frustrations against the ruling establishment – the techniques of fascism. Jabotinsky's youth movement wore uniforms – brown shirts, to symbolize the soil of Palestine – long before those of Mussolini and Hitler.

The idea of forming his own youth movement and political party occurred during a speaking tour of Latvia and Lithuania in late 1923. His brand of Zionist activism was enthusiastically received by the Jewish student association in Riga, and he in turn was fired by their youthful militancy. Betar, an acronym for Brit Trumpeldor (Covenant of Trumpeldor), named after his erstwhile colleague in the Jewish Legion, was founded in Riga. It was Jabotinsky's first, and most blatant, example of myth appropriation. Trumpeldor and six comrades had been killed in 1920 at Tel Hai in Upper Galilee, defending the isolated settlement against marauding Arabs, and his death quickly became the stuff of legend. Jabotinsky had opposed sending help to Tel Hai, because he did not approve of piecemeal colonizing. Three years later, he was happy to purloin Trumpeldor's memory as an example of heroic sacrifice, with the symbolic bonus that Betar was also the place-name of the last futile stand by Simon Bar-Kochba[1] against the Romans in AD 135.

---

1. Simon Bar-Kochba (d. AD 135). Leader of last Jewish revolt against Roman rule, AD 132–5, which left Judea destroyed and its population annihilated.

In Jabotinsky's strategy, fighting for a lost cause could have more potent appeal than a mundane victory.

The tenets of Betar were simple. Discipline was its key principle. At a command from the centre, recruits were to carry out an order with synchronized efficiency, because 'it is the highest achievement of a multitude of free human beings to be able to act together with the absolute precision of a machine.' The cult of the leader was extolled. 'We all have one will, we all build one structure, and therefore we have all responded to the call of the one architect whose building abilities have been accepted by us.' Betar members should be ready to fight for their national independence and expect to be called at any time to serve in a new Jewish Legion. Finally, they were required to comport themselves with the quality of *hadar*, a Hebrew word denoting 'grace', 'pride', 'dignity'. Jabotinsky defined it as 'dignified beauty and harmony of manner, gesture, speech and attitude'. It pained him that so many of his young followers lacked social graces, so he lectured Betar members on the rules of etiquette, 'Eat noiselessly and slowly, do not protrude your elbows at meals, do not sip your soup loudly. Walking upstairs at night, do not talk – you awaken the neighbours . . . in the streets give right of way to a lady, to an elderly person . . .'

His next step was to form the nucleus of a political party. With his backers, a circle of Russian Zionists who supported the Jewish Legion idea, Jabotinsky gained control of *Razsvet*, the weekly newspaper of Russian Zionism. He now had a forum for publicizing his views, and in March 1924 an office was opened in Paris to co-ordinate the activities of fifty local groups, from Canada to Harbin in Manchuria. A year later, in April 1925, the first conference of Zohar, the Zionist–Revisionist party, was convened in Paris. As its title implied, its manifesto was to 'revise' Zionism by returning to the original principles of Herzl: a Jewish homeland guaranteed by international law as the prerequisite for mass colonization, leading to a Jewish majority in Palestine and the establishment of the Jewish state. The programme was expressed with beguiling simplicity, 'The aim of Zionism is a Jewish state. The territory – both sides of the Jordan. The system – mass colonization. The solution of the financial problem – a national loan. These four principles cannot be realized without international sanction. Hence the commandment of the hour – a new political campaign and the militarization of Jewish youth in *Eretz Israel* and the Diaspora.'

A pliant nonentity, Vladimir Tiomkin, was elected president of the new party, but Revisionism was, and always would be, dependent on the personality, moods and whims of Jabotinsky, and it was he who drew up the battle lines and identified the targets in the policies of official Zionism. His first quarry was Weizmann, 'dean of the impressionistic school of Zionism'. Jabotinsky's animus was personal as much as political; each man thought himself uniquely qualified to understand the British character and interpret Whitehall policy. Both were anglophiles, Weizmann's affection stemming from the years he lived in England and mixed with the liberal stratum in politics and society, Jabotinsky's admiration based on his respect for hierarchy, institutions and empire.

It was evident to most, Weizmann included, that Britain's geostrategic interests in the Middle East since the First World War had lessened enthusiasm for promoting a Jewish homeland in Palestine. The Balfour Declaration – Weizmann's personal triumph and Zionism's tangible political charter – was being whittled away. The 1922 White Paper had detached the Emirate of Transjordan from the area of potential Jewish settlement, and mandate officials, led by the high commissioner, Sir Herbert Samuel, a Jew, who as a consequence bent over backwards to appear even-handed, seemed keener to appease the Arabs than to facilitate the creation of a Jewish national home. Weizmann clung to his belief in British good faith, without which Zionist success was doomed, and emphasized the need to build up the Yishuv cautiously, settlement by settlement, immigrant by immigrant, while negotiating with the mandate authorities in the way he understood best: a word in a sympathetic ear here, an understanding there, a communality of interests based on the implicit assumption that both belonged to the same club and spoke the same language.

Jabotinsky had no patience for this 'little' Zionism, insisting that Britain should be forced to clarify her commitment to the Balfour Declaration. His confidence in British good faith was as touching as Weizmann's. 'I believe as firmly as ever that there is a real coincidence of interests between Zionism and the British in the eastern Mediterranean ... Furthermore, I believe that no British government will break the Balfour pledge,' he had written in a confidential memorandum to the Zionist executive in 1922. It was only because of meek and vacillating Zionist leadership (i.e. Weizmann) that Britain was reneging on her mandate responsibilities. Zionism was the best safe-guard of Britain's imperial interests in the Levant. 'Moreover, in the Mediterranean, that corridor of England to the Orient, on whose east-ern and southern shores anti-European dangers coalesce – there the Jews build the only sustaining basis which belongs morally to Europe and will always belong to it.' He had no qualms about being associated with imperialism, at a time when liberal opinion was questioning the morality of colonialism and the left was urging subjugated peoples to revolt against European dominance: 'In its eyes this dominance is "imperialist" and exploitative; in my view European dominance makes them into civilized peoples.'

Jabotinsky's, and Revisionism's, second target was Labour Zionism. It had taken over the World Zionist Organization, he charged, and was subsidizing labour institutions at the expense of private settlers. His new party had been founded with a clear constituency in mind, the immigrants of the Fourth Aliyah, predominantly Polish and middle-class, who came to Palestine between 1924 and 1928. Squeezed by the deflationary policies and increased taxation of the Polish government, they came to a Yishuv in the throes of an economic crisis. There were scores of bankruptcies, the collapse of the construction industry, large-scale unemployment and more Jews leaving the country than entering. Ben-Gurion placed the blame on middle-class immigrants who had tried to transport their European ways of making a living 'and didn't understand that the Land of Israel was not Poland'. 'My dear man,' Jabotinsky wrote to his adoring colleague Joseph Schechtman three months after the opening convention in Paris, 'don't delude yourself; though many workers are tempted to accept our programme, our true field of action is the *Mittelstand*.' It was as champion of the dis-enfranchised bourgeoisie that Jabotinsky trained his guns on Labour Zionism, the Histadrut, the kibbutz movement, and the attempted syn-thesis of nationalism and socialism, which he mockingly compared to *sha'atnez*, the admixture of wool and linen in the same garment, prohibited by biblical law.

He had a field day knocking down the shibboleths of 'The Left' in a 1925 article of that title. The Labour movement was merely a socialist reincarnation of Chibbat Zion, which had been superseded by Herzl's political Zionism. The Palestinian co-operatives were islands of that utopian socialism which Marx had ridiculed; they were not even self-sufficient. Their workers relied on national capital to subsidize them, making them dependent on the other social strata whose contributions to the Zionist cause created that capital. This proved that class collaboration, not the class warfare enshrined in socialist ideology, was essential for the realization of Zionism. In another article, 'We the Bourgeoisie', he extolled the achievements of the shopkeeper and the merchant in carrying progress forward. Labour's stress on the role of the worker was countered by his specific recommendations: redistribution of the Zionist Organization's budget away from the socialist bastions in favour of private settlers, artisans and small business enterprises. A broad Zionist vision was the need of the hour, Jabotinsky insisted, not Labour's 'cult of the cow'. Monism, concerned with the nation rather than one class, was the way forward. His message touched a chord, and the Revisionist movement grew steadily. Starting with four delegates at the Fourteenth Zionist Congress of 1925, by the Sixteenth in 1929 it had become the third largest party, and at the crucial Congress of 1931, which ousted Weizmann from the presidency, the Revisionists gained a quarter of the votes.

From his headquarters in Paris, Jabotinsky travelled far and wide to woo supporters. Revisionism became especially strong in Poland, the largest reservoir of Zionist sentiment once Stalin's Russia had been sealed off, and Betar soon equalled the well-established rival youth movement Ha-Shomer Ha-tza'ir in numbers, especially when the latter moved left politically, turning from scouting to socialism. As the message was the man, Jabotinsky deliberately fostered the cult of the charismatic leader to whose will the disciplined multitude gladly submits. The image of marching battalions parading with machine-like precision at the behest of a supreme orchestrator occurs frequently in his writings. In his 1927 historical novel *Samson the Nazirite* Samson watches a pagan festival at the temple of Gaza. Several thousand young men and girls all dressed in white, the young men in short, belted tunics, the maidens in close-fitting dresses cut away to show their bare breasts, are led in dance by a priest. Jabotinsky lingeringly describes a scene which would not need Freud to interpret as a metaphor for collective orgasm. When the music starts, the vast crowd watches in silence, the only sound that of the surf beating against the quayside. 'Not a fold moved on the dancers' dresses, and scarce a sign of breathing could be seen on the bared breasts of the girls. The beardless priest turned pale and seemed to submerge his eyes in those of the dancers, which were fixed responsively on his.' The dance builds to a climax so intense that the watching Samson bites through his lip and feels he will choke if the suspense lasts a moment longer. 'Suddenly, with a rapid, almost inconspicuous movement, the priest raised his baton, and all the white figures in the square sank down on their left knee and threw their right arm toward heaven — a single movement, a single, abrupt, murmurous harmony. Then tens of thousands of onlookers gave utterance to a moaning sigh . . .' Samson is 'profoundly thoughtful', as well he might be, having participated in the largest sexual congress in human history, but the lesson he deduces is that 'here, in this spectacle of thousands obeying a single will, he had caught a glimpse of the great secrets of builders of nations.'

Occasionally, the anomaly between claiming to be an advocate of nineteenth-century liberal values and living in a time when peoples 'discover within them the God-chosen leader with the stamp of Caesar imprinted on his forehead', occurred to Jabotinsky, but not enough to deflect him from his role.

By 1931, his goal was to oust Weizmann, defeat the Labour movement and take over the World Zionist Organization, or secede from it. A few weeks before the Seventeenth Zionist Congress opened in Basel at the end of June, Jabotinsky had indicated that his patience was exhausted, '. . . unless this Congress satisfies my Revisionist conscience, Revisionism must become independent and I, for one, will no longer adhere to any organization even theoretically subordinate to the Zionist Organization.' He put it more bluntly in a private letter, saying that he 'would not finish my days as "opposition" to the crowd of spiritual bastards which calls itself the ZO'.

The riots of 1929, in part deliberately fuelled by Betar provocations over praying rights at the Wailing Wall, in which 133 Jews were killed and 339 wounded by Arab mobs before the mandate military restored order; the response of the new Labour government in London to the riots; and the frantic attempts of Weizmann and the Jewish Agency to retrieve something of the Balfour Declaration from the conflagration — these were the issues that precipitated Jabotinsky's open revolt. To previous criticisms that he was subverting the authority of the duly constituted leadership he had replied that it was the duty of every true Zionist to participate in the 'hygienic work' of 'purging' the organization of assimilationists; now he judged to be the time, the more so since his popularity was at a peak, the mandate authorities having banned him from Palestine as a threat to public order.

The Shaw commission of inquiry into the riots, appointed by the colonial secretary, Lord Passfield, published its findings in March 1930. While laying responsibility for the bloodshed squarely on the Arabs, it stressed that their underlying motives were disappointed national aspirations and economic fears as a consequence of Jewish immigration and land purchase. The commission recommended that His Majesty's government should issue a clear definition of the mandate's provisions for safeguarding the rights of the Arabs. The colonial secretary despatched Sir John Hope Simpson, a retired Indian civil servant, to prepare a report on economic conditions in Palestine. This was a further blow to Zionist hopes, because it specified that no extra land was available for agricultural settlement, that there would be room for only 20,000 new immigrant families and that prospects for industrialization were poor. The Hope Simpson report was published in London in October 1930, at the same time as the Passfield White Paper, which reiterated that Britain's obligations to Jews and Arabs were of equal weight, that the Jewish Agency had no privileged political status, and strongly implied that building of a Jewish national home would depend on Arab consent.

The White Paper, Weizmann wrote, was intended 'to make our work in Palestine impossible', and in despair he tendered his resignation from the Jewish Agency. Fortunately for Zionism, British parliamentary opposition to the White Paper united Liberal and Conservative spokesmen with uneasy Labour Party members, and Passfield (the Fabian Sidney Webb, who with his wife Beatrice had never been enamoured of Jewish nationalism) was obliged to beat a tactical retreat. The hiatus enabled the Jewish Agency to extract from Prime Minister Ramsay MacDonald a public letter to Weizmann which reaffirmed his government's intention to fulfil the terms of the mandate and to maintain the criteria laid down in the 1922 White Paper for permitting Jewish immigration to Palestine in line with the absorptive economic capacity of the country. Zionist anxieties were barely allayed. During the months of uncertainty, Revisionism's unequivocal demands that Britain must fulfil her obligations or face the threat of boycott, non-co-operation, protest demonstrations and litigation at the League of Nations had contrasted with the haverings of the Zionist executive.

The 1931 Congress was, Ben-Gurion wrote to his wife, the most difficult, nerve-racking and critical one he had attended. In the middle of it, Weizmann, under pressure from all sides, gave an injudicious interview to the Jewish Telegraph Agency in which he was reported as saying, 'I have no sympathy or understanding for the demand for a Jewish majority [in Palestine]. A majority does not necessarily guarantee security . . . A majority is not required for the development of Jewish civilization and culture.' Weizmann complained bitterly afterwards, neither the first nor the last person to do so, that he had been misquoted, that it was 'sloganeering' about a Jewish majority he objected to; but the damage had been done. Weizmann defended his policy of gradualism, in collaboration with Britain: 'If there is another way of building a country save dunam by dunam, man by man and farmstead by farmstead – I do not know it.' An American delegate, Rabbi Stephen Wise, sarcastically retorted that Weizmann had supped too long at English feasts, the Labour Zionist delegation withdrew its support, and a vote of no confidence in Weizmann's leadership was passed by 123 votes to 106.

This was Jabotinsky's golden opportunity to gain control of the Zionist Organization, but, like another demagogue, General Boulanger[1] after the Franco-Prussian war, he fluffed it. Confident that the Congress would endorse his resolution about Zionism's *endziel* ('The aim of Zionism, which is expressed in the terms "Jewish State", "National Home" or "National Home secured by public law", is the creation of a Jewish majority on both sides of the Jordan'), he let it be known that the Revisionists would consent to sit on the Zionist executive, provided they were given 50 per cent of the seats. When a majority show of hands decided not even to put such an explosive resolution to the vote, Jabotinsky climbed on a chair, shouted, 'This is no longer a Zionist Congress,' tore up his delegate card and stormed from the hall – a disastrous tactical blunder. His maximalism, so baldly stated with no consideration of diplomatic repercussions, had alarmed many delegates. A coalition of Mapai, the General Zionists and Mizrachi deposed Weizmann, installed Nahum Sokolow, a veteran from the Herzl era

1. Georges Ernest Jean-Marie Boulanger (1837–91). French general and populist politician who in 1889 might well have effected a *coup d'état* but flinched from the opportunity, fled Paris, was condemned for treason, and committed suicide in Brussels.

who wore spats and affected a monocle, as president, and blocked Revisionist representation on the new executive. Jabotinsky had snatched defeat from the jaws of victory, and would never again be so close to democratically elected power. Congress ended with the Labour movement becoming the decisive faction and Ben-Gurion the pivotal politician.

For a while, Jabotinsky sulked in his tent, brooding on his rejection. 'I don't try to conceal from myself that this may prove the beginning of the end of my work and of me as a public man.' His authority within his party had been eroded; previously loyal subordinates opposed his threat to secede from the Zionist Organization and pursue independent initiatives. A formula was cobbled together in September 1931, the 'Calais Compromise': the World Union of Revisionist Zionists would withdraw from the Zionist Organization, but not yet, and in the meantime individual Revisionist members were free to belong or not to the WZO. It was too patently absurd to hold up. The Zionist executive issued a strongly worded statement that allegiance to its rules and decisions took precedence over external loyalties; a reminder unacceptable to Jabotinsky, but which effectively cowed the wavering members on his party's council. In March 1933 he resolved the deadlock in a manner Hitler, Mussolini and other men of destiny would have appreciated; he took sole control of the Revisionist party, suspending his opponents and replacing them with a new executive, but declaring that he would be attending the next Zionist Congress in person. It was, according to his hagiographer Joseph Schechtman, a master-stroke, brushing aside a tiresome opposition while neutering their complaints by refraining from immediate secession. The deposed courtiers spluttered with indignation. 'It is hard for me to grasp,' huffed Meir Grossman, one of his earliest disciples, 'how democratic principles can be reconciled with the dictatorship of a single person . . .'

Jabotinsky was steadily shedding his liberal scruples. The unqualified loyalty of his marching, brown-shirted Betarim was compensation for the wheeler-dealing of Zionist politics and the timidity of his former confidants. For all that he waved away the calls of his Palestinian admirers to make him Führer, and told a Betar convention in Vienna that there was no place in the movement for totalitarianism, a 1933 article, 'By the Fireside', was a truer indication of the direction he was taking. The title was taken from a Yiddish song about a rabbi teaching the

Hebrew alphabet to children. Jabotinsky gave it a contemporary moral: 'The alphabet now has a more simple ring: young people, learn to shoot!'

Betar in Palestine had come under the dominance of an extremist group, Brit ha-Biryonim (League of Outlaws), named after a sect at the time of the first Jewish revolt against Rome and led by three former Labour movement supporters – Abba Achimeir, a journalist; Yehoshua Yevin, a physician; and Uri Zvi Greenberg, a poet. They embraced fascism and denounced Marxism with the proselytizing zeal peculiar to the convert. Achimeir's column in the Betar newspaper was titled 'From a Fascist's Notebook'. A mood of profound nihilism permeated their writings. Despair, sacrifice, blood-letting, death were recurring motifs. Mankind was evil and politics a jungle. 'We see that those movements which have adapted to the concepts of our cruel era are triumphant among mankind,' pontificated Achimeir. 'We will not engage in mourning nineteenth-century Europe.' The efforts of Mussolini to transform a weak-willed people into a vital nation were proof of his political genius, and Hitler's national socialism, despite its anti-Semitic overtones, had saved Germany from civil war and the dictatorship of the Soviet secret police. The inevitable war with the Arabs, a clash between two irreconcilable cultures, would be a therapeutic purging for the Jewish people, out of which the true Zionist revolution would emerge. 'We are destined for power, force, the Kingdom of the House of David, or a hellfire of shame, an Arab kingdom,' keened Greenberg, the former bard of kibbutz pioneering.

Jabotinsky watched over his brood like an indulgent grandparent, occasionally chiding their excesses. 'I demand an unconditional stop to this outrage,' he wrote to the editor of *Do'ar ha-Yom* after a series of positive articles about Nazi Germany. 'To find in Hitler and Hitlerism some feature of a "national liberation movement" is sheer ignorance. Moreover, and under present circumstances, all this babbling is discrediting and paralysing my work . . .' More typically, he expressed admiration for their activist spirit, defending 'impulsive maximalist tendencies in our movement' as the excusable enthusiasm of youth. They might use robust language to anathematize Marxists and leftists – Chaim Arlosoroff, the rising star of the Labour movement was 'Foreskinoff' and 'The Red Diplomat' – but could claim that they had learned at their leader's knee. Jabotinsky's collection of essays, *Problems of Labour*, published in 1933, included titles like 'Yes, Let Us Smash Them!' and 'The Red Swastika', and none of his progeny could match his elegant invective against 'the obese sarcoma called Histadrut which grows daily fatter and fatter on middle-class gifts' and would stifle Zionism were it not for 'a stream of healthy blood, Betar, fighting this malignant tumour . . . a handful of young people, for whom Zionism is everything . . . [fighting] the red banner – a rag, and alien at that – and defending their right to serve the Jewish state ideal'.

Betarim in Palestine were 'his boys', the militant arm of Revisionism in its struggle with Labour Zionism. Matters came to a head over the Histadrut's control of the work force in a country that lacked adequate labour legislation. The Histadrut dominated the labour exchanges set up to regulate relations between workers and employers, acted as an agent of collective bargaining, protected the interests of the Jewish worker against cheaper Arab labour, and tried to establish closed shops. Revisionists demanded instead that there should be a national arbitration authority under the neutral auspices of the Zionist executive. Betar immigrants began strike-breaking. Employers unwilling to meet the Histadrut's wage demands took on Betar workers. The Histadrut was bested in two rowdy clashes with Revisionists over strike-breaking in Jerusalem in 1932, and in February 1933 in the Petach Tikvah building industry. Verbal and physical violence escalated. On May Day 1933, Mapai posters branded Revisionists 'the students of Hitler' on 'the Jewish street'. The Revisionist press assaulted Labour in turn, urged on from abroad by Jabotinsky.

In June 1933, Chaim Arlosoroff, the thirty-four-year-old political secretary of the Jewish Agency, was shot dead by two assailants while strolling along the Tel-Aviv beach with his wife. A highly regarded Mapai theoretician and *bête noire* of the Revisionists, Arlosoroff had recently returned from delicate negotiations with the Nazi leadership to allow German Jews to emigrate to Palestine with some of their wealth. The Revisionists, conveniently overlooking Jabotinsky's negotiations with Petliura, denounced it as a pact with the devil. On the morning of the shooting, Achimeir's newspaper had editoralized that 'Jews have always known how to deal with those who trade on the honour and beliefs of their people'. Several Brit ha-Biryonim members, including Achimeir, were charged with planning and committing the murder. The Yishuv was riven by the assassination, Labour politicians quick to point out the tragic consequences of right-wing, anti-socialist chauvinism, Revisionists insisting that the accused were innocent victims of a Mapai 'blood libel'. Jabotinsky rose above such vulgar epithet-hurling. In a letter pleading for leniency for Avraham Stavski, sentenced to death for the murder but released for lack of corroborating evidence (only to be killed on board the *Altalena* in 1948), Jabotinsky grandly declared, 'Stavski belongs to Betar, a youth organization of which I am head; no member of Betar would lie to me. I pledge my honour that Stavski is innocent.'

Public opinion was more sceptical, and in the elections for the Eighteenth Zionist Congress that summer, Mapai garnered 44 per cent of the votes (71 per cent in Palestine), while Jabotinsky's threat to make it his final appearance was vitiated by Revisionism's humiliating decline from 25 per cent two years previously to 14 per cent. With Mapai firmly in the driving seat, Ben-Gurion summarized his future modus operandi in Zionist (and later Israeli) politics: 'I have always favoured a broad coalition – everyone apart from the Revisionists.' A series of Congress resolutions effectively quarantined them; they were forbidden to conduct independent negotiations with governments or the League of Nations, reminded of the paramountcy of the Zionist Organization, condemned for strike-breaking and arraigned before a commission of inquiry established, at Mapai's request, to investigate violence in the Zionist movement. Revisionism had been reduced, politically speaking, to an isolated rump. Despite Jabotinsky's widespread support in the Yishuv and the Diaspora, his party had failed to harness its resources and realize its vision democratically. Direct action, the politics of gesture, was the only option left.

In the lexicon of Italian fascism, cutting a *bella figura* was an admired trait. The figure Jabotinsky cut in his final years was increasingly bathetic, more Charlie Chaplin's great dictator than Nietzsche's man of iron. His grandiose gestures and bombastic statements rang hollow, all style and little substance, beside the all-too-solid achievements of serious contemporaries like Salazar in Portugal, Franco in Spain, Hitler and Mussolini. They mobilized battalions, Jabotinsky brandished petitions. His first campaign was in 1934, to collect 600,000 signatures for an appeal to the governments of all civilized states drawing attention to the worsening plight of Jews in Europe. Only by mass immigration to Palestine, declared the signatories, could they rebuild their lives. The

Zionist executive repudiated the petition as a Revisionist publicity stunt, politically worthless.

The Revisionist Labour Union was founded in the spring of 1934, to challenge the Histadrut's monopoly. Relations between Betar and Labour Zionism had worsened since Arlosoroff's murder. The Betar leadership had instructed its members abroad who wished to emigrate not to do so under the aegis of the Jewish Agency. The Agency retaliated by refusing to grant any of its precious entry permits (only 5500 that year, against the 24,700 requested from the mandate government) to Betarim. The Revisionists claimed discrimination against their workers, and clashes with Histadrut members followed. It was to avert the fear of worsening violence that secret talks, brokered by Pinhas Rutenberg, founder of the Palestine Electrical Corporation, were held in London in the autumn of 1934 between Ben-Gurion and Jabotinsky. The situation was delicate. Ben-Gurion customarily referred to Jabotinsky as 'Vladimir Hitler', and Jabotinsky had made fun of 'Ben Bouillon', the boastful Mapai leader. In fact, the two men got on well. Ben-Gurion called Jabotinsky 'friend' and 'comrade' – they had, after all, been in the Jewish Legion together – and Jabotinsky responded to his warm words with the wistful admission that perhaps he was at fault for having long forgotten how to use such polite language. Their cordiality produced remarkable results. They initialled a draft agreement to present to their respective organizations which banned violence and insults in public debate, restored Betar immigration permits and provided a united labour framework for the 60,000 members of the Histadrut and the 7000 belonging to the Revisionist Union. Even more ambitiously, they outlined an agenda for the eventual inclusion of Revisionist representation on the Zionist executive.

To symbolize their accord, Jabotinsky suggested that a spectacular joint project should be undertaken. The Labour leader agreed, and proposed a new settlement in Palestine. Jabotinsky countered with his pet scheme, a worldwide petition on behalf of Zionism, saying, 'You underestimate the value of a gesture and a slogan. The word, the formula, possess enormous power.' Commenting later, Ben-Gurion reflected, 'I felt that here we came to the fundamental conflict.' Their parting had the poignancy of two medieval knights bidding farewell before being forced by circumstances to take opposing sides in a war. Nevertheless, their correspondence continued. 'Whatever comes, the

London chapter will not be erased from my heart,' wrote Ben-Gurion. 'Should it be that fate leads us to battle, know that among your "enemies" there is one who appreciates you and for whom your pain is his pain.'

They could not refrain from jousting over their contrasting views of Zionism, but with courtesy rare in the annals of Zionist polemic. Jabotinsky complimented Ben-Gurion and the Labour movement on having fashioned a delicate blend of socialism and Zionism, 'a work of art which only artists can understand and cherish', but one which modern youth, inclined to 'a direct, simple, primal, brutal Yes or No' rejected. 'This generation is exceedingly monistic.' Ben-Gurion repudiated the taunt of *sha'atnez* Zionist socialism; 'the necessary aspiration of the workers, and all those for whom Zionism comes before class politics, is to a united and free Jewish nation with equal rights, within which there are no class differences and contradictions, but rather the economic and social equality proper to a free nation.' Jabotinsky's reply was a blithe echo of glad confident mornings from his nobler past: 'If I were assured that there was no road to a state but through socialism, or even if this would hasten its creation in one generation, I'd be ready and able. Even more than that: if an Orthodox state in which I would be forced to eat *gefilte* fish morning after morning was what is necessary – I'd agree to it (if there is no other way). Even worse: a Yiddish state, which for me would end the charm of the thing – if there is no other way – I agree to it. And I will leave a will to my children telling them to make a revolution. But I'll write on the envelope: To be opened five years after the Hebrew state is established.'

He was not called upon to make good his promise. In February 1935, the Revisionists announced that they would insist on the right of independent action whatever the Zionist Organization decided, and a month later the Histadrut rejected the draft agreement between the two leaders. Secession from the World Zionist Organization and the Jewish Agency was now inevitable, and Jabotinsky made overtures to those same Orthodox whose obscurantism he despised to gain the support of religious circles in eastern Europe. In September 1935 the founding congress of the New Zionist Organization was held in Vienna. Delegates were elected by 713,000 voters from thirty-two countries, a computation mysteriously arrived at and less than the round one million Jabotinsky had hoped for, but still a significant tally to set against the claim made at the Nineteenth Zionist Congress earlier in the summer of 1.2 million subscribers to the WZO.

Jabotinsky, at last, was the undisputed leader of his own, unfettered Zionist organization. Its principles bore the hallmarks of his gift for potent simplification: the redemption of Israel and its land, the revival of its sovereignty and language; implanting in Jewish life the sacred treasures of Jewish tradition (a nod to Orthodox supporters and his new-found discovery of Judaism's eternal verities); a Jewish state on both sides of the Jordan; social justice without class struggle in Palestine; and a Ten Year Plan to settle one and a half million Jews in Palestine within a decade. From headquarters in London, Jabotinsky travelled the world on behalf of his new movement in the role of alternative leader-in-exile to Weizmann, who had been re-elected to the Zionist presidency in 1935. He gave interviews, addressed large crowds – according to Arthur Koestler, once keeping an open-air audience of thousands spellbound for five hours in Vienna – met with presidents and ministers and members of parliaments. His mass emigration plan, denounced by most sections of the Jewish public who feared it would give credence to the anti-Semitic slur that Jews are aliens in their countries of residence, was, predictably, given a sympathetic hearing in those east European countries not averse to shedding their 'surplus' Jews. He had no difficulty in obtaining audiences with the Polish cabinet, King Carol of Romania, and the presidents of Czechoslovakia and Lithuania.

To a Jewish newspaper in Warsaw which had regularly published his articles but now attacked his scheme editorially, he sent a farewell message, 'I regret that you do not see the dark clouds that are gathering over the heads of the Jews in Europe.' But Jabotinsky did not prophesy, as his admirers would later claim, the magnitude of the impending Holocaust. Right up to September 1939, he was certain that there would be no war. His forebodings were prompted by the current fate of German Jewry under Hitler, and his anxiety about an endemic anti-Semitism in the heart of Europe, which could nevertheless be exploited to bring about the *endziel* of a Jewish majority and a Jewish state in Palestine 'independently of what we Jews do or do not do'.

Over 164,000 Jews had poured into Palestine between 1933 – the year of Hitler's rise to power – and 1936, a sudden and dramatic influx which almost doubled the Yishuv's population. The Arab response was equally dramatic: a six-month general strike and economic boycott, demonstrations and guerrilla warfare. All the Arab political groupings united on a common platform calling for an end to Jewish land purchases and immigration, the termination of the mandate and the proclamation of an independent Arab state. In scale, widespread support, severity and duration, the Arab Revolt of 1936–9, as it came to be called, dwarfed all previous anti-Jewish disturbances. According to the report of the mandate administration, nearly 10,000 violent incidents were perpetrated by Arab nationalists, including 1325 attacks on British troops and police, 1503 acts of sabotage and 930 attacks on Jewish population and settlements; 2850 Arabs were killed and several thousand injured in riots quelled by British forces, and 9000 Arabs were interned. Nearly 1200 Jews and 700 British were killed or wounded in the uprising.

Jabotinsky, still *persona non grata* in Palestine, was forced to watch from the sidelines. During the first year of the riots, official Zionist policy was to refrain from retaliation and practise *havlagah* (self-restraint). The maturity with which the Jewish self-defence force, the Haganah and even Jabotinsky's paramilitary cadres responded to Arab violence won favourable notices for Zionism in the European press. When Arab attacks intensified in 1937–8, the policy of non-retaliation was abandoned by the Haganah in favour of selective retaliatory action. But they were faced by a rival military organization, substantially Revisionist in personnel, the Irgun, an abbreviation of its full title Irgun Z'vai L'umi (National Military Organization). The Irgun had been formed in 1931, after an acrimonious split in the Jerusalem Haganah, but half of its 3000 members returned to the fold in April 1937. Those who stayed outside declared their loyalty to Jabotinsky as their commander and rejected the obligation of *havlagah*. Once again, the threat of civil war was real.

Jabotinsky could barely control his Palestinian fighters from afar. The liberal who cited as his heroes Garibaldi, Lincoln, Gladstone and Victor Hugo had spawned a brood of terrorists who attacked Arabs passing through Jewish quarters and indiscriminately threw bombs into Arab markets and bus stations. They quoted his 'iron wall' morality at him – that just aims justified violent measures. Generally speaking, he preferred not to hear about specific actions. 'Man fregt nit den Taten' ('Don't bother father') he once answered Menachem Begin, when the future leader of Irgun wanted instructions. The old man was growing soft.

Avraham Stern, leader of a splinter group within Irgun, contemptuously referred to him as an 'ex-activist leader'. When he inquired if Arabs could be warned in advance to evacuate an area under impending attack, Irgun commanders replied that such a warning would endanger the lives of their own troops, as they similarly responded in defence of the massacre of 254 Arab civilians at Deir Yassin in 1948.

Jabotinsky's last significant contribution to the Zionist cause which, under Ben-Gurion, was determined to marginalize his brand of adventurism and weed out his undisciplined followers was to give evidence before the British Royal Commission on Palestine in February 1937. The Peel Commission, chaired by an experienced colonial negotiator and grandson of Robert Peel, had been set up to investigate the causes of the disturbances in Palestine and make recommendations. Its report, published in July 1937, was the fairest and most realistic of the several commissioned during the years of the mandate, and concluded with the momentous proposal that Palestine should be partitioned into a sovereign Jewish state, an Arab state linked to Transjordan, and British mandatory zones controlling the main holy places and seaports. The commission spent two months in Palestine interviewing Zionist and Arab spokesmen, then reconvened in London, where Jabotinsky was called before it representing his New Zionist Organization. It was a setting and situation to his liking, recognition conferred on the outsider from Odessa in the palace of Westminster by the Mother of Parliaments. He rose to the occasion superbly. His testimony, an hour and a half long (modest by his standards), was a magnificent piece of oratory: eloquent, subtly flattering to British culture and imperial pride, emotional but dignified, a sustained '*J'accuse*' against mandate policy but delivered with the dignity of one for whom suffering was the badge of his tribe.

He painted a vivid picture of imperilled European Jewry and asked that it be given what every normal nation had, 'beginning with the smallest and the humblest who do not claim any merit, any role in humanity's development' – a state of its own. If that was asking for too much, then Oliver Twist had been guilty in asking for 'more', meaning a normal portion. Jabotinsky had every respect for reasonable Arab claims, even though their economic progress as a result of Zionist colonization was the envy of their neighbours; nor would he deny that eventually they would become a minority in Jewish Palestine. What he did deny was that for a fraction of the Arab nation to live in somebody else's state represented hardship. Of course he understood their preference for Palestine to become Arab state number four, five or six, 'but when the Arab claim is confronted with our Jewish demand to be saved, it is like the claims of appetite versus the claims of starvation'. And so on in similar vein, with a plea for the Jewish Defence Force to be legalized, a side swipe at the Jewish Agency, and reminders of Britain's imperial responsibilities, from which he was confident she would not flinch in implementing the Balfour Declaration, because 'I believe in England, just as I believed in England twenty years ago when I went, against nearly all Jewish opinion, and said "Give soldiers to Great Britain!" because I believed in her. I still believe.'

Perhaps being in London stirred memories of the moral values he had once proclaimed. A few months later he dismissed a Betar resolution which called for 'liberating Palestine by force of arms' with the stinging rebuke, 'If you, Mr Begin, have stopped believing in the conscience of the world, then my advice to you is to go and drown yourself in the Vistula River.' In December 1938 he approached the editor of the London *News Chronicle* offering to write a series of articles on liberalism, 'the old-fashioned creed . . . [that had] made the nineteenth century great' and that he was convinced was destined for a spectacular renaissance within five years, 'with enthusiastic crowds of youth to back it', repeating its catchwords as they had those of communism or fascism, 'only the effect will be deeper, as liberalism has its roots in human nature which all barrack-room religions lack'.

The world of his Italian student days, of idealistic enthusiasm for Garibaldi and his liberating Red Shirts, had long since passed Jabotinsky by. The Zionist executive was not interested in welcoming the prodigal back. He died suddenly of a heart attack in August 1940, while visiting a Betar summer camp in upper New York state, an exile to the end. In his will, written in 1935, he stipulated, 'My remains will be transferred to *Eretz Israel* only on the instructions of a Jewish government.' Twenty-five years after his death, in a symbolic gesture of reconciliation, Jabotinsky and his wife Johanna were reinterred in a state funeral on Mount Herzl, watched, among thousands of other spectators, by David Ben-Gurion. Since then, his reputation has been reassessed by a number of Zionist historians at pains to refute the fascist label and point out where his ideas on nation-building, the corporate state, economic policy and trade unionism differed from those of Hitler or Mussolini. To the impartial observer these seem to be picayune distinctions; the similarities are more disturbing than the divergences, for all that Jabotinsky was infinitely more sophisticated, intelligent and personable than either of his fascist contemporaries.

Flags, parades, sloganeering, excitation of mass enthusiasm – those were Jabotinsky's distinctive, and transient, contributions to the Zionist debate. Of all the major political creeds and parties in the Yishuv during the twenties and thirties, the Revisionist movement alone failed to establish any settlements, any economic enterprises, any lasting institutions. A political party claiming Jabotinsky as its ideological mentor, Herut, did eventually emerge from the turmoil of establishing a state after the Second World War, and with it a leader, Menachem Begin, who slavishly imitated his former Betar chief in gesture, speech cadences, emotive rhetoric and outpourings of elaborate charm to disarm criticism. It has to be said in favour of Begin, however harshly his years as prime minister of Israel are judged, that once he had discarded his terrorist image he displayed a punctilious regard for parliamentary procedure and the responsibilities of a loyal opposition. Jabotinsky, in contrast, frequently chafed in a subordinate role and had little patience for democratic niceties.

Perhaps the last word on him should go to someone in the best position to know: 'For Zionism to succeed you must have a Jewish state with a Jewish flag and a Jewish language. The man who really understands this is your Jewish fascist, Jabotinsky.' The man who spoke those words to the chief rabbi of Rome in 1935 was Benito Mussolini.

14

David Ben-Gurion – From Class to Nation

On the afternoon of 14 May 1948, the People's Council convened in a drab museum hall in Tel-Aviv and issued the Declaration of Independence proclaiming the establishment of 'a Jewish state in Palestine, the State of Israel'. The proclamation was read in a voice occasionally breaking with emotion by a short, stocky man with a shock of white hair; in deference to the occasion, he was wearing a tie instead of the open-necked shirt he customarily sported.

If any one person deserved to set the seal on the adventure in state-building begun by Herzl fifty years previously, it was David Ben-Gurion. By force of personality and single-minded (but flexible) pursuit of the ultimate goal, he had destroyed sophisticated opponents while appropriating their ideological baggage, gained the allegiance of cleverer colleagues, and reduced Chaim Weizmann to honorific status, to splutter impotently from the sidelines of his presidential residence that Ben-Gurion was not fit to be a shoemaker, let alone to run a country. And that was just within Zionist politics. On the wider playing field of diplomacy, he had precipitated Britain's humiliating withdrawal from her League of Nations mandate and out-manoeuvred the Palestinian Arab community. He had won crucial American support and, for the time being, necessary Soviet approval; soon he would mastermind the defeat of the invading armies of neighbouring Arab states.

The young man who began his career as a rigid, small-town Marxist never stopped mouthing the jargon of revolutionary socialism, but transcended the limitations of Po'alei Zion class politics in the interests of the wider Yishuv, all the while with a singleness of purpose Jabotinsky would have envied, subordinating every dogmatic consideration to the overriding imperative of *raison d'état*. From the amalgamation of Achdut Ha-Avodah with Ha-Po'el Ha-tza'ir in 1930 to form the Mapai party, until his death in 1973, his presence dominated first Yishuv, then the Zionist Organization, then Israeli politics. As the leader, he showed inspirational qualities of vision, courage and generosity and ended his days as a respected international statesman; the man could be stubborn, petty and relentlessly vindictive and left damaged and in disarray the unified political base he had laboured to build over forty years.

Ben-Gurion has been the subject of several biographies and controversial reappraisals. His roles as socialist theoretician, secretary-general of the Histadrut, leader of the Labour movement, chairman of the Jewish Agency and first prime minister of Israel, have been analysed exhaustively and unflaggingly, so powerful is his imprint on the Israeli collective psyche. A wide-ranging analysis is impossible in this brief portrait, which concentrates on three areas of his thought: the consolidation of national unity over class struggle; relations with the British; and responses to the Arab problem.

David Ben-Gurion was born David Gruen in Plonsk, Poland, in 1886. His father Avigdor was an ardent member of Chibbat Zion, and used his home as the meeting-place for Zionist activity in the town. Most of the town's 8000 inhabitants were Jews. David's mother died when he was eleven years old, and he had a Haskalah-influenced schooling, with additional lessons from private tutors (a polite euphemism for hungry students earning pocket money). His earliest memory was learning Hebrew on his grandfather's knee, and the books he claimed most influenced him as a child were Abraham Mapu's *Love of Zion* – the first Hebrew novel, a historical romance set in ancient Palestine – Harriet Beecher Stowe's *Uncle Tom's Cabin*, which taught him to despise slavery and dependence, and Tolstoy's *Resurrection*, a tale of spiritual regeneration; such a happy congruence between childhood reading and his adult role of reviving the Jewish people in its ancient homeland may appear neatly contrived to suspicious minds. 'When I was ten years old,' wrote Ben-Gurion, 'the word spread through town that the Messiah had come, that he was to be found in Vienna, that he had a black beard, and that his name was Dr Herzl.'

At the age of seventeen he joined Po'alei Zion, was briefly arrested during the 1905 revolution, and a year later emigrated to Palestine as a farm worker. The mythic status of the pioneer was so ingrained in his thinking that over forty years later, as prime minister, he registered himself in the new state's first census as 'agricultural labourer'. When he retired for the first time in 1953, it was to S'deh Boker, a pioneering kibbutz in the heart of the Negev, to encourage Israeli youth to follow his example of building up the land. 'The settlement of the land is the only true Zionism, all else being self-deception, empty verbiage and merely a pastime.'

The Palestinian branch of Po'alei Zion, with all of sixty members, held its first conference (how the early Zionists loved conferences!) in Ramleh in October 1906, and duly produced its platform. The Borochovian document declared that 'the history of mankind is the history of national and class war' and called for a Jewish state in Palestine to promote the cause of international socialism. Ben-Gurion was elected to the central committee, but soon disagreed with colleagues who planned to publish a party newspaper in Yiddish, the mother tongue of most immigrants. David Gruen, like many other Second Aliyah pioneers, had changed his name, to Ben-Gurion (Son of Lions), to signify repudiation of Diaspora inferiority. Only Hebrew, he claimed, not the language of the exile, should be used in the new society being created. It was his first doctrinal battle, and he won. By 1910, a party weekly, *Achdut*, was being produced in Hebrew by an editorial board that included Ben-Gurion, Yitzchak Ben-Zvi and the novelist Y. H. Brenner. Ben-Gurion, a fiery orator, tended to write bluntly and repetitively, hammering home a message. Not for him the dialectical subtleties of his friend Ben-Zvi or the political nuances of Berl Katznelson, the trade union leader. Ben-Gurion had no time for circumlocution. The destiny of Zionism did not depend on the diplomatic machinations of the Diaspora-based World Zionist Organization, but on realities in Palestine 'here, in the land of the Turk'. The emerging Jewish working class would become the universal class of the Jewish nation. 'The interests of the workers and the general national interests are one and the same,' he declared in 1911, confidently identifying a socialist future for Zionism.

With Ben-Zvi and Israel Shohat, head of Ha-Shomer, the self-defence organization, he went to Constantinople to study law. Their ulterior motive was to establish ties with the more liberal ruling circles in the Ottoman empire and advance the cause of Jewish autonomy in Palestine. For their pains, they were arrested when the First World War broke out on the charge of conspiring against Ottoman rule, and expelled from Palestine. By no means convinced of an Allied victory, Ben-Gurion paused in Egypt, where with Ben-Zvi he opposed Trumpeldor's formation of the Zion Mule Corps as inimical to the Yishuv's interests. He then crossed to America to lecture and win recruits for Labour Zionism. He constantly disabused his audiences of the notion that the patrimony of a Jewish state would be gifted to the Zionist Organization by victorious allies: 'We are seeking something very different in Palestine – a homeland. And a homeland cannot be taken just like that, like a gift, it cannot be acquired by concessions or political agreements, it cannot be bought, neither can it be seized by force. A homeland has to be built by the sweat of your brow . . .' For Ben-Gurion, a presumptuous newcomer on the Zionist scene, the key to statehood lay with the pioneers in Galilee, not in overtures to the great powers by the bourgeois dilettantes of the Zionist executive. The great bonus of the Balfour Declaration did not change his view:

England has not given Palestine back to us. It is not in England's power to give Palestine back to us . . . A country is not given to a people except by its own toil and creativity, its own efforts in construction and settlement . . . The Hebrew people itself, body and soul, with its own strength and its capital must build its national home and make good its national redemption.

The seeds were being sown of friction with the architect of the Balfour Declaration. Weizmann, basking in his triumph, let slip that the years between Herzl's death and his diplomatic coup had been uneventful for Zionism: the very years in which, with his young comrades, Ben-Gurion had been laying the social and economic foundations of a Jewish state. But he was quick enough to grasp the significance of Balfour's letter, and call for the formation of a Jewish army to liberate Palestine. It was as a soldier in the Jewish Legion and a recently married husband that Ben-Gurion returned to Palestine in 1918.

His role over the next dozen years as a Labour movement apparatchik was to push, badger, cajole and coerce the factions of the left into a semblance of unity in order to promote socialist Zionism. In February 1919, Po'alei Zion voted to dissolve itself and merge into Achdut Ha-Avodah (the Unity of Labour), intended as part political party, part trade union. His main allies in effecting the merger, as they were in all subsequent efforts to extend the scope of Labour hegemony within the Yishuv, were Ben-Zvi, Katznelson and Yitzchak Tabenkin. The most important decision taken by Ben-Gurion and his colleagues was to form the Haganah; their most serious failure was in persuading the pacifist and settlement-building members of Ha-Po'el Ha-tza'ir to overcome their misgivings about international socialism and join the new association. But a greater prize was in store: in December 1920, after months of complicated negotiation between Ben-Gurion and the leaders of Ha-Po'el Ha-tza'ir, the two parties joined in forming the Histadrut, which became the foremost instrument of the pioneer movement, dedicated to the national vision of large-scale, organized immigration and land settlement, and the socialist vision of a self-sufficient workers' commonwealth. Ben-Gurion and Berl Katznelson were appointed joint general secretaries.

His steady success in building what he called 'constructive socialism' – eschewing the mechanistic class warfare of Marxism for the primary task of creating a co-operative Jewish infrastructure – reached its apogee in 1930, with the formation of Mapai. In placing Labour unity above factionalism, he had learned from the Soviet experience. In 1923 Ben-Gurion was Histadrut's representative at the Moscow Agricultural Exposition. What impressed him most was the will-power and determination of the Bolsheviks in the face of adverse circumstances. He was particularly taken with Lenin:

Indeed this man is great. He possesses the essential capacity of looking life straight in the face. He doesn't think in concepts or words, but reflects on the fundamental facts of reality. His eye looks afar towards the forces that will dominate the future. However, before him he sees one direction, that which leads to his goal, and he turns neither left nor right, whilst he remains ready to use different routes as the situation demands. For he pursues one path – to his goal.

Too young to have known Herzl, too provincial to trust Weizmann or Jabotinsky, too practical to fall for the Gordon brand of mystical pioneering, Ben-Gurion had found his role-model. But hero-worship did not blind him to the weaknesses of Soviet communism. The Bolshevik attempt to create socialist structures without the advanced capitalist development posited by Marx's original paradigm had failed in Russia as it surely would in Palestine, where a Jewish working class did not exist to throw off the shackles of a capitalist bourgeoisie. Ben-Gurion's bold way out was simply to leapfrog class warfare in favour of creating – through Histadrut control of primary production and the economy – a self-sufficient proletariat that would become the truly 'national class' in the sense Marx meant when he wrote that the dominant class is the one whose interests 'must genuinely be the aims and interests of society itself, of which it becomes in reality the social head and heart'.

Ben-Gurion encapsulated his programme in the slogan 'From Class to Nation', the title he gave to a volume of essays published in 1933. Socialism and Zionism were two sides of the same revolutionary coin. Socialism was not only an end but the means through which Zionism would fulfil its mission of reshaping the social and economic contours of previous Diaspora history: 'The very realization of Zionism is nothing else than carrying out this deep historical transformation occurring in the life of the Hebrew people. This transformation does not limit itself to its geographical aspect, to the movement of Jewish masses from the countries of the Diaspora to the renascent homeland – but in a socioeconomic transformation as well; it means taking the uprooted, impoverished, sterile Jewish masses living parasitically off the body of an alien economic body and dependent on others – and introducing them to productive and creative life, implanting them on the land, integrating them into primary production in agriculture, in industry and handicraft – and making them economically independent and self-sufficient.'

The embodiment of constructive, nation-building socialism was the Jewish worker who came to Palestine 'not as a refugee, clutching at any reed offered to him. He came as a representative of the whole people, and as an avant-garde pioneer in the grand enterprise of the Hebrew revolution did he capture his position in the labour market, in the economy, and in settlement activities.' The Jewish worker was a Renaissance figure in his capabilities; creating agricultural and industrial structures, learning a new language and culture, sharing in defence duties, fighting for class and national interests through the agency of the Histadrut: 'in all this the Jewish worker was conscious of the historical task destined to be carried out by the working class . . . The Hebrew worker combined in his life work national redemption and class war, and in his class organization created the content of the historical aims and needs of the Jewish people.' That worker, representing dominance, class and party, would bear out Marx's axiom in *The Communist Manifesto* that 'the ruling ideas of each age have ever been the ideas of its ruling class'. Labour Zionism articulated the ideas of the ruling class for national redemption and social equality. To propagate those aims, Ben-Gurion was ready to lead any broad-based coalition, except with the

Revisionists, meaning except anyone who challenged the hegemony of the Histadrut and Mapai socialism.

He could afford to be assertive; the newly created Mapai party commanded nearly 30 per cent of the votes in Zionist Organization elections. At the 1921 Zionist Congress in Carlsbad, there had been 306 General Zionists, 97 Religious Zionists and only 34 Labour delegates. After the 1931 Congress which ousted Weizmann, Ben-Gurion wrote in the Mapai newspaper, 'Our movement has always maintained the socialist idea that the party of the working class, unlike the parties of other classes, is . . . also a national party, responsible for the future of the entire nation and viewing itself not just as a particular party but as the nucleus of the future nation. In this Congress, this idea became political reality. The Labour movement, which fifteen years ago hardly existed as a visible entity, has today become a corner-stone of Zionism, qualitatively and quantitatively . . . In the Land of Israel we are turning from a party to the mainstay of the community.'

Revisionism had been stopped in its tracks, the guiding control of the Histadrut and its affiliates confirmed. Labour Zionism was ensconced as the major partner in future national coalitions, its leadership, particularly Ben-Gurion and Katznelson, accepting that 'compromise equilibrium' was the price to be paid for heading as broad a coalition as possible in the Yishuv and the World Zionist Organization. Labour would no longer be able to function as if working-class interests and national interests were automatically identical – a sea change Ben-Gurion recognized. He continued to use the rhetoric of socialism and the class struggle, but adapted it as the situation demanded: Lenin's tactic of choosing different routes to the ultimate goal. He regarded his election to the Zionist executive in 1933 with mixed feelings. The challenge of Jabotinsky to organized labour still had to be quashed and party work for Mapai had been neglected in his involvement with the Histadrut. But fate now played its part in elevating him to leadership in the power vacuum created by Weizmann's deposition.

Ben-Gurion might have been *primus inter pares* in the Labour movement in Palestine, but he had formidable challengers. Katznelson preferred organizing the Histadrut to national politics, perhaps Ben-Zvi was too narrowly doctrinaire, Tabenkin too radical, Moshe Shertok (later Sharett) too prone to compromise; the most effortlessly brilliant of them all was Chaim Arlosoroff. Born in the Ukraine in 1899, he had come to Palestine in 1924 with a doctorate from the University of Berlin for his thesis on Marx's theory of class war, and rose quickly in the Labour movement, its most acute theoretician and most powerful mind. He was Weizmann's 'favourite son', a sophisticate at ease in European culture, bookish but dashing, a superb orator, and at the time of his assassination head of the political department of the Jewish Agency – the quasi foreign minister of the Yishuv. In the judgement of many shrewd observers, he was the man most likely to emerge as prime minister of a future Jewish state. In the event, Ben-Gurion benefited from his shocking death.

Ben-Gurion's election to the chairmanship of the Jewish Agency in 1935 confirmed his role as the most important figure in Zionism. Although under the formal control of the World Zionist Organization, the Agency was effectively the government of the Palestinian Jewish community and its representative in negotiations with the mandate authorities. Weizmann, reinstated that same year as president of the WZO, had greater prestige than Ben-Gurion and was the person with whom the mandate administration preferred to negotiate, but he was a statesman without a party, whereas Ben-Gurion had the apparatus of the Histadrut and Zionist socialism behind him. In his dealings with the British, he displayed the calculated pragmatism that had welded Labour Zionism into the dominant force in Yishuv society. He distrusted the Colonial Office with the inherent suspicion of every Russian-born Jew for officialdom. By upbringing and experience he was temperamentally incapable of sharing Arlosoroff's subtle analysis, expressed in a 1928 essay, 'The British Administration and the Jewish National Home', that it was simplistic to ascribe every disagreement between British officials and Zionism to anti-Semitism. Arlosoroff identified three groups among mandate administrators: the first category, perhaps 10 per cent, comprised people of high intelligence and culture who had come to Palestine with a broad knowledge of the Jewish problem and were sympathetic to the Zionist enterprise, 'though this still does not cause them to speak out and act as though they were members of the Zionist Actions Committee'; the second category was equally cultured and intelligent, but less well-versed in Jewish affairs, and understood its colonial responsibility as safeguarding the welfare of the 'natives' – in this case, the Arabs. The vast bulk of British officials, including police officers, NCOs and bureaucrats, belonged to the third category, which based its decisions on practicality, prudence and keeping order, not sympathy (or lack of it) towards Zionism. These minor officials happened to have been posted to Palestine 'and before coming here they have probably never heard of Zionism. The worldwide Jewish question interests them as much as last year's snow . . .'

Ben-Gurion was not concerned with a sociological typology of the mandate administration; he applied a simpler test. Was working with the British in Zionism's interests or not? Opposition to imperialism was one of the central tenets of Achdut Ha-Avodah's platform, yet when he was asked in 1921 why he had followed Weizmann in calling for co-operation with the British, Ben-Gurion replied, 'so long as we were few and weak, co-operation with the mandatory government was of vital importance for increasing our strength and numbers in the country.' He recognized that an alliance between Zionism and a great power was essential for its success, and while Britain held the reins he would forgo any scruples about colonialism to achieve the priority of accelerated Jewish immigration. A relatively small and weak Yishuv necessitated an accommodation with the mandate authorities:

Not because I don't know what the Colonial Office and the British Empire mean, but because we have the right to exist, to work, and to live, even in this corrupt world and this corrupt regime; we don't have to wait until a new world emerges before we can breathe. We have the right to come to this country today . . . We have to make use of all the forces in the world in order to settle a maximum number of Jews in Palestine and build our life there . . . As long as Russia – czarist or communist – and a Labour Britain or the Britain of Balfour, make it possible for us to work here in the task of creation, to strike roots as a nation in this country, we have to make use of all our opportunities and we are not responsible for anything that occurs outside our sphere of work.

Unlike Weizmann, he had no faith in the essential decency of British diplomacy or her inviolable commitment to the Balfour Declaration. 'The declaration is a broken reed. Since the issuance of the Balfour Declaration, the Versailles Treaty has been torn to shreds, the Covenant of the League of Nations, signed by thirty-four nations, has been rendered valueless . . . the Assyrians and Armenians have been deceived, and the Locarno Pact nullified . . .' As long as Britain was the external factor in making or breaking Zionism, he made the correct noises about long-term interests, without taking seriously, as Jabotinsky did, the suggestion floated by Josiah Wedgwood, a British Labour MP, that the Yishuv should be granted dominion status in the British empire.

A few months before his death, at a meeting of the Mapai Labour Party Council, Arlosoroff had provocatively queried one of socialist Zionism's obdurate convictions: its reluctance to participate in the administrative structures of the mandatory government, preferring to develop its own self-governing network of Histadrut enterprises, the kibbutz movement, marketing societies and loan associations. A consequence was not only opposition to the administration's pet scheme of a Legislative Assembly but also to extending government taxation and control of land usage and water resources. The result was that the state apparatus emerging in Palestine was becoming heavily biased in favour of the Arabs, due to deliberate Jewish non-involvement. The very success of the Yishuv in catering for its own education, health and economic requirements was creating a situation in which the mandate administration addressed itself almost exclusively to the needs of the Arab sector. Arlosoroff's conclusion, after listing instances of Mapai's obstructionism and equivocation, was to call for more Zionist representation on such government bodies as boards of education, water supply and land development, and to urge Jews to influence the administration from within, by joining it as officials and civil servants. The reaction to a speech from a Labour Zionist calling for more participation in the state machinery of a colonial administration (and one that had recently issued the discouraging Passfield White Paper) was implacably hostile. Ben-Gurion accused Arlosoroff of nurturing '*étatist*' ideas – a particularly heinous crime in the vocabulary of the Labour movement. Yet within three years, Ben-Gurion was willing to espouse the formula of parity between Jews and Arabs on a Legislative Assembly, because the Arab Revolt was affecting the British government's attitude towards Jewish immigration into Palestine. He explained his change of tactics: 'England is not wholly in accord with our enterprise . . . she is hesitant, apprehensive. She wants the friendship not only of the Jewish people, but the Muslim and Arab world . . . If we succeed in removing the growing obstacle of Arab opposition we will immensely strengthen our political position with England.' By the temporary expedient of appearing reasonable about the issue of parity, he hoped to mollify British public opinion 'only as long as the Mandate lasts'.

A year later, and persuaded by his reading of events in the wider world that the days of the mandate were numbered, he campaigned pugnaciously for Zionist acceptance of the Peel Commission's partition recommendation. For Weizmann and Ben-Gurion, the essential point about the Peel Report was that it recognized the principle of Jewish sovereignty; arguments about boundaries could come later. Ben-Gurion felt able to declare that 'The independence of the Jewish people was inconceivable without Palestine as an independent political unit, that is, a Jewish state', and to remind listeners that Achdut Ha-Avodah had been the first party to formulate this explicit demand. He had always been as uncompromising as Jabotinsky about Zionism's *endziel* – a Jewish state – but had refused to spell it out until the time was ripe, rejecting the Revisionists' bluster as reckless and politically inept when Jews were less than 20 per cent of the Palestinian population. That had altered with the substantial immigration of the thirties, but canny considerations still led him to dissimulate about statehood in evidence before the Royal Commission: 'We did not say it at the time and we do not say it now.' Britain was still the power on whose good-will Zionism depended.

It was a measure of Ben-Gurion's maturity, his ability to eschew the distant peaks of socialist dogma for realistic attainment, that he could draw up a fair assessment of Britain's discharge of her mandate responsibilities. In a 1936 article, 'Our Balance Sheet with the English', he wrote, 'England allowed 350,000 Jews into the country. She built a harbour at Haifa, and Haifa became a city with a Jewish majority. She built roads connecting the Jewish settlements, and she supported, albeit not sufficiently, Jewish industry. The English are not a nation of angels, and I know only too well the terrible things done by them in Ireland and other places; but the English have also done many positive things in the countries under their rule. They are a great nation, with a rich culture, and not a people of exploiters and robbers. And to us, the English were far from being just bad. They recognised our historical right to this country – they were the first to do so – proclaimed our language an official language, permitted large-scale immigration – and if we are to judge, let us judge justly and fairly.'

Because his co-operation with the British was dictated by practical self-interest, not ideology, several twists and turns in the relationship were still to come. In the event, the recommendation of the Peel Report was rejected as unworkable by the London government.

Instead, the Colonial Office convened an Arab–Zionist conference in London in February 1939, also inviting representatives from neighbouring Arab states to participate – a fateful precedent which encouraged rival Arab regimes to become involved in the future disposition of Palestine. That conference too ended in failure, and the British government determined to impose its own solution. The MacDonald White Paper was issued in May 1939. Effectively, it abrogated the Balfour Declaration and terminated the mandate. It proposed Arab self-government with minority exercise of authority for the Jewish community, limitation of Jewish immigration to a total of 75,000 newcomers over the next five years and thereafter subject to Arab consent, and the curtailment of land sales by Arabs to the Zionists.

Condemnation of the White Paper was universal. Zionists were appalled that immigration should be slashed when hundreds of thousands of Jews were trying to escape from Nazi Europe; the Arabs rejected self-government which acknowledged Jewish rights. The Permanent Mandates Commission of the League of Nations considered the White Paper and expressed the view that it was contrary to the provisions of the Palestine mandate. The British government was due to present its case in September 1939, but by then the Second World War had broken out and Ben-Gurion summed up the Zionist response to hostilities in a pithy slogan: the Yishuv would fight the war against Hitler as if there were no White Paper, and would fight the White Paper as if there were no war against Hitler.

15

Ben-Gurion – The Primacy of the State

Ben-Gurion's conduct during the Second World War was characterized by pursuit of two consistent yet divergent goals: a strategic orientation away from Britain towards America, the global superpower, to
enlist the support of its large Jewish community in the post-war
demand for Jewish statehood; and participation in the war effort and
active partnership with the British authorities – even to the extent of
handing over to them Irgun terrorists and sympathizers – in so far as
it strengthened and safeguarded the institutions of the Yishuv and
developed the capabilities of the Haganah for post-war confrontation with the Arabs. That armed conflict was inevitable had been
Ben-Gurion's conviction at least since the 1929 disturbances. He was
already privately counting the manpower potential of the Arab states
in the event of war. No single aspect of his political strategy reveals
more clearly than his dealings with the Arabs his ruthless suppression
of moral niceties and ideological theory for the imperative of state-
building.

His experience of the Arabs went back to his early days as a watchman in the Galilee, where 'I saw for the first time the acuteness and
danger of the Arab problem . . . Jews being murdered simply because
they were Jews.' He had come to Palestine with the doctrinal assumptions of Po'alei Zion: Jewish pioneers were the vanguard of European culture, bringing economic and scientific benefits to the native
population; class solidarity between Jewish and Arab workers would
break down antagonism towards Zionism. 'Like all workers, the Arab
labourer hates his oppressor and exploiter, but since in addition to the
class clash there is in this case a national difference between workers
and farmers, this hatred takes the form of national hostility,' Ben-
Gurion wrote in 1910. At that stage, he was unwilling to concede a
fundamental incompatibility between the socialist clarion call of class
unity and Labour Zionism's purpose of creating an autonomous infrastructure in Palestine; the Arab worker could be weaned away from

nationalism by the advantages of economic co-operation with his Jewish counterpart.

At the second conference of Achdut Ha-Avodah, after the riots of May 1921, he called for 'friendly relations between Jewish workers and the Arab working masses on the basis of joint economic, political and cultural activity'. He cited acceptance of Arab workers into the Histadrut Sick Fund, joint public-work projects on conditions of equal pay, and the organization of Arab trade unions, as immediate areas of potential co-operation. Moshe Shertok, then studying in London, wrote to him that the proposals were impractical, since neither Jews nor Arabs were ready to consider them and it was wishful thinking to imagine that Arab workers could be won over: 'Who is more likely to find a response: we, the hated foreigners, or the *mukhtar* and the sheikh who dwell in the midst of their people . . . For the sake of self-delusion we have made it all sound easy and simple – a handful of *effendis* against the masses of workers.'

It is unlikely that someone as clear-sighted as Ben-Gurion was hiding behind rose-coloured spectacles. He had already remarked after the May riots that 'what we had suffered at Arab hands was child's play compared with what we might expect in the future,' and it was precisely because he saw no likelihood of compromise in the political sphere that he looked for economic palliatives. When the joint secretariat of the two Labour parties gathered eight years later in the shocked aftermath of the 1929 riots, Ben-Gurion summed up their tortuous semantics with curt dismissiveness, 'The debate as to whether or not an Arab national movement exists is a pointless verbal exercise; the main thing for us is that the movement attracts the masses. We do not regard it as a resurgence movement and its moral worth is dubious. But politically speaking it is a national movement.' The Arabs would never become pro-Zionist, because they would never want the Jews to become the majority. 'Herein lies the true conflict between us and the Arabs. We both want to be the majority.'

Two weeks later he presented to the joint secretariat his own blueprint for future relations, 'Plans for establishing a Political Regime in Palestine'. The plan was predicated on four assumptions: that Palestine belonged to the Jewish people and the Arabs living there; that Jewish rights were not conditional on external will or consent, but derived from the ties of the Jewish people to their national homeland; that the

Jewish demand for self-determination was justified by the criteria of universal justice; and that the moral validity of Zionism stemmed both from the Jewish predicament in the Diaspora and from the settlers' determination to cultivate a barren country for the sake of all its inhabitants. That, essentially, would henceforth be the defence of Zionism against its critics. Ben-Gurion proposed a constitutional regime in Palestine in which Jews and Arabs would enjoy equal rights as individuals and communities on the principle of non-domination irrespective of majority—minority numbers, both peoples guaranteed the opportunity of undisturbed development towards full national independence. The scheme would be implemented in three stages. In the first, municipal autonomy would be introduced under a joint Jewish—Arab ruling council of equal representation, the high commissioner remaining the final arbiter of national affairs and Jewish immigration rights. The second stage would extend municipal autonomy to regional autonomy and the ruling council would be elected directly by the two peoples. The third stage would commence when the Jews and Arabs had reached numerical parity, which would signify the fulfilment of the Balfour Declaration and the termination, therefore, of the mandate. Its authority would be replaced in an independent Palestine 'constituting [two] autonomous states within the federal Palestinian commonwealth'.

Criticism of Ben-Gurion's plan was widespread among his colleagues, not least because it required co-operation with the existing Arab leadership, which was deemed — in socialist parlance — reactionary, corrupt and exploitative. That no Arab would fall for such a barefaced attempt to create a Jewish majority in Palestine as soon as possible was beside the point. Nevertheless, he persisted with the plan, or aspects of it, such as the parity principle, throughout the worsening situation of the thirties. It offered, he averred, an answer to the plight of the Jews of Europe, the apprehensions of the Arabs in Palestine, the predicament of the mandate government, and the ethical concerns of enlightened world opinion.

In fact, his own concerns were more urgent and practical, motivated not by idealism but by demographic reality. Jewish society would always be surrounded by the great Arab Muslim world, and being in Palestine alone was not 'an amulet protecting us against assimilation'. Majority status was the only guarantee of a national, and socialist, future. 'The majority is but a stage along our path, albeit an important and decisive stage in the political sense. From there we can proceed with our activities in calm confidence and concentrate the masses of our people in this country, and its environs.' To justify bringing that majority into Palestine required the insistent re-iteration that whereas a Jewish *nation* sought to live there, it was only an Arab *community*, which was part of the larger Arab nation spread-ing from the Atlantic to the Indian Ocean. Jewish immigration would not endanger the social, political or national status of the Arabs, since the significance of the Palestinian Arabs 'was merely a question of a land less than 2 per cent of the total area occupied by the Arabs in the east, and containing 3 per cent of the total number of Arabs in the world . . . There was no comparing the value of *Eretz Israel* for the Arabs with the importance it held for the Jewish people.' Jewish necessity took precedence over Arab free choice, or as Jabotinsky would have put it, the demands of hunger over the options of appetite.

Unlike the Revisionists, Ben-Gurion did not denigrate the Arabs, nor was he condescending, like some of the well-meaning Brit Shalom supporters. In the winter of 1933, when renewed immigration, if main-tained at that level, held out the rosy prospect of a Jewish majority within two decades, he warned the Mapai central committee that Arab protest demonstrations showed clear features of a national movement: 'This time there are truly national heroes and it is this that inspires a movement, and particularly the young generation. This time we are witnessing a political movement that must arouse respect.' It was be-cause he took the Arabs seriously, recognized the plausibility of their complaints and was haunted all his political life by the spectre of a tiny and isolated Jewish entity adrift in an Arab sea that he deliberately promoted the concept of pan-Arabism in an effort to vitiate the thrust of Palestinian nationalism. A solution to the Zionist–Palestinian Arab impasse lay in an agreement with a wider Arab federation. 'In this limited area there is indeed a conflict which is hard to overcome,' he told George Antonius, a Christian Arab historian and a senior civil ser-vant in the mandatory government, shortly before the Arab Revolt of 1936, 'but we must perceive the Jews as a worldwide unit and the Arabs as well.' The Jewish people demanded only a small part of the vast territ-ory over which the Arab people claimed sovereignty, and if the Arabs would agree to a Jewish return to their homeland, 'we would help them with our political, financial and moral support to bring about the rebirth and unity of the Arab people.'

Ben-Gurion held a series of meetings, on his own initiative, with Mussa Alami, the Arab nationalist leader, Antonius, leaders of the Syrian national movement, and other figures in the ruling circles of Arab countries, throughout the crisis years of 1936–9. He always dangled the prospect of Jewish economic and technical assistance, and did not disabuse them of their exaggerated notion of international Jewry's power. 'The legend of the domination of the world by the Jews is for them a fact . . . This is the source of the fear that grips all the Arab leaders. And although this fear causes us a lot of trouble, it may also serve as a stimulus and an incentive for an agreement,' he reported to the Jewish Agency executive. He was as lavish with his assurances as Herzl had been. Several Arab notables complained of Ben-Gurion's 'arrogant superiority', but it was the studied bluntness of a plain-spoken farmer confident of the worth of his produce: 'On the basis of our settlement experience and detailed scientific research, we are convinced that there was room in the country for both Arabs and large-scale Jewish settlement,' he told Mussa Alami. The Arabs would benefit spectacularly; they would be taught modern work methods and intensive farming, and health and education would improve out of all recognition. On another occasion he told Alami, 'If we formed an alliance and invested manpower, organization, technology and money in the development of the Arab economy, the entire economic and cultural situation of the Arabs might change . . . we would assist not only in the development of Palestine and Transjordan, but in that of Iraq. That country offered tremendous possibilities . . .'

Calculating his strategy 'on the basis of what we want and what they seek. If not, there is no possibility of accord and we must rely solely on the British,' he was not averse to encouraging Hashemite religious pretensions of becoming guardians of the Muslim holy sites in Palestine. To Moshe Shertok, who had taken over Arlosoroff's post at the Jewish Agency and was almost alone among the Zionist leadership in speaking fluent Arabic and understanding Arab society, he wrote, 'I would suggest that Abdullah be given supreme religious authority over all Muslims in *Eretz Israel*, in return for opening up Transjordan to us.'

Immigration, settlement and consolidation of the Yishuv's economic and military self-dependence were his order of priorities as the

European situation deteriorated throughout the thirties and Axis propaganda fomented unrest in the Middle East. His fear that centuries of Jewish vulnerability would be duplicated in Palestine unless the Jewish people was allowed to concentrate there en masse governed his choice, at different times, of constitutional parity, a Jewish state within a greater Arab federation, ties with the British Commonwealth, or partition, as the solution best fitted to promote Zionism's aims while neutralizing Arab opposition. It was not dark humour, but his assessment of how a numerically weak Zionism had to counter Arab demands, that led him to say during the Arab Revolt, 'There is no conflict between Jewish and Palestinian nationalism because the Jewish nation is not in Palestine and the Palestinians are not a nation.' A year later, when partition was on the agenda, he was hopeful that Arabs who chose to remain within the future Jewish state as 'a small fragment of the great Arab nation' would serve as bridge-builders to the Arab world.

To what extent did Ben-Gurion believe in his conciliatory noises towards the Arabs? To the same extent that he believed in socialism; both were paths to the final goal, means to an end. More clearly than most of his colleagues, because less ideologically hidebound, he recognized the justice of Arab opposition and its fundamental intransigence to Zionism. He never lapsed into the pious rhetoric of Weizmann and European-based members of the Zionist executive, whose expressions of good faith sounded like echoes of *Manchester Guardian* liberalism. Let us dispel the illusion, he told the Mapai central committee in July 1938, that the Arab Revolt was the handiwork of a few gangs financed from abroad. 'We are facing not terror but a war. It is a national war declared upon us by the Arabs . . . to what they regard as a usurpation of their homeland by the Jews – that is why they fight.' Behind the terrorists stood an Arab national movement 'not devoid of idealism and self-sacrifice'. It was all very well to minimize Arab opposition in the propaganda argument abroad, but respect for truth among themselves led to sobering conclusions. The Arabs could be portrayed as aggressors, while the Zionists were simply defending themselves, but that was only half the case. Morally and physically the Yishuv was in good shape, and were it allowed to mobilize would speedily prevail, but the fighting was only one aspect of an essentially political conflict, 'and politically we are the aggressors and they defend themselves'. The Arabs were fighting for their country against newcomers wanting to take it, and, however unpalatable it might be to acknowledge, that was the nub of their revolt.

In all his monumentally prolix speeches and writings about the Arab question, and his efforts over thirty years to grapple with the problem analytically, two significant passages seem to confirm that from the time he was elected chairman of the Jewish Agency, Ben-Gurion directed the movement with the realization that only war, not diplomacy, would resolve the conflict between Zionism and the Arabs. As early as January 1935 he foresaw, with great prescience, the stages of a European conflagration. 'The disaster which has befallen German Jewry is not limited to Germany alone. Hitler's regime places the entire Jewish people in danger, and not the Jewish people alone . . . Hitler's regime cannot long survive without a war of revenge against France, Poland, Czechoslovakia and the other neighbouring countries with German communities, and against Soviet Russia . . . there is no doubt that we now stand before the danger of war not less than in 1914 . . . The Jewish people is not a world factor with the ability to prevent or delay this danger or to weaken or diminish it. But there is one corner of the world in which we are a principal factor if not yet the decisive one, and this corner determines our whole national future as a people. What will be our strength and our weight in this corner on the day of judgement, when the great world disaster will begin? Who knows, perhaps only four or five years, if not less, stand between us and that awful day. In this period of time we must double our numbers, for the size of the Jewish population on that day may determine our fate at the post-war settlement.'

That paramount consideration put negotiations with the Arabs into perspective. After his round of meetings with Arab notables, he summed up his guiding principle,

We need an agreement with the Arabs, but not in order to create peace in the country. Peace is indeed vital for us – a country cannot be built in a state of permanent war. But for us peace is only a means. Our aim is the complete and absolute fulfilment of Zionism. It is only for this that we need an agreement.

For Ben-Gurion, 'the complete and absolute fulfilment of Zionism' became identified and coeval with the achievement of statehood. In May 1942, over 600 American Zionists meeting at the Biltmore Hotel in New York adopted an eight-point programme more outspoken in its recommendations than anything previously resolved at Zionist congresses. Demanding the fulfilment of the Balfour Declaration's 'original purpose' and repudiating the 1939 White Paper, the conference specifically called for a Jewish commonwealth (rather than Zionism's euphemisms of 'homeland' or 'national home') to be established in the whole of Palestine as part of the structure of the democratic world after the defeat of fascism. Ben-Gurion enthusiastically endorsed the Biltmore Programme as the new blueprint for Zionism's goals, and from his successful lobbying for its adoption by the Zionist Actions Committee in November 1942 until his rancorous final departure from politics in 1970, he was the supreme personification and orchestrator of Jewish statehood.

His growing estrangement from Weizmann, who still favoured the British connection, and his successful strategy after the war to render continuation of the mandate untenable have been amply chronicled elsewhere, as have his leadership during Israel's War of Independence and his tenures of office as prime minister. They belong to the history of politics and international relations rather than a study of Zionist thought. Here, it needs briefly to be recorded that Ernest Bevin, foreign secretary of the new Labour government after the landslide British election of 1945, was committed to implementing the recommended quotas of the 1939 White Paper, even though some 250,000 Jewish survivors of the Holocaust were languishing in European displaced persons camps, and the Yishuv was anxious to resettle them.

The magnitude of European Jewry's destruction was vaster than anyone, Zionist or otherwise, had dared to believe. At Biltmore, Weizmann had estimated that 25 per cent of central European Jewry would perish under German occupation. Six months later, news reached Palestine that a systematic extermination programme was being implemented, and in December 1942 the American State Department confirmed that two million Jews had already perished. It is not possible to determine the total number of Jews gassed, murdered, starved, worked to death or driven to suicide during the Holocaust, but by the war's end only 3.1 million Jews remained in Europe, out of a total of about 9.2 million before 1939; broadly calculated, two out of every three European Jews did not survive.

There were victory parades in Jerusalem, Tel-Aviv and Haifa on VE day, but jubilation was mingled with pain. The Zionist movement had been incapable of fulfilling its *raison d'être*, to provide a haven for persecuted European Jewry. Over one 100,000 people took to the streets of Tel-Aviv, shouting, 'Open the gates of Palestine!' Feelings against the British ran high. The World Zionist Conference of September 1945, meeting in London, passed a resolution endorsing the demand for a Jewish state. Ships carrying illegal immigrants tried to evade the naval blockade of the Palestinian coast. Incidents involving Haganah actions against British military installations and personnel escalated, as did those of the outlawed Irgun, culminating in the blowing up of the King David Hotel in Jerusalem, with the loss of nearly 100 British, Jewish and Arab lives. A war-exhausted Britain, with neither the will nor the manpower to maintain an indefinite mandate and needled by President Truman's reiterated requests (with an eye on the Jewish electorate) that 100,000 immigration certificates be granted immediately, turned the question of Palestine's future over to the United Nations. International sympathy, including that, most importantly, of the Soviet Union, sided with the Yishuv's struggle for independence, and on 29 November 1947 the General Assembly voted by thirty-three votes to thirteen to partition Palestine. Jewish celebrations were countered by a three-day Arab protest strike and attacks on Jews.

Britain announced that she would leave Palestine by 16 May 1948. The intervening months were filled with overt preparations for war. The day after Ben-Gurion read out the Proclamation of Independence, the armies of five neighbouring Arab countries attacked the Yishuv. Despite being outnumbered and poorly equipped, a series of Jewish victories meant that by the time armistice agreements were signed between February and July 1949, the Israelis had established themselves over 8000 square miles of Palestine rather than the 6200 square miles allocated by the UN partition plan. A more troublesome legacy for the newborn state was the continuing moral and humanitarian dilemma posed by up to 700,000 Palestinian refugees, whose exodus, either voluntary or forced, was, in Weizmann's notorious remark, 'a miraculous simplification of the problem'.

Ben-Gurion's pugnacity, daring and flair for the unexpected had come to typify the new state of Israel for the outside world. And it was his insistence on the concept of *mamlachtiyut* – the primacy of the state – and his zeal in pursuing it regardless of criticism or offence, that defined the character of the young state and its distinctive qualities. In his mind a new priority, Zionism and statism, had replaced the old synthesis of Zionism and socialism. 'The state has become the principal and driving force of the achievement of Zionist aims,' he declared in 1949, adding that he hoped 'the day will come when a socialist state will be built in Israel in our generation'. Ben-Gurion frequently stressed that the state was only in a first stage – but usually when he wanted to avoid awkward questions about the implementation of socialism.

Disenchanted veterans of Achdut Ha-Avodah, Po'alei Zion and Tabenkin's radical kibbutz movement, Kibbutz Ha-M'uchad, had split from Mapai in disappointment with its lukewarm socialism, to form the Mapam (United Workers) party. Ben-Gurion was unmoved. Immigration, defence and building the land were truer, more urgent expressions of Zionism than planning for the socialist millennium. 'A Zionism which is not wholeheartedly bound up with the state is no Zionism . . . the state and Zionism are one and the same thing. For we must realize that the state to which the Zionist Movement and the Jewish people looked forward does not yet exist.' As a young man, he had said that his communism derived from his Zionism; in old age, he would date his abandonment of the epithet 'socialist' to the Second World War years. He had found a new source of inspiration, more relevant than Marx or Herzl: the Bible. 'The stories of our forefathers 4000 years ago; the wanderings of Israel in the desert after the Exodus from Egypt; the wars of Joshua and the Judges that followed him . . . all these have more actuality, are closer, more edifying and meaningful for the younger generation maturing and living in the Land of Israel than all the speeches and debates of the Basel Congresses.' The universal prophetic message of justice, brotherhood and peace was more attractive to a nation in the process of redeeming itself than sterile notions about class struggle: 'The redemption of one nation is inconceivable without the redemption of all humanity and all humanity will not be redeemed if one of its members is not redeemed.'

Ben-Gurion's emphasis on *mamlachtiyut* stressed the unifying role of the army and education in integrating immigrants, at the expense of the sectarian concerns of the Histadrut and Labour movement. The army, especially, took over the mythic values of those Second Aliyah pioneers who had ploughed the land with one hand, holding a rifle in the other – but without their socialist preoccupations. In 1948,

Ben-Gurion disbanded the Haganah's élite brigade, the Palmach, which was composed mainly of kibbutz members, and steadily purged the Haganah of its left-wing elements in favour of Mapai loyalists and non-partisan professional officers, to create a new people's army, the IDF (Israel Defence Forces), as the embodiment of the universal state. The army, he told its high command in 1950, had become 'the creative force of the nation's pioneers, the cultural instrument for the assimilation of the returnees'. The IDF 'must serve as a school of civic good comradeship and fraternity, a bridge between different Jewries and different generations. It is, and must remain, a unique army, because it will be, as it was, the instrument of a unique enterprise of pioneering and state-building.' His definition of pioneering would not have been recognized by former Po'alei Zion comrades: 'What is pioneering? It is recognition of a historic mission and offering oneself in its service without conditions or flinching from any difficulty or danger. Pioneering is the moral ability and the spiritual need to live each day according to the dictates of one's conscience and the demands of the mission. Pioneering is what man demands of himself. It is the personal realization of destiny and values, the values of truth, justice and love of one's fellows. It is the will and ability to perform deeds of creation *ex nihilo*.'

Service in the state's needs was the new pioneering, and Ben-Gurion grew steadily less enamoured of the kibbutz movements, accusing them of becoming a socialist aristocracy that failed to employ immigrants from Arab lands because of their outworn dogma that wage labour was a form of exploitation. His next great battle was to extend state education at the expense of Histadrut, Labour or religious schools. Each tendency maintained its own institutions, from central funding, and jealously preserved its educational ethos. Ben-Gurion pressed for a unified state educational system throughout the country and in the transit camps of new immigrants. It was a bitter and prolonged struggle, triggered by disturbances in two transit camps of Yemenite Jews, whose agitators handed out leaflets warning that the 'evil instructors and clerks' of the Education Ministry planned 'to turn your children, of holy seed, over to the Devil, who will train them to abandon the ways of the righteous and become part of the unclean life in Israel'.

Eventually, after the fall of a government coalition and blatant horse-trading with the religious parties, Ben-Gurion forced through an education law which granted recognition to religious schools in return for their acceptance of the goal of a national education based on 'the values of Jewish culture and the achievements of science, on love of the homeland and loyalty to the state and the Jewish people, on practice in agricultural work and handicraft, on pioneer training, and on striving for a society built on freedom, equality, tolerance, mutual assistance, and love of mankind'. To those in Mapai and the Histadrut who accused him of dismantling the workers' educational system, he retorted that the issue at stake was 'When do we appear as a nation and when do we appear as a class?' Unified education, he told a meeting of Mapai-affiliated teachers in July 1953, was third in the nation's priorities, ranking only behind the establishment of the state itself and the IDF.

In transforming the Haganah into the IDF, he had nationalized it, so to speak, from a Labour army into a state army. By abolishing sectarian education for a unified state system, he had elevated *mamlachtiyut* above class. Labour values were still identified with state values because Mapai and its affiliates were the ruling coalition in the Israeli Knesset (Parliament), but the country was shedding its socialist hue of pre-state days. Loans from foreign governments and banks, capital raised from the sale of Israel bonds, private enterprise, investment from Jewish contributors abroad and – most controversial of all – large-scale German reparations, were turning Israel into a pro-western, anti-Soviet, mixed-economy social democracy.

One bastion of perceived privilege remained: the Histadrut. In taking on the vast workers' co-operative which he had been instrumental in founding, Ben-Gurion destroyed himself. Initially, the relationship between the Histadrut and the Mapai-led government had been one of wary partnership in extending *mamlachtiyut* under Ben-Gurion's direction. Nationalization of the Histadrut's water company and labour exchanges was effected without much opposition. Ben-Gurion had told the 1956 Histadrut conference some home truths which it appeared willing to accept: the state was neither socialist nor capitalist but the comprehensive tool, the universal structure, above the particularist interests of the working class. 'The Histadrut is neither the state's rival nor competitor, but its faithful aid and loyal supporter . . . Every service benefiting the entire public should be under state control.' Health care, in the form of its Kuppat Cholim (Sick Fund), was the jewel in the Histadrut's crown, a non-profit insurance scheme that offered its members an array of clinics, hospitals, laboratories and rest homes throughout the country. It was a major inducement for joining the Histadrut, 'a most admirable example of mutual aid' to supporters, but 'control by illness' to critics, because newly arrived immigrants automatically received three months' Kuppat Cholim insurance, which subtly recruited them into the Labour movement. Whether or not to prise the Kuppat Cholim from the Histadrut and bring it under state control — a politically contentious and financially complex issue on which Ben-Gurion was ready to compromise — soon became a much wider debate about policies and personalities, the generation gap and the future direction of Labour Zionism.

Ben-Gurion had retired for the first time to his desert kibbutz in 1953, emotionally and physically exhausted by the tensions of office. Within fifteen months he was recalled by his nominated successor, Moshe Sharett, to take over the defence portfolio, following the resignation and return to his post at the Histadrut of Pinchas Lavon after a bungled intelligence operation in Cairo. During his brief reign as defence minister, Lavon had managed to alienate most of the Mapai establishment, and in particular two of Ben-Gurion's favourite protégés, Shimon Peres, director-general of the Defence Ministry, and Moshe Dayan, the IDF chief of staff. He had been assiduously grooming a younger succession in his own image — efficient technocrats and practical state-builders for whom the how of solving a problem was more important than the ideological why. Eight years after independence, he declared with satisfaction, 'There is no need to prove to the generation growing up in Israel the necessity for a Jewish state. It wants to know how to build the state, to maintain it, to strengthen it, develop it, to mould its character.'

The *Tze'irim* (young ones), as they became known, brash, self-confident, devoted to Ben-Gurion, their credentials proved in the Haganah and the War of Independence, increasingly came to question the old guard who ran Mapai and the Histadrut. 'The people who crawled with their rifles among the rocks of Israel for the past twenty years know as much of their country's needs as those who have spent their time sitting on the fifth floor of the [Histadrut] headquarters,' Dayan stingingly rebuked Labour movement veterans. For their part, the founding generation, represented by the familiar faces of Levi Eshkol, Golda Meir, Zalman Aran and Pinhas Sapir, felt threatened by the

growing presumption of young men who, owing to Ben-Gurion's patronage, had sidestepped the party apparatus in their political advancement. Pinchas Lavon became the catalyst for the simmering ideological
and generational tension within the Labour movement. Dayan, the
hero of the 1956 Sinai campaign against Egypt, and Peres had both
entered the Knesset on the Mapai list in 1959, their candidature vigorously championed by Ben-Gurion. Part of their appeal to voters lay in
the iconoclasm with which they attacked vested interests, chief among
them the Histadrut. Lavon forcefully defended his fiefdom, backed by
the Labour old guard. He served notice that the Histadrut would transfer no more of its functions to the state, and on the fortieth anniversary
of its founding warned a press conference of 'the spread of the dangerous philosophy of *étatism* among certain circles'. Ben-Gurion was not
invited to address the anniversary celebrations.

Lavon's calculated snub to 'the Old Man' and his young statists
had been occasioned by more than renewed calls from Peres for the
nationalization of Kuppat Cholim. The Lavon Affair, hushed up six
years previously, had become public knowledge in September 1960,
following revelations that perjury had been committed in the original
investigation into the failed intelligence operation. Lavon demanded a
formal exoneration from the prime minister, and his evidence before
the Knesset Foreign Affairs Committee, in which he insinuated that
Dayan and Peres had exploited the security mishap to incriminate
him, was leaked to the press. The controversy absorbed the country
for the next four months. Ben-Gurion refused to accept the verdict of
a commission of seven ministers that acquitted Lavon of any responsibility for the botched operation, and demanded a judicial inquiry. On
31 January 1961, he submitted his resignation as prime minister, and
requested Mapai to choose between him and Lavon. A week later his
increasingly disarrayed party, split between loyalty to Ben-Gurion the
vote-winner and sympathy for Lavon the innocent scapegoat, voted
to dismiss Lavon from his Histadrut post by a majority of 159 to 96,
after which Ben-Gurion withdrew his resignation. The summary
treatment of Lavon and a growing public perception that Ben-Gurion
was conducting a vendetta damaged his authority and crucially
undermined his relations with the old guard of Mapai. The party lost
10 per cent of its votes at the general election in August 1961, and
within two years, depressed and disillusioned, Ben-Gurion retired

for a second time to S'deh Boker, recommending Levi Eshkol as his successor.

In his seventy-eighth year, an international figure secure in the affections of a grateful nation, it was a good time to bow out. Those who sought his monument had only to look around at a rapidly developing and exuberant young country, its industry, farming and scientific progress the envy of the Third World, since the proclamation of statehood its population swollen a mammoth 211 per cent by the successful absorption of one and a half million new immigrants from eastern and western lands. A statesman who rubbed shoulders on the world stage with Adenauer, Kennedy and de Gaulle and had grown sentimentally attached to the British *in absentia*, enjoying visits to Oxford to buy his books from Blackwell's, Ben-Gurion had outgrown his Israeli colleagues who still spouted socialist jargon. Physically fit and intellectually vigorous, he now had the chance to write the history of the rebirth of Israel that he had been promising, to pursue his interests in the Bible, Greek philosophy and Buddhism, and to give photo opportunities to the world's press as he went about the menial tasks of a simple kibbutz member or stood on his head in yoga positions.

Unfortunately, an old man's vanity proved stronger than his prudence. In his absence the Mapai old guard tried to reassert socialist values rather than *mamlachti* inclusiveness, and Dayan and Peres came under increasing pressure in the Cabinet. Less than a year later, Ben-Gurion was back in the fray, reiterating his demand for a judicial inquiry into the Lavon Affair and criticizing Eshkol and the Mapai leadership. In response, Eshkol, Golda Meir and a dying Moshe Sharett turned furiously on their former leader for sundering the party with his Lavon fixation. At the tenth Mapai Conference in January 1965, his motion to endorse a judicial inquiry was decisively rejected and one critic wondered aloud, 'How could Churchillian greatness suddenly appear in the guise of provincial pettiness, vindictiveness and rancour?' Ben-Gurion organized his followers, including Dayan and Peres, in an independent list for the Histadrut and Knesset elections that summer, but the Israel Workers' List (Rafi) did poorly. Rafi, minus Ben-Gurion, rejoined the government on the eve of the Six Day War in June 1967, and a year later merged with Mapai and Achdut Ha-Avodah in the reunited Israel Labour Party. Solitary, outcast and embittered, Ben-Gurion continued with his crusade for an inquiry into the Lavon Affair and patched together a 'State List' to contest the October 1969 elections. It won just four seats, and a year later Ben-Gurion resigned from the Knesset.

So totally had Ben-Gurion's exaltation of *mamlachtiyut* emphasized statism above ideology and reduced the function of the Histadrut and Labour movements to supporting pillars in the society they had largely created that the irony was barely remarked upon when in 1977 his Rafi remnant entered the government as part of Likud, the right-wing alignment which traced its ancestry to Revisionism. Dayan opportunistically became foreign minister to Menachem Begin, Jabotinsky's heir, and Labour, now led by Peres, was left to adapt to a role it had not played since the Zionist Congress of 1931 – minority opposition party.

Ben-Gurion regularly justified *mamlachtiyut* by pointing to the Jewish inexperience of self-government, of centuries trying to survive under hostile regimes. The Jews had learned stratagems of survival, but not the disciplines of good citizenship. 'The law calls for fostering loyalty to the state. In every other state, this is self-evident and expected, but not with us. For two thousand years we did not cultivate a state ideal, and the mere proclamation of the state does not grant a sense of statehood to a people. This is a quality that demands nurturing in Israel more than in any other new country . . .' The lack of civic responsibility shocked him: 'In our country, even personal manners are deficient. Many of our inhabitants, including Israeli youth, have not learned how to respect their fellow-citizens and treat them with politeness, tolerance and sympathy. Elementary decency is lacking among us, that decency which makes public life pleasant and creates a climate of comradeship and mutual affection.' During the stormy debates of January 1952 on negotiating financial compensation with West Germany for the victims of Nazism, and the ensuing riots against accepting German reparations, incited by Begin's shameful demagogy, he feared for the state's future. 'Yesterday the hand of evil was raised against the sovereignty of the Knesset and the first steps in the destruction of democracy in Israel were taken.'

Ben-Gurion made it clear that the state would take whatever action necessary, as it had at the time the *Altalena* was sunk, to protect itself and safeguard democracy. Opponents charged him with worshipping the state as a golden calf, of subordinating socialism, even Zionism, to the state's needs. He did not demur, if thereby the state was more firmly established and its institutions strengthened. Under his leadership and before his Lear-like attempts to assert a lost authority, Labour was reified into the national movement of the state, and the all-pervading influence of *mamlachtiyut* came to signal the demise of partisan Zionist ideology. To his socialist critics, that was Ben-Gurion's greatest sin; to those who had longed to see the creation of a state in which all Jews would share equal citizenship and national, not class or ethnic, identity, it was his greatest achievement.

16

Zionism – The End of Ideology

In 1960, Shimon Peres, the most thoughtful inheritor of Ben-Gurion's mantle, told a meeting of Young Mapai that the problem of his generation was 'not to know what we want to be, but what we want to *do*'. Ben-Gurion had already asserted, in an important summation of his views, entitled *Terms and Values*, that there was little to be learned any longer from the classic socialist and Zionist texts, since nobody could continue to accept seriously Marx's claim that all history was about class struggle, and now, in Israel, Jewish society was being built from new beginnings. Faithfully echoing his master's voice, Peres declared, 'The world has evolved beyond the social patterns that fashioned the generation of early Zionists, and Israel entering the second decade of her political existence must look beyond the romantic ideas of her founding fathers.' It was a theme that Peres, the realistic, unromantic practitioner of *mamlachtiyut*, would reiterate:

The last generation was a generation of aspirations; the new generation must take up planning. The previous generation had dreams and visions, the present one will have to realize concrete tasks. Though there is no contradiction between vision and concrete tasks, there is a difference in emphasis . . . Action is required, the writers and ideologists will come later.

Or would be rendered superfluous by the practical demands of nation-building. Twenty-five years later, in the unaccustomed role of leader of the Labour party opposition to a right-wing government, Peres defined science, technology and efficiency as the most pressing issues facing the country, and pointed to the Japanese system – hardly a bastion of social-ism – as the best contemporary example for Israel. Before Israeli in-dependence, he argued, there had been no contradiction between party and state. Mapai was *the* party, and the Histadrut was the draft of the state-in-the-making, but that had long ceased to be applicable. 'The ideology that leads to the creation of a state cannot remain after the state is created.'

The sheer scope and magnitude of the challenges facing Israel in her formative years, and her success in meeting them under Ben-Gurion's leadership, had relegated ideological considerations to secondary importance. In the first three years of statehood, the population more than doubled by immigration alone, and the character of Yishuv Palestine was transformed almost beyond recognition. Bald statistics give some idea of the task involved: the first mandate census in 1922 had calculated the number of Jews in the Yishuv at 84,000; by 1938, it had grown to 412,500. During the Second World War, and until the declaration of statehood in May 1948, nearly 250,000 Jews had entered Palestine. Between 1948 and 1966, the Jewish population exploded from 650,000 to almost 2.5 million, 68 per cent due to immigration, 32 per cent to natural increase. The composition of the new immigrants had altered radically. Whereas during the mandate period almost 90 per cent came from Europe, in Israel's first fifteen years 55 per cent of the newcomers were from Asia, Africa and the Middle East. The entire Iraqi community of more than 120,000 had been joined by nearly 50,000 Yemeni Jews, flown to Israel in a massive airlift. In North Africa, Syria, Turkey and Iran, Jewish communities that had lived there for centuries were substantially reduced, in most cases because of the ongoing state of war between Israel and neighbouring Arab countries. Coming from Middle East, religiously traditional, non-democratic backgrounds, these new Israelis were remote from the social and cultural influences that had nurtured Zionism's founding fathers. By the mid 1980s, Jews of Sephardi (eastern) origin comprised 55 per cent of the population of a state built by Ashkenazi (European) pioneers to provide a homeland for the east European masses.

Israel's first priority had been to bring in the refugee remnant of the Holocaust: 220,000 survivors from Poland and Romania, the entire Bulgarian community of nearly 40,000 Jews, smaller numbers from Czechoslovakia and Hungary, and the inmates of DP camps came to Israel between 1948 and 1951 – some 320,000 new European immigrants. Memories of the British blockade to prevent illegal immigration were still vivid when, in July 1950, the Knesset passed the 'Law of Return', granting every Jew, whatever his citizenship, and wherever his domicile, the right to settle in Israel. The *raison d'être* of Zionism as the movement for ending Jewish 'homelessness' was given legal validation. In the same year the Knesset enacted the Absentee Property Law, to legalize the major expropriations of Arab land – about 1.5 million acres – that had accrued to Israel as a result of the War of Independence. The Nationality Law, passed by the second Knesset in April 1952, provided for acquisition of Israeli citizenship for both Jews and non-Jews by birth, naturalization or residence. In its application to non-Jews (that is, Arabs for the most part), residence was defined as having been a Palestinian citizen immediately before the establishment of the state and registered as living there on 1 March 1952; legal confirmation of the 'miraculous' solution that Weizmann had detected in the flight from their homes and villages of 600,000–700,000 Arabs. Absorbing the vast influx of immigrants required a decisive restructuring and expansion of the Israeli economy. Socialist aspirations had to be sacrificed to the imperatives of economic growth. The major sources of new capital were Jewish donations from abroad; German reparations and personal restitution payments; loan capital from foreign governments, banks and investment companies; private loan capital raised by the sale of Israeli bonds; the personal assets and remittances of immigrants; and private investment.

Ben-Gurion personally launched the sale of Israeli bonds in the United States, harnessing the wealth and sentimental attachment to Zionism of that country's six million Jews. Other Jewish communities throughout the world responded with consistent generosity to the task of absorbing new immigrants and supporting Israel financially during the years of threat from hostile Arab countries. In 1950–67, the amounts raised by Diaspora Jewish philanthropy, including contributions to public institutions and the main sums channelled through the Jewish Agency for housing and land settlement, totalled approximately $1735 million. During the same period the sale of Israeli bonds realized some $1260 million. The German Reparations agreement, ratified in 1953, provided for the payment of $820 million over a period of twelve years. Loans, direct American aid, private foreign investment and the personal assets of immigrants added over $4000 million to the total capital import during this period.

As a result, Israel managed to feed, house and provide work for her new immigrants without undergoing economic disintegration or a drastic decline in living standards. They were years of austerity, but for the sake of state-building were readily borne by most citizens, buoyed by high morale, a shared sense of purpose and wry humour. The needs of the moment took precedence over theory. 'Don't be a Zionist' was the curt dismissal of young Israelis to veterans who spouted socialist rhetoric rather than concentrating on the immediate tasks of immigration, defence and *mamlachtiyut*. Indeed, piqued by the reluctance of comfortable western Jews to immigrate into their new homeland, Ben-Gurion had declared that he was no longer a Zionist, but almost every Jew in the world would have called himself a Zionist, even if it went no deeper than Salvador Dali's famous put-down of Picasso, 'Picasso is a Spaniard, and so am I. Picasso is a genius, and so am I. Picasso is a communist, and neither am I.'

Calling oneself a Zionist – meaning, paying lip service to the concept of a strong Jewish state and giving it every financial and moral support short of actually going to live there – was a label worn proudly by all but a fringe minority of ultra-Orthodox, assimilated, or far-left Jews in the Diaspora, tinged with guilt at not having taken the ultimate step of making Aliyah and throwing in their lot with the generation of state-builders. Every visiting delegation of fund-raisers and supporters was welcomed by government ministers with the ritual invocation that next year may they too be living in Jerusalem and participating in the rebuilding of Zion. Israel's public relations, propaganda and educational agencies assiduously peddled the line to well-entrenched western communities that not going to live in Israel was a dereliction of Jewish duty and a wilful misreading of Diaspora history, especially after the horrors of the Holocaust. But the leaders, educators and opinion-formers of the new state were having to grapple with a perplexing paradox; despite pride in, and popular support for, reborn Israel, despite universal recognition that the Jews needed their own homeland as a refuge, Zionism was still, as it had always been, a minority option among Jews with the freedom to choose.

According to Zionism's early adherents, the Jews comprised a nation. Broadly speaking, they meant the Jews of the Russian empire; eastern Jewries were beyond the experience of thinkers like Pinsker, Herzl and Borochov. The bulk of people they would have expected to compose the human reservoir for a Jewish state had been slaughtered by the Nazis, and the vast majority of 1950s immigrants, European or eastern, had come to Israel under pressure, not from choice. They lived in Zion, but were not Zionists. Derivatives of European political thought that had been transplanted to Palestine by the early pioneers, and had fashioned the Yishuv, were incapable of sustaining a national ideology to embrace millions of new citizens from east and west. The state took over that function. In its early years, Israel's mass absorption of immigrants was often compared to the American 'melting-pot' experience, but given the relatively small size of the country and its centralized institutions – especially education, the army and the Histadrut – the exercise in turning assorted immigrants into proud Israelis and welding a new nation was more pressure cooker than melting-pot.

In theory, the new state could make choices about its orientation: socialism or capitalism; secular democracy or theocracy; neutrality or a western-leaning foreign policy; attempted conciliation of the Arab world or military deterrence. In practice, the exigencies of the hour dictated the commitments. Thus Mapai-led government coalitions talked the language of socialism, while having to promote a capitalist economy. The religious parties called for an Israel governed by rabbinic law, while squabbling for portfolios in a succession of secular cabinets. The urgent need for resources to fund mass immigration ruled out neutrality, and made a United States-oriented foreign policy inevitable. If the option ever seriously existed of conciliation of the Arab world, its unremitting hostility intensified reliance on a strong military posture.

The constant feature of Israeli politics for the first thirty years of statehood was coalition government, led by Mapai, in alliance with Orthodox religious parties and additional representation of the near left or acceptable right, as circumstances dictated. Apart from ephemeral splinter groups, the political parties in post-1948 Israel, and the constituencies they appealed to, were a continuation of Yishuv and World Zionist Organization configurations from the thirties. Political parties to the left of Mapai still indulged their fondness for Marxian analysis, while protecting the market interests of their kibbutzim. The heirs of Revisionism dusted down their chauvinist rhetoric and geared a populist appeal to the less privileged in a society dominated by the ethos and vested interests of the Labour movement. Three new parties did emerge, but they too were directly descended from the politics of the pre-state period. Mapam, founded in January 1948, was an alliance of Ha-Shomer Ha-tza'ir and Achdut Ha-Avodah–Po'alei Zion, which had broken from Mapai as keepers of the flame of pure socialism. Herut, established six months later on the initiative of Irgun, with Menachem Begin as its leader, was supported by most of the former

Revisionists living in Israel, and formally adopted Jabotinsky's political programme. At its conference in August 1948, the General Zionist party that throughout the twenties and thirties had supported Weizmann and the executive of the Zionist Organization split and reformed as the Progressive party, a liberal grouping which appealed mainly to professional immigrants from central Europe.

Broad-based coalition government necessarily entailed centre-ground compromise on social and economic issues. Mapai wore its doctrinal clothing ever more lightly, no longer the socialist vanguard but a pragmatic governing party of respectable social-democratic hue which did not cause alarm in Washington or scare off American-Jewish investors fearful of the red menace. Personal rivalry and jockeying for position, particularly between Golda Meir, Shimon Peres, Moshe Dayan, Yigal Allon and Yitzchak Rabin, became the hallmark of Labour Zionism in the decade after Ben-Gurion's retirement, rather than projection of a socio-political vision. Efficiency in managing the economy and competent government were the main points at issue with opposition parties. John Stuart Mill's comment, in *On Liberty*, that without vigorous contesting a political doctrine becomes inefficacious, its meaning 'in danger of being lost, or enfeebled, and deprived of its vital effect on the character', came to apply to the ageing, complacent, corruption-ridden Israeli Labour movement, and contributed to its surprising downfall in the 1977 elections which brought to power the Herut–Likud coalition led by Begin.

That stunning electoral swing ushered in the most traumatic period in the state's brief history. For the first time since independence, a fundamental ideological issue took precedence over the *mamlachtiyut* consensus that had sustained Israel. Now in power was a party that, as custodians of Jabotinsky's political testament, was explicit both in its definition of the state's desirable borders and in its response to Zionism's longest-lasting, most complex and intractable problem: dealing with the Palestinians.

Labour Zionism, like the Zionist Organization at large, had never been able to formulate a consistent Arab policy. The Yishuv leadership's lofty principles and pious hopes of economic co-operation and federal partnership had always foundered on the intractable reality of Palestinian opposition. But if one stubborn illusion persisted among the pre-state Zionist politicians and was taken over as the paradigm for its strategic diplomacy by Israel's Foreign Ministry, it was that Palestinian nationalism might be neutralized by an accommodation with the Hashemite dynasty of Mecca. In January 1919, Weizmann had reached an understanding with Emir Faisal, eldest son of the sheriff of Mecca and leader of the Arab uprising against Turkey, that, in return for Zionist aid to a Greater Syria, Faisal would cede Palestine for Jewish colonization. Afterwards, Weizmann talked wistfully of this great lost opportunity for a Jewish–Arab settlement, but he was deluding himself. Faisal was as much a pawn of Great Britain's strategic intentions as were the Zionists, and in 1920 he was expelled from Syria, with British connivance, by its new overlords, the French. A fresh kingdom, Transjordan, was created by the British in 1922, to compensate the Hashemites for their loss of Syria. Faisal's brother, Emir Abdullah, ruler of the new kingdom, was regularly courted by the Zionist leadership before and after the 1937 Peel Royal Commission, since Transjordan stood to gain most from the partition of Palestine into a Jewish and an Arab state; but Abdullah was so unpopular in the Arab world that he was a dubious asset. He reached a secret agreement with the Jewish Agency in November 1947 to divide up Palestine on the basis of the proposed United Nations partition frontiers, was distrusted with good reason by the other Arab League countries which sent forces to fight against Israel in 1948, but honoured his promise that his Arab Legion army of 6000 men, the best-trained and best-equipped force in the Middle East, would operate only defensively against the Haganah; in 1950 he unilaterally annexed the West Bank, proclaimed himself ruler of the Hashemite kingdom of Jordan, and was assassinated in Jerusalem a year later, allegedly at the instigation of the mufti.

The succession passed to his young grandson Hussein, who maintained the family tradition of regular, discreet contact with Israeli officials. But his overriding concern was to maintain his precarious kingdom, dependent on financial support from other Arab states and with 65 per cent of its population hostile Palestinian refugees from either the 1948 War of Independence or the Six Day War of 1967. These considerations made him cannily reluctant to accept the poisoned chalice of an agreement with Israel by breaking Arab ranks. The elusive 'Hashemite connection' was the Labour government's increasingly forlorn attempt to find some solution to Palestinian nationalism and the maintenance of order over an additional 1.1 million Arabs in Gaza and the West Bank who had come under Israeli military rule as a result of her overwhelming victory in 1967.

In contrast to Labour uncertainty, Likud promised a clear alternative for the conquered territories. Under their biblical designation of Judea and Samaria, they were part of 'Greater Israel', land historically envisaged for the Jewish state on both sides of the Jordan. Whereas Golda Meir had notoriously dismissed claims of a distinctive identity by asking, 'Who are the Palestinians?', Menachem Begin knew full well who they were, and was determined to bring former Palestine under permanent Israeli control; its Arab residents would be granted limited autonomy under Israeli jurisdiction. An 'iron wall' of Jewish settlements and new towns, strategically linked by a road network that bypassed Arab villages, would transform Judea and Samaria into a permanent part of *Eretz Israel*.

In the heady aftermath of the 1967 victory, it was not only Likud supporters who dreamed of a *pax Hebraica* throughout the region. Within two weeks of the war's end, the Israeli government, reflecting public consensus, announced the annexation of East Jerusalem. By the end of the year, the first settlers were established on the Golan Heights and the West Bank, which Dayan declared would never be 'abandoned'. A new highway linking Jerusalem to Tel-Aviv had been cut through the Latrun salient. The various territorial proposals (such as the Allon Plan) put forward over the next few years by the Labour coalition as part of any projected peace settlement, all presupposed Israeli retention of anything between 30 and 70 per cent of the West Bank. The obdurate refusal of defeated Arab states to recognize Israel or talk peace with her – until Anwar Sadat of Egypt paid his visit to Jerusalem in November 1977, followed by the Camp David Accords – seemed to confirm Jabotinsky's original diagnosis and Begin's repetition of it: that negotiations with the Arabs would succeed only from a position of overwhelming Jewish superiority. Begin was re-elected in 1981 with an enlarged majority. His most enthusiastic support came from voters of the Second Israel – the unskilled, the low-waged, disaffected Sephardim resentful of Histadrut paternalism and Labour indifference, retailers, taxi drivers, petty clerks, stall-owners – the sans-culottes of Tel-Aviv, Haifa and Jerusalem, who hailed him at his rallies as 'Begin, King of Israel'. Likud's free-market economics offered a respite from the Histadrut's closed-shop syndicalism, and Begin's tough stance on the territories had reaped the reward of peace with Egypt.

Given his mandate, West Bank settlement accelerated. Low-interest mortgages and other inducements attracted thousands of Israelis to forsake the crowded suburbs of the coastal plain for pioneering life in Judea and Samaria – the new Zionism of Greater Israel. Religious fundamentalists, typified by the zealots of Gush Emunim (Block of the Faithful), reverently established themselves on sites mentioned in the Bible, impervious to the local residents. A demoralized Labour opposition was too involved in self-analysis to offer a coherent repudiation of Likud's expansionist policy, and those who did, in the Knesset or outside, were branded with standard Revisionist insults – 'traitors', 'self-hating Jews', 'Arab-lovers'. Arab terrorist attacks, under the banner of the PLO, increased, as did civilian unrest. In response, Israeli military rule, operating under British emergency regulations from 1946, became more draconian; preventive detention, expulsion and censorship more arbitrary; the blowing-up of Arab houses and closing of schools and universities more frequent; the curtailment of civil liberties more widespread. The mood of large sections of the Israeli public hardened into an ugly xenophobia, exploited by the new defence minister, Arik Sharon, who warned darkly that the Arabs of Greater Israel should 'not forget the lessons of 1948', when 700,000 of them had left either voluntarily or under intimidation, never to return. Annexation of the West Bank to follow that of the Golan Heights was called for, as was the euphemism of 'population transfer' to their 'natural homeland' in Jordan of Palestinians in the occupied territories who would not accept Israeli citizenship.

With few exceptions, Israel's Diaspora supporters barely demurred. Whatever reservations they had were voiced privately. Anti-Zionist criticism was decoded as anti-Semitism in disguise, and Begin's speeches and interviews brooded increasingly on memories of past Jewish persecutions and their lessons for modern Israel. Yasir Arafat, the ineffectual PLO chairman, was demonized as a second Hitler. The tenor of official pronouncements from Jerusalem was a blend of paranoia (tiny Israel against the world), strident self-justification and manipulation of the Holocaust to condone government policy. The population was deeply divided between those who queried the cost to morality and democracy of continued occupation and its corrosive effect on the young soldiers policing the West Bank and Gaza, and those who endorsed Likud's hard line as vital to Israel's security needs. It was to stop the shelling of her northern borders, destroy the PLO infrastructure in Lebanon and stifle Palestinian nationalism that Israel launched an invasion of Lebanon in June 1982, under the deceptive codename 'Operation Peace in Galilee'. The stated aim of clearing a forty-kilometre cordon sanitaire speedily turned into a three-month siege of Beirut and a disastrous sucking into the murk of Lebanese politics. International sympathy for the Palestinian cause increased in proportion to condemnation of Begin's and Sharon's brutal adventurism.

The aftermath of Israel's misconceived foray was mass public demonstrations against the war, violent clashes between Peace Now and Herut supporters, the evacuation of some 10,000 PLO fighters to Tunisia, and the slow and costly withdrawal from Lebanon of a bitter citizens' army questioning why it had been there in the first place. A broken Begin retired into seclusion, to be replaced by Yitzchak Shamir, as obdurately opposed to Palestinian self-government but lacking his predecessor's flamboyance. Sharon was forced to resign as defence minister. The cost to the country of its flirtation with delusions of *pax Hebraica* hegemony over the region was a collapsing economy, damaged international standing, wavering Diaspora support and mounting unrest within the Israeli Arab community and in the occupied territories. Yet so raw were the divisions within Israeli society, and so extreme the reactions, that the election of July 1984 did not produce the expected Labour Alignment victory, after a campaign which its leaders had considered it prudent to fight on the issue of superior competence rather than its fundamental differences with Likud over the future of the West Bank. Labour and Likud won almost the same number of seats and formed a government of national unity, with the bizarre spectacle of Peres and Shamir rotating the posts of prime minister and foreign minister.

Such a recipe for foreign policy inertia at least slowed the pace of Jewish expansion on the West Bank and ensured that the domestic economy was brought under control after a period of 400 per cent inflation. But in 1988, Palestinian frustration at the restrictions of military rule erupted in a movement of resistance throughout Gaza and the West Bank; the *intifada* bore all the hallmarks of a spontaneous national movement that Ben-Gurion had identified in the Arab Revolt of 1936. It was Shamir's turn as prime minister when the *intifada* broke out. His inflexible and unimaginative response, and the army's incapacity to quell stone-throwing rioters and threatening crowds save by disproportionate use of force ensured widespread support for the *intifada* among the inhabitants of the occupied territories. The PLO was forced to watch impotently from exile in Tunis and respond to the wishes of those in the territories whom it claimed to represent. Unable to suppress the uprising, on the defensive against foreign criticism, and faced with a dispirited and perturbed public, Shamir reacted negatively, as was his wont, when the Palestine National Council, meeting in Algiers, issued a charter which, for the first time, acknowledged the existence of Israel and expressed readiness to negotiate a final settlement with her.

The international situation was propitious for a compromise. The new-found amity between the United States and the USSR in the wake of *perestroika* meant not only that both superpowers had an interest in resolving Middle East tensions but it gave Israel the unexpected bonus of some 200,000 highly qualified Jewish immigrants now allowed out of Russia. Israel's restraint during the Gulf War was rewarded by her American patron; but given the fluid Middle East strategic reappraisals resulting from the alliance against Iraq, she could no longer rely on tacit acquiescence for West Bank settlement in return for her role as the region's most important outpost of Capitol Hill foreign policy. It was to barely concealed Washington satisfaction (and that of the bulk of Diaspora Jewry) that a Labour coalition, committed to territorial compromise in the search for peace, was decisively returned to power in the next election, with Yitzchak Rabin, the arch-pragmatist, as prime minister, and Shimon Peres, the practical but flexible technocrat, as foreign secretary. The dream of a Greater Israel, Zionist ideology's last fling, was well and truly over.

By the beginning of 1996, under the provisions of the Israel–PLO agreement on interim self-government for Gaza and Jericho, the Israeli army had withdrawn from the six largest Arab towns on the West Bank, prior to local elections. There was a peace treaty with Jordan, in addition to that with Egypt, and negotiations were proceeding with Israel's most implacable neighbour, Syria. Rabin, Peres and Arafat had been the unlikely recipients of the 1994 Nobel Peace Prize. There were still many obstacles to a comprehensive regional peace, among them fundamentalist Islamic hostility to a Zionist state in its midst, fundamentalist Jewish reluctance to cede any part of biblical land and Israeli security anxieties about an independent Palestinian entity in immediate proximity. Shocked Israeli soul-searching in response to Rabin's assassination (by a fellow Jewish citizen) gave way to public outrage after two Hamas suicide bombs killed sixty civilians. The May 1966 election was fought on a single issue – how to achieve peace with security – and the desperately close result demonstrated that the electorate was deeply and passionately divided about an answer. When the campaign rhetoric has been forgotten, the more sobering lesson for Likud and Labour to ponder is that both of them lost considerable ground to right-wing religious parties; not a comforting thought for a country that regards itself as a secular democracy.

What can be said with confidence is that the enduring reality of Israel's existence is finally conceded by her neighbouring Arab states, whatever revanchist dreams they and the Palestinians might secretly harbour, and in Israel the attainables of realpolitik have replaced the illusions of grand design. Progress towards a settlement may be slowed, but not reversed, by Binyamin Netanyahu's unexpected electoral success. Cautious optimism is still permissible that the twentieth-century's longest, bitterest, most intractable conflict may be winding down at last in an atmosphere of fatigued realism, wary mutual acceptance and widespread Arab and Jewish acknowledgement of Abba Eban's observation, after many fruitless years as Israel's foreign minister, that people tend to behave sensibly once they have exhausted all other possibilities.

Over 100 years since Zionism's inception, and more than four and a half decades of Israeli statehood, it is possible to attempt a balanced assessment of the Jewish national movement. The first thing to say, neither in praise nor condemnation, is that Zionism's founders were as spectacularly mistaken about the course their movement would take as was Karl Marx about the future of communism. Whatever they proposed was beyond their power to control – at the mercy of larger historical currents and subject to the fluctuations of international politics. In that, they were true to the pattern of 1900 years of Jewish existence, which since the obliteration of Judea by the Romans had been on the fringes of larger, settled societies, adapting circumspectly to the host culture and learning stratagems for survival without power.

Zionism sought to break this mould of Jewish existence in the Dia-spora, to restore Jewish self-respect and dignity by rebuilding the ancient homeland so that Jews, in Herzl's words, could 'live as free men on their own soil, to die peacefully in their own homes'. Nationalism succeeded in achieving this, where assimilation, patriotism, religious reform and traditional Orthodoxy all failed to alleviate the condition of European Jewry. But to promote Jewish nationalism meant the propagation of myths which became enshrined in Zionist ideology, some successfully, others to its detriment. The first myth was that the Jews were one nation, in von Herder's definition of an identifiable group sharing language, culture and historical memories. The Jews were not, and are not. They were, and are, *several* Jewries, widely diversified culturally and geographically, but bound in a strong sense of *k'lal Yisrael* (the com-munity of Israel), because they share religious identity in common. It was fidelity to the teachings and practices of their religion, Judaism, in however devoted or attenuated a manner, that enabled a Sephardi Jew of Spanish origin to find common ground with the Ashkenazi Jew of Russian ancestry, or for an assimilated Berliner to be made welcome in a Polish ghetto. So long as the Jewish sabbath was on Saturday, not Sunday or Friday, and Jews congregated in a synagogue, not a church or a mosque, that – not nationhood – was the link that bound them. They shared a theology and religious traditions stretching back to the first patriarch, Abraham, and incorporating the Exodus from Egypt, the Giving of the Law on Mount Sinai, the Promised Land, prophetical teachings of brotherhood and social justice, the destruction of the two Temples, exile and the promise of messianic redemption.

By sifting these motifs and appropriating the most suitable, Zionism, the newcomer and outsider among Jewish sects, laid claim to being in the authentic mainstream of Jewish history. Every new religious or pol-itical movement needs to validate itself by proving its credentials as a fulfilment of, not a rupture with, the past, and it was Herzl's genius to make the Zionist Organization into almost all things for almost all Jews. Secularists, ardent socialists, agrarian populists, cultural revivalists, re-ligious conservatives – all found in the Jewish national movement satisfy-ing confirmation of their particular proclivity. Under its broad wings and quasi-religious terminology, Zionism could shelter those who wanted to prepare the ground for the proletarian revolution, and those who wanted to pave the way for the coming of the Messiah. A second, and more harmful, myth was fostered to justify the Zionist enterprise: that the return to the barren and sparsely populated Jewish homeland was being undertaken by enlightened bearers of western culture to the backward orient. Zionism never recovered from the shock of finding in Palestine a large Arab population that had lived on the land for centuries and was indifferent to the benefits of colonization. Zionism had to adjust its rationale: it was in Palestine by 'historic right' (whatever that might mean, and a strange proof of divine sanction to be advanced by secular nationalists); it was morally justified as an answer to pressing Jewish needs; Zionists came not as colonizers but as co-partners in building the country.

None of those vindications is satisfactory or has withstood the evidence of events. 'Historic right' might reasonably be thought to have lapsed after 2000 years, even if remembered daily in the prayer book. An unbroken Jewish presence in Palestine over centuries, however contingent, was a stronger but still flimsy justification for return, the incoming pioneers having little in common with the pious Jewish mendicants of Jerusalem, Tiberias and Safed. Secondly, Zionism is as defensible as any other national movement – given the insecurities of European Jewish existence when it emerged, probably more so – but nationalism per se is morally neutral. In Syrkin's phrase, it is a 'category' of history, not an absolute. Answering a collective need is its impetus. It is a mistake to judge political actions, as Machiavelli warned, by criteria of morality rather than efficacy. Surveying the course of the Zionist–Arab conflict, the most forbearing moral judgement one can pass on it is that here was a tragic dilemma of Jewish need against Palestinian rights; a just solution being impossible, only the most generous restitution to the dispossessed could begin to compensate for the injustice done to them. That did not happen, for reasons which reflect little credit on Israel and less on neighbouring Arab countries, which kept the Palestinian refugees in squalor and misery as a handy *casus belli* for decades to come. Finally, the pretext of co-partnership did not survive the doctrinaire insistence of Second Aliyah pioneers on performing all their own tasks. Jabotinsky pointed out that never in history had one people voluntarily welcomed another into its land; he might have added that never in history had they gone on to work together, except as master and servant.

To encourage the mass immigration on which it depended, Zionism promulgated a third myth: that Jewish history between the destruction of the Second Temple and the Zionist return had been one prolonged weeping by the waters of Babylon, an endless saga of persecution and pogrom. It was, in the words of the scholar Salo Baron, 'the lachrymose view of Jewish history'. In fact, Diaspora Jewish life east and west knew many periods of security, toleration and cultural efflorescence. First-century Alexandria, third- to tenth-century Babylonia, the golden age of Spanish Jewry, are just three examples of large and flourishing Jewish communities which successfully adapted to dispersion from Zion. Even in medieval Europe under the shadow of Christianity, there were instances of vibrant Jewish creativity, notably in Italy and southern France. Taking a broad perspective of 2000 years, it can be said that the Jews in Islamic countries rarely experienced the anti-Semitism and exclusion which characterized the existence of their co-religionists in Christian Europe, but the Jews of Christian Europe were able to rise to positions of wealth and influence rarely afforded to their brethren in the east.

Zionism's lack of success in attracting significant numbers of immigrants from the countries of the western hemisphere would suggest that after two millennia of learning to survive without a state, integration abroad and not nationality in Israel is the normative aspiration of most Jews. Prudence, timidity, material affluence, lack of Jewish commitment – whatever the accusation levelled against them, the fact remains that for the Jewrys of North and Latin America, Great Britain, France, Australia and South Africa, which among them comprise two-thirds of the world's fourteen million Jews, the state of Israel represents a last resort rather than a first choice. Zionists point to the ephemerality of even the greatest Diaspora communities of history; Diasporists respond that the continued existence of a small state exposed to the expansive designs of hostile neighbours is not assured either. There have always been more Jews in America than in all the Jewish homeland. The Jews remain essentially a Diaspora people, as they have been since the sixth century BC.

Zionists claim that only in their own land can Jews lead a full, 'normal' life without fear of anti-Semitism. But the irony of Israel's geopolitical situation is that the average Jew walking the streets of Los Angeles, Golders Green or even Moscow is physically safer than the average Israeli walking in Jerusalem or Tel-Aviv. Nor has Zionism's ambition of turning Israel into the cultural lodestar of Jewry, radiating its light from the centre to the periphery, been realized. A distinctively *Jewish* culture has yet to emerge in Israel. National art, music, literature and dance are derivative, their several distinguished practitioners firmly in the tradition of the European or eastern cultures from which they and their parents emerged. Israelis are a well-informed, literate, politically aware, book-buying, theatre-going, music-loving public, whose emphasis on higher education is testimony to the abiding Jewish stress on learning. But such is the all-pervasive influence of cultural imperialism in the modern world of mass communication that a small country like Israel can only imitate the tone set by London, Paris or Hollywood. As everywhere else, English is the language of diplomacy, commerce, science, technology and ideas.

Significantly, the only specifically Jewish features that distinguish Israeli culture from that of most western societies are atavistic: biblical archaeology; the revival of spoken Hebrew; a proliferation of *yeshivot*, the traditional Talmudic academies. The Jew who is stimulated by pluralism, and would cite Maimonides, Einstein and Kafka as three out of thousands of similar examples of Jews enhanced by their contact with wider culture, will still prefer to take his chances in the United States or Europe. The Israeli who feels constrained by cultural particularism of the Zionist or religious Orthodox variety will envy and seek to emulate him. Rather than light radiating from the centre to the circumference, as Achad Ha-Am hoped, the eventual relationship between Israel and the Diaspora will more likely come to resemble that between Palestinian and Babylonian Jewry from the third century onwards. The larger community – in numbers, prestige, influence and scholarly attainment – lived and prospered in Babylonia but deferred respectfully to the residue who remained loyal to the Holy Land.

Thus far, the summation of Zionism has been grudging and cautionary. What of the positive achievements? It was a unique attempt to alter the course of 2000 years of Jewish history and, partially, it succeeded. Those Jews who wanted to, and those who had no alternative, could now live as citizens of their own state, governed by laws passed by a Jewish parliament, protected by a Jewish army. No door was closed to them, as had been the case in Europe when Zionism was first mentioned. They could become farmers, entrepreneurs, mechanics or artists, socialists or capitalists, in control of their own destiny, not at the whim or behest of alien legislatures. The kind of society they chose to fashion was their own responsibility, dependent on how they exercised the novel circumstances of Jewish self-rule. To an extent, Zionism's high hopes of creating a model society were bound to be clouded by disappointments; only those social and political movements which do not advance beyond the manifesto stage retain their pristine idealism. Nevertheless, the end result of more than fifty years of Zionist struggle was a Jewish state, built on will, bravery, pioneering determination, daunting feats of labour and fierce ideological clashes that mirrored the wider political conflicts of the twentieth century.

Undoubtedly, Zionism's most important achievement, after winning its state, was to provide a haven for the escapees and survivors of Hitler's Holocaust, where, in the words of the novelist Philip Roth, 'Jews could begin to recover from the devastation of that horror, from a dehumanization so terrible that it would not have been at all surprising had the Jewish spirit, had the Jews themselves, succumbed entirely to that legacy of rage, humiliation and grief.' That alone justified Zionism's patient and frequently derided construction in the inter-war years of a Jewish state-in-embryo, which a guilty world sanctioned into being more speedily than it otherwise would have done, as atonement for its indifference to the Nazi death camps. Zionism became the bond uniting Diaspora Jewry, and the birth of Israel its source of pride, hope and consolation. If it was no longer possible to write lyric poetry after Auschwitz, as Theodor Adorno lamented, and if God had died there, as more than one theologian insisted – then Israel, to an important extent, filled the spiritual vacuum. Modern Jewry identified with and shared vicariously in the triumphs and tribulations of the Jewish state, a symbol of the perennial Jewish will to survive, even after the loss of the six million Holocaust victims. Without the focus of Israel, or if Israel had been overthrown, as many feared might happen in 1967, it is a moot point whether the Jewish people could have withstood two such tragedies in succession and gone on proclaiming itself Jewish.

In the four-thousand-year saga of Jewish history, Zionism is but one, and the newest, manifestation of Jewish resilience and adaptability. Born of the Emancipation, it was a radical response to the prevalence of anti-Semitism beyond the ghetto, and the problems for the east European masses still within the ghetto. Only time will tell whether state-building was Zionism's correct and most far-sighted adjustment to modernity. The striking feature about contemporary Jewish demography is that few people today live where their grandparents did a century ago. Will the existence of a Jewish state provide the stability that previous generations lacked, or is it Jewish destiny to be forever supranationalist, a cosmopolitan and universal people, the leaven in other nations wise enough to recognize their talents and energies?

Those are questions that history will answer. For the present, critical analysis of Zionism is as old as Zionism itself, and has come from many directions: religious and secular, Orthodox and Reform, liberal and socialist, right and left. Many critics would claim, pointing to communism as an analogous example, that once the state was established Zionism had fulfilled itself, and thereafter served only a rhetorical and symbolic function, its myths a link to the past but irrelevant and even harmful to national development in the future. If that is so, most Jews in the world today would be tempted to paraphrase the old cry and say: Zionism is dead. Long live the State of Israel!

GLOSSARY

Achdut Ha-Avodah (Unity of Labour). Jewish workers' party, 1919–30, formed from merger of Po'alei Zion* and other socialist groups.

Aliyah (Ascent). Immigration to the Land of Israel. There were five major 'ascents' in pre-state years.

FIRST ALIYAH (1882–1903), numbering about 25,000 immigrants, mainly from eastern Europe and influenced by the Chibbat Zion* movement.

SECOND ALIYAH (1904–14), 20,000–30,000 immigrants, including key figures in the development of Labour Zionism.

THIRD ALIYAH (1919–23), approximately 35,000 immigrants, mainly influenced by Marxism and radical socialism.

FOURTH ALIYAH (1924–8), 60,000–80,000 immigrants, largely middle class and from Poland.

FIFTH ALIYAH (1929–39), 230,000 immigrants, prompted by the rise of Nazism and the spread of European anti-Semitism.

Balfour Declaration. British policy statement supporting the establishment of a Jewish national home in Palestine (1917).

Betar (Brit Trumpeldor). Youth organization of Revisionist* party, founded 1923.

Brit ha-Biryonim (League of Outlaws). Extremist group within Betar.*

Brit Shalom (Peace Covenant). Association advocating Jewish–Arab understanding, established 1925.

Bund. Jewish socialist party, founded in Vilna in 1897.

Chibbat Zion (Love of Zion). Collective name for group of small societies founded in Russia after the 1881 pogroms, to colonize in Palestine. Supporters were called *Chovevei Zion* (Lovers of Zion).

Eretz Yisrael (The Land of Israel). Biblical designation for the territory 'promised' to the Children of Israel.

Haganah (Defence). Jewish defence force, formed originally by Achdut Ha-Avodah.*

Ha-Po'el Ha-tza'ir (The Young Worker). Zionist Labour party, influenced by the writings of Nachman Syrkin and A. D. Gordon, founded 1905.

Haskalah (Enlightenment). Late eighteenth- and nineteenth-century Jewish modernization movement in western and central Europe. Its followers were called *maskilim*.

Herut (Freedom). Political party founded by the Irgun★ after the creation of the state of Israel, led by Menachem Begin.

Histadrut. The General Federation of Trade Unions in Palestine (later Israel), founded in 1920 by the merger of Achdut Ha-Avodah★ and Ha-Po'el Ha-tza'ir.★

Irgun (Z'vai L'umi) (National Military Organization). Right-wing military group, predominantly Revisionist, formed in 1931, after breakaway from the Haganah.★

Jewish Agency. The 'appropriate Jewish agency' designated by the terms of the mandate, to work with the British authorities in creating the Jewish national home in Palestine.

Kibbutz(im) (Ingathering). Collective agricultural settlement(s) established by Zionist Labour movement.

Labour party. Social democratic party established in 1968 after the merger of Mapai,★ Achdut Ha-Avodah★ and Rafi.★

Mamlachtiyut (Statism) (derived from the Hebrew word for 'kingdom'). Ben-Gurion's policy of the primacy of the state in all aspects of Israeli public life.

Mapai. The Israel Workers' party, founded in 1930 by the merger of Achdut Ha-Avodah★ and Ha-Po'el Ha-tza'ir.★ Dominated politics until it merged into the Labour party in 1968.

Mapam. Left-wing United Workers' party, founded 1948.

Mizrachi. Religious Zionist party, founded in Vilna in 1902.

Po'alei Zion (Workers of Zion). Socialist Zionist party, established 1903, strongly influenced by the writings of Borochov; its Palestinian branch was founded in 1905.

Rafi (Israel Workers' List). Ben-Gurion-led breakaway from Mapai★ in 1965; rejoined Labour party★ in 1968, without Ben-Gurion.

Revisionism. Right-wing, ultra-nationalist expression of Zionism that sought to 'revise' the movement. A Revisionist party, led by Jabotinsky, was founded in 1925 and split from the World Zionist Organization★ in 1935 to form its own New Zionist Organization.

World Zionist Organization (WZO). Umbrella organization of the Zionist movement, founded by Herzl at the Basel Congress in 1897; responsible for policy-making, fund-raising and colonization.

Yeshivah (pl. yeshivot) (Assembly). Academies for the study of Talmud and rabbinic codes.

Yishuv (Settlement). Term used to describe the Jewish community of Palestine prior to statehood.

The material on and about Zionism is enormous, but only relatively recently – in the last twenty-five years or so – has it been studied dispassionately by serious students seeking an approximation to historical truth beneath the layers of myth, legend, polemic and self-justification which previously enveloped the subject. The reasons for this distortion were touched on in the Introduction and concluding chapter of this book. Any new movement makes grandiose claims for itself and glorifies its founders. Early accounts of Herzl, Achad Ha–Am and Jabotinsky are now embarrassing to read for their uncritical adulation, and the autobiographical writings of Weizmann, Ben-Gurion and other Zionist figures tend to show their subjects, like most politicians' reminiscences, only in flattering profile.

Zionism is a controversial and highly charged political creed, but the creation of the modern state of Israel, living in constant danger and born under the shadow of the Holocaust, prompted circumspection from even the acutest Jewish observers, whatever their private reservations. To be critical was to be disloyal to the memory of Jewish suffering and indifferent to the miracle of Jewish renewal. (The word 'miracle' was freely used by religious and secular Jews alike to describe both the rebirth of Israel and her triumph in the Six Day War.) The Arab world's hostility towards the new state, supported by the virulent propaganda of the Soviet bloc, intensified commitment to the Zionist version of history. As a result, so much that was written about and on behalf of Zionism in Israel's first thirty years was partisan and tendentious, recalling Yeats' words, about Irish nationalism, that 'The best lack all conviction, while the worst are full of passionate intensity'. Scholarly detachment seemed impossible to achieve or maintain in such a fraught atmosphere. Not that the necessary sources for a temperate analysis of Zionism's aims and achievements were lacking. There is a wealth of indispensable archival material in Hebrew, Yiddish, Russian, English, German and French, and no serious problems of access to any of the major collections in Jerusalem, Tel-Aviv and New York. It was simply that every historical evaluation or hindsight judgement of Zionism's successes and failures had contemporary implications in the context of the on-going Arab–Israel conflict. Truth, or at least objectivity, is usually the first casualty of war.

In recent years, though, and influenced in large part, it has to be acknowledged, by the research of Israeli scholars and historians, a more balanced appraisal of Zionism is emerging. Much of this work is now available in English, as are the writings of most of those whose contribution to Zionist thought is discussed in this book. Although it helps to have a knowledge of Hebrew to study original sources published and edited in that language, the English-speaking reader will acquire an adequate basis of information about Zionism from the works listed below. The list is selective and is intended as an introductory guide to further reading.

The most accessible single-volume history about the evolution of Zionism to statehood is *The Modern History of Israel* (Weidenfeld & Nicolson, London, 1974) by Noah Lucas. I am particularly indebted to its chapters on immigration and economic and social development in Israel since 1948. Walter Laqueur's *A History of Zionism* (Weidenfeld & Nicolson, London, 1972) is usually described as 'magisterial', but the casual reader may be deterred by its length and confused by its unsystematic, non-chronological approach. An earlier, more discriminating study is Ben Halpern's *The Idea of the Jewish State* (Harvard University Press, 1969). Still useful for its wealth of detail, if one disregards its naive tone, is Nahum Sokolow's *History of Zionism 1600–1918* (2 vols., London, 1919), but the most scholarly introduction to Zionism's early development and growth is by David Vital in his two volumes, *The Origins of Zionism* (Oxford University Press, 1975) and *Zionism: The Formative Years* (Oxford University Press, 1982).

Overdue attention is being paid by historians to Zionist–Arab relations before and during the mandate period. Two valuable source books are *Zionism and the Palestinians* (Croom Helm, London, 1979) by Simha Flapan, and Yosef Gorny's *Zionism and the Arabs 1882–1948* (Oxford University Press, 1987), a particularly lucid exploration of Zionist attitudes to the Arabs from the arrival of early settlers to the foundation of the state.

There have been several compilations of Zionist writings, most of them uncritical and superficial. Two worthy of attention are Arthur Hertzberg's *The Zionist Idea* (Atheneum, New York, 1959) and *The Making of Modern Zionism* (Basic Books, Inc., New York, 1981) by Shlomo Avineri. Hertzberg's reader is an anthology of Zionist writings from Judah Alkalai to David Ben-Gurion, with an interesting introductory essay on the intellectual origins of Zionism, but brief portraits of the chosen writers are sometimes careless with biographical detail. Avineri's book is a series of expanded political science lectures that analyse central aspects of Jewish nationalist thought.

There are Hebrew but no English editions of the writings of Alkalai and Kalischer. However, excerpts from Alkalai's *Minchat Yehudah* (The Offering of Judah) and Kalischer's *D'rishat Zion* (Seeking Zion) are included in Hertzberg's *The Zionist Idea*, and Avineri's book has a brief chapter on both.

Full translations of *Rome and Jerusalem* by Moses Hess can be found in English, but the most recent is a 1943 edition published in New York. A major extract is included in *The Zionist Idea*. The best introduction to Hess's thought and career is an affectionate essay by Isaiah Berlin in *Against the Current* (The Hogarth Press, London, 1979).

An English edition of *Auto-Emancipation* and some other writings by Leo Pinsker can be found in *Road to Freedom* (ed. B. Netanyahu, New York, 1944), substantially reproduced in *The Zionist Idea*. There is no biography of Pinsker in English, but he receives detailed attention from David Vital in *The Origins of Zionism*.

Small libraries have been devoted to Herzliana, most of it of ephemeral quality. The truest source for an assessment of his character and career remains his diary, begun in May 1895 and continued until May 1904, just two months before his death. An unabridged English version is *The Complete Diaries of Theodor Herzl* (ed. Raphael Patai, trans. Harry Zohn, Herzl Press, New York, 1960, 5 vols.), but the less devout reader will find *The Diaries of Theodor Herzl* (ed. and trans. Marvin Lowenthal, Dial Press, New York, 1956) an adequate introduction and selection. Other original works by Herzl translated into English are *The Jewish State* (trans. H. Zohn, Herzl Press, New York, 1970), *The New Ghetto* (trans. H. Norden, Herzl Foundation, New York, 1955), *Old-New Land* (trans. L. Levensohn, Bloch, New York, 1960), and *Zionist Writings: Essays and Addresses* (trans. H. Zohn, Herzl Press, New York, 1975, 2 vols.). For many years the standard biography was Alex Bein's *Theodor*

Herzl (JPS, Philadelphia, 1941) a work of reverent hagiography. *Herzl* by Amos Elon (Schocken, New York, 1986) is less romanticized and more concerned to trace the influences on Herzl of *fin-de-siècle* Vienna, but rather too flowery for most tastes. As shrewd an analysis as any of the man and his thought is Steven Beller's brief monograph *Herzl* (Peter Halban, London, 1991).

Achad Ha-Am is well represented in English, although his biographer, Leon Simon, suffers (like Alex Bein with Herzl) from a surfeit of awed admiration. *Selected Essays* (JPS, Philadelphia, 1912), *Ten Essays on Zionism and Judaism* (London, 1922), and *Essays, Letters, Memoirs* (Phaidon Press, Oxford, 1946), all edited and translated by Simon, contain most of his published writings.

The early activities of socialist Zionists have received scant attention in English, but an edition of Nachman Syrkin, *Essays on Socialist Zionism*, was published in New York in 1935. Marie Syrkin, his formidable daughter, wrote a warm biography of her father, *Nachman Syrkin* (New York, 1961). The best version in English of Ber Borochov's thought is *Nationalism and the Class Struggle: A Marxian Approach to the Jewish Problem* (New York, 1937), with an excellent introductory essay by A. G. Duker. A selection of A. D. Gordon's writings is conveniently presented in *Selected Essays* (trans. F. Burnce, New York, 1938). Dan Leon's *The Kibbutz* (Pergamon, Oxford, 1969), is a useful survey of the cooperative farming movement. There is no collected edition in English of Rabbi Abraham Kook's writings, but a brief selection from *Orot* (Lights) (2nd ed., Jerusalem, 1950) is translated by the author and included in *The Zionist Idea*.

The papers of Arthur Ruppin, founder of Brit Shalom and a key figure in the history of Zionist colonization, are translated in *Memories, Diaries, Letters* (Weidenfeld & Nicolson, Jerusalem, 1971). A valuable study of the binational movement is by Susan Lee Hattis, *The Bi-National Idea in Palestine during Mandatory Times* (Tel-Aviv, 1970), and both Flapan and Gorny deal with the activities of Brit Shalom in *Zionism and the Palestinians* and *Zionism and the Arabs* respectively.

Vladimir Jabotinsky's diffuse writings comprise eighteen volumes in Hebrew, of which only random selections from his autobiography, speeches and political essays have appeared in English translations. It is worth noting that the *right*-arm salute of the Philistines in *Samson the Nazirite* (trans. Cyrus Brooks, London, 1930) becomes, in the Hebrew version (*Shimshon*, Tel-Aviv, 1930), a *left*-handed gesture, presumably because the obvious parallel with fascist salutes was too uncomfortable to accept. Jabotinsky is sycophantically served, and widely quoted, in Joseph B. Schechtman's *The Vladimir Jabotinsky Story* (New York, 1956 and 1961, 2 vols.). The same author collaborated with Y. Benari to produce a *History of the Revisionist Movement* (Tel-Aviv, 1970), and O. K. Rabinowicz's *Vladimir Jabotinsky's Conception of a Nation* (New York, 1946) is another admirer's tribute to his philosophy. A useful corrective is Yaacov Shavit's *Jabotinsky and the Revisionist Movement 1925–1948* (London, 1988), which defines Jabotinsky's role in the political and intellectual history of the Zionist right.

David Ben-Gurion has been the subject of several Hebrew biographies, but is less well represented in English. The most authoritative treatment of his career is Michael Bar-Zohar's *The Armed Prophet: A Biography of Ben-Gurion* (trans. Peretz Kidron, London, 1978). A more recent, overwhelmingly detailed and less digestible account is *Ben-Gurion: The Burning Ground 1886–1948* (Boston, 1987), by Shabtai Teveth. *Rebirth and Destiny of Israel* (New York, 1954), *Ben-Gurion Looks Back in Talks with Moshe Pearlman* (Weidenfeld & Nicolson, London, 1965), and *Israel: A Personal History* (New English Library, London, 1972) are characteristic, occasionally candid examples of the statesman in reflective mood. *My Talks with Arab Leaders* (trans. Aryeh Rubinstein and Misha Louvish, Keter Books, Jerusalem, 1972) is an important record of his unsuccessful attempts over thirty years to reach an accommodation with representatives of the Palestinian community and the Arab world.

Israeli friends bridle indignantly when I insist that there has been no new Zionist thinking worth serious attention since 1948; either it has been a rehash of outworn attitudes and humanitarian sentiments from the left, or back-to-the-Bible territorialism from the right. Friends respond with obscure names, usually on the fringes of the Labour party or the kibbutz movement. Yet it is significant that the two best-known modern Zionist advocates, certainly in the western world, are not politicians but writers: Amos Oz and A. B. Yehoshua. They are proud to call themselves Zionists, are principled, perplexed liberals, but have no more in common with the classic sources of the Zionist movement than have the policies of the modern Israeli Labour party with the theories of socialist Zionism. How the revolutionary intentions of

Zionism's founders were constrained by the realities of state-building is the theme of Mitchell Cohen's *Zion and State* (Basil Blackwell, 1987), a turgidly written but well-researched examination of the journey from pioneering socialism to Shimon Peres. The Revisionist response, culminating in the Herut party's electoral successes under Menachem Begin, is analysed by Yonathan Shapiro in *The Road to Power* (State University of New York Press, 1991), an illuminating study of the character, roots and myths of Revisionism.

Finally, *Jews Among Arabs: Contacts and Boundaries* (eds. Mark R. Cohen and Abraham L. Udovitch, The Darwin Press, Princeton, 1989), a selection of papers from a scholarly colloquium at Princeton University, is a heartening reminder that Jewish–Arab relations have been cordial and mutually enriching in the past, and could conceivably be again in the future.

REFERENCES

pp. 4–5, *happier . . . sufferings*: Heinrich Graetz, *History of the Jews*, 11 vols., Germany, 1853–76

p. 5, *Let us . . . counts*: J. G. Herder on *Social and Political Culture*, trans. F. M. Barnard, Cambridge, 1969, p. 188

pp. 9–10, *which . . . home*: *Neujudäa*, Berlin, 1840

p. 10, *All . . . truth*: Benjamin Disraeli, *Tancred*, Book 2, ch. 14

pp. 13–14: Isaiah Berlin, 'The Life and Opinions of Moses Hess', *Against the Current: Essays in the History of Ideas*, London, 1979, p. 214

p. 14: *Die heilige Geschichte der Menschkeit von einem Jünger Spinozas*, Stuttgart, 1837

p. 14, *speculative . . . literature*: 'Manifesto of the Communist Party', in R. C. Tucker, ed., *The Marx–Engels Reader*, New York, 1972, p. 341

p. 15, *I wanted . . . Europe*: *Rom und Jerusalem, die Nationalitätsfrage*, Leipzig, 1862; translated by, and quoted from, A. Hertzberg, *The Zionist Idea*, New York, 1986, p. 119

p. 15, *a body . . . centuries*: Quoted in Theodor Zlocisti, *Moses Hess*, Berlin, 1921, p. 257

pp. 16–17, *German . . . origin*: *Rom und Jerusalem*, Letter IV, p. 14

p. 17, *Jewish . . . conversion*: ibid., Letter IV, p. 15

p. 17, *with . . . phenomena*: ibid., Letter IV, p. 16

p. 17, *Without . . . others*: ibid., Letter XII, p. 110

p. 18, *I myself . . . fast days*: ibid., Letter VII, p. 50

p. 18, *What I . . . same time*: ibid., Letter VIII, p. 67

p. 19, *an almost . . . Jews*: Abraham Geiger, *Jüdische Zeitschrift für Wissenschaft und Leben*, I (1862), 252

p. 19, *. . . we are . . . Jews*: *Allgemeine Zeitung des Judenthums*, 26 (1862), 610

p. 24, *Autoemancipation; ein Mahnruf an seine Stammesgenossen, von einem russischen Juden*, Berlin, 1862

p. 24, *For the living . . . rival*: *Auto-Emancipation: A Warning to His People by a Russian Jew*, trans. D. S. Blondheim, ed. A. S. Super, London, 1932, p. 13

p. 26, *We probably . . . repeatedly*: ibid., p. 25

p. 30, *. . . almost choked . . . Zionism*: Dan Vittorio Segre, *Memoirs of a Fortunate Jew*, London, 1987, p. 109

p. 32, *. . . so well-written . . . German*: Diary, 9 February 1882

p. 32, *the whole performance . . . candour*: Herzl–Leitenberger (Baron Friedrich) correspondence, 1893

p. 35, *If the romance . . . Land!*: Diary, 2 June 1895

p. 35, *a mediocre philosopher*: Anton Chekhov, *Ariadne*, published in *Russian Thought*, December 1895

p. 36, *The Jewish State: An Attempt at a Modern Solution of the Jewish Question*, English translation of 500 copies, trans. Sylvia d'Avigdor

p. 37, *A small enterprise . . . vessels*: ibid., ch. 1

pp. 37–38, *When . . . or not*: ibid., ch. 2

p. 38, *conducted . . . together*: ibid., ch. 3

p. 39, *is our . . . homeland*: ibid., ch. 2

p. 39, *an outpost . . . barbarism*: ibid., ch. 2

p. 40, *Here . . . parliaments*: Letter to Colonel Goldsmid, 27 February 1896

p. 41, *I have read . . . practical*: Zadoc Kahn to Herzl, 11 May 1896

p. 41, *cold and comparatively uninviting*: *Jewish Chronicle*, 29 April 1896

p. 42, *this single pamphlet . . . all times*: Nordau to Herzl, 26 February 1896

p. 43, *A majestic . . . museums*: Quoted by Walter Laqueur, *A History of Zionism*, New York, 1976, p. 98

pp. 46–7, *As I sat . . . walk*: Diary, 15 July 1896

p. 48, *The Jews . . . help them*: Letter to David Wolffsohn, August 1896

p. 48, *My name . . . published*: 'My Literary Testament', 12 February 1897

pp. 48–9, *It is . . . funds*: Letter to Jacob de Haas, 15 December 1896

p. 49, *internationally . . . matters*: Sir Samuel Montagu to Herzl, 14 July 1897

p. 50, *extremely difficult*: Zadoc Kahn to Herzl, 30 April 1897

p. 50, *efforts . . . Congress*: Press statement, 6 July 1897

p. 52, *It would have been . . . activities*: Circular letter signed by S. P. Rabbinowitz, Willy Bambus and P. Turow, 30 July 1897

p. 52, *Perhaps . . . understanding*: Achad Ha-Am to Michelson, 29 July 1897

p. 53, *Before us . . . beauty*: Ben-Ami, pseudonym of Mordecai Rabin-owicz, Russian and Yiddish author (1854–1932)

p. 56, *I am . . . way*: German Foreign Office Archive (Turkey 195K; 175903–10)

p. 57, *becomes . . . forward*: Diary, 23 September 1897

p. 58, *Yes . . . march*: Diary, 12 May 1898

p. 59, *I cannot . . . feet*: Chaim Weizmann, *Trial and Error*, London, 1949, p. 62

p. 62, *It is . . . realization*: Letter to Wolffsohn, 7 October 1898

p. 62, *Life . . . character*: Diary, 7–8 October 1898

p. 63, *Truly . . . soul*: Diary, 19 October 1898

p. 63, *expressive . . . thought*: *Kaiser's Memoirs*, Hauptarchiv, Berlin-Dahlem, p. 8

p. 64, *musty . . . cleaning it up*: Diary, 31 October 1898

p. 65, *will live . . . consequences*: Diary, 2 November 1898

p. 65, *These people . . . thing*: Quoted in Herzl's Diary, 29 March 1899

p. 65, *The results . . . colossal*: Letter to Nordau, 29 November 1898

p. 66, *Everything . . . dry*: Diary entries for 16 January, 11 February, 23 May 1899

p. 67, *No . . . bread*: Letter to Nordau, 6 March 1900

p. 67, *How well . . . jingoist!*: Diary, 22 April 1900

p. 70, *We have . . . money*: Diary, 21 May 1901

p. 70, *In fifty years . . . money*: Letter to Mandelstamm, 18 August 1901

p. 71, *We venerated . . . soul*: Quoted by Ernst Pawel, *The Labyrinth of Exile: A Life of Theodor Herzl*, New York, 1989, p. 453

p. 72, *He stood . . . gone*: Diary, 10 June 1902

p. 73, *It must . . . Palestine*: Letter to Joseph Cowan, 13 November 1901

p. 73, *I should . . . Christians*: Letter to Herzl, 18 August 1901

p. 74, *If you . . . again*: *Old-New Land*, trans. L. Levensohn, New York, 1960

p. 78, *Would you . . . them?*: ibid., pp. 137–41

p. 79, *To copy . . . too*: *Ha-Shiloah*, September 1902

p. 80, *No . . . there!*: Diary, 23 October 1902

p. 81, *We are . . . ground*: Letter to Otto Warburg, 22 December 1902

p. 82, *He . . . enthusiast*: Cromer to Sir Thomas Sanderson, Foreign Office Papers, 78/5479

p. 86, *merited . . . thanks*: Diary, 22 August 1903

p. 88, *fearful . . . horror*: Letter to Wolffsohn, 30 September 1903

p. 89, *It was . . . years*: Stefan Zweig, *The World of Yesterday*, London, 1940, pp. 40–41

p. 90, *Let us not . . . curtain*: To Dr Nissan Katzenelson, 9 May 1904

pp. 90–91, *. . . It is hard . . . them*: *Jewish Chronicle*, 8 July 1904

p. 91, *He died . . . Sixth Congress*: Quoted in *Herzl Year Book*, 2:151, New York, 1960

p. 92, *At Basel . . . wedding feast*: 'The First Zionist Congress', *Ha-Shiloah*, September 1897

p. 93, *to make clear . . . affairs*: 'Reminiscences', *Essays, Letters, Memoirs*, trans. L. Simon, Oxford, 1946, p. 333

p. 93, *spectacles . . . heart*: Isaac Babel, *Collected Stories*, trans. W. Morison, Harmondsworth, 1961, p. 18

p. 94, *I went . . . people*: 'The Truth from the Land of Israel', *Complete Works of Achad Ha-Am* (Hebrew), Tel-Aviv, 1946, p. 30

p. 94, *We tend . . . fallow*: ibid., p. 23

p. 95, *The Arab . . . easily*: ibid., p. 24

p. 96, *A single . . . Palestine*: Introduction to *Al Parashat D'rachim*, 1895

p. 96, *Perhaps . . . generation*: ibid., p. 6.

p. 97, *If I undertook . . . promise*: To S. Z., Novograd, 13 June 1897

pp. 97–8, *rabble . . . understanding*: Achad Ha-An to Michelson, 29 July 1897

p. 98, *All . . . communicate*: Letter to Dr J. Tchlenow, Moscow, 7 October 1898

p. 98, *the emancipation . . . in us*: 'The First Zionist Congress', *Ha-Shiloah*, September 1897

p. 98, *salvation . . . diplomats*: ibid.

p. 99, *The meeting . . . perfect*: 'The Jewish State and the Jewish Problem', *Ten Essays on Zionism and Judaism*, London, 1922, p. 33

p. 99, *The Congress . . . Hebrew*: ibid., p. 33

pp. 100–101, *because . . . inferiority . . .*: ibid., p. 41

p. 101, *In the west . . . Jewish*: ibid., p. 42

p. 102, *Then . . . Jews*: ibid., p. 44

p. 102, *though . . . error*: ibid., p. 55

p. 103, *the haze of legend*: Letter to R. Brainin, Charlottenburg, 26 December 1898

p. 103, *buy . . . Turk*: Letter to Dr Z. Michelson, Eupatoria, 17 March 1899

p. 103, *followed . . . criticism*: ibid.

p. 104, *fifteen years . . . work*: 'Pinsker and Political Zionism', *Ten Essays on Zionism and Judaism*, p. 58

p. 104, *mostly . . . rechauffés*: ibid., p. 59

p. 106, *Herzl . . . build!*: Shmaryahu Levin (1867–1935), quoted in Bernard Avishai, *The Tragedy of Zionism*, New York, 1985, p. 62

p. 106, *henceforth . . . used to be*: Letter to M. Hacohen, Homel, 15 December 1902

p. 106, *one of . . . humiliation*: Letter to Ahiasaf, Warsaw, 15 December 1902

p. 106, *In Basel . . . interpretation*: 'Those Who Weep', *Ha-Shiloah*, September 1903

p. 107, *A cemetery . . . tombstones*: Letter to Dr J. Klausner, Odessa, 28 February 1908

p. 107, *Judaism . . . Russia*: Letter to Simon Dubnow, St Petersburg, 18 December 1907

p. 108, *For us . . . near*: 'Summa Summarum', *Ten Essays on Zionism and Judaism*, pp. 130–161

p. 109, *The man . . . reach*: Letter to Dr A. Kasteliansky, Rotterdam, 10 May 1915

p. 109, *now . . . loathing . . .*: Letter to S. B. Maximon, New York, 12 April 1916

p. 109, *In these . . . line*: Letter to M. Hacohen, Jaffa, 15 January 1918

p. 110, *an act . . . suicide*: Letter to Chaim Weizmann, 5 September 1917

p. 111, *I am . . . spirit*: Letter to Simon Dubnow, Berlin, 28 March 1923

p. 111, *Do not . . . tomorrow*: Introduction, *Complete Works* (Hebrew), June 1920

p. 114, *It is not . . . souls*: 'Wrecking and Building' (1900), in A. Hertzberg, *The Zionist Idea*, New York, 1986, p. 294

pp. 114–115, *some . . . them*: ibid., p. 294

p. 115, *cease . . . nationality*: ibid., p. 294

p. 115, *We are . . . nation*: ibid., p. 295

p. 118, *a blend . . . Palestine*: 'The Jewish Problem and the Socialist Jewish State' (1896). See Hertzberg, *The Zionist Idea*, p. 333

p. 119, *Do I . . . multitudes*: Walt Whitman, *Song of Myself*, 1855

p. 119, *the wound . . . Bastille*: Hertzberg, *The Zionist Idea*, p. 336

p. 119, *Jewry . . . lived*: ibid., p. 337

p. 120, *dregs . . . passions*: ibid., p. 339

p. 121, *the socialists . . . heritage*: ibid., p. 343

p. 121, *The socialism . . . socialism*: ibid., p. 344

pp. 121–2, *he has no . . . countries*: ibid., p. 346

p. 122, *which has . . . life*: ibid., p. 347

p. 122, *can . . . problems*: ibid., p. 348

p. 122, *From the humblest . . . greatest*: ibid., p. 350

pp. 122–3, *He will . . . peoples!*: ibid., p. 350

p. 123, *more than . . . Europeans*: *Essays on Socialist Zionism*, New York, 1937

p. 126, *In order . . . production*: *The National Question and the Class Struggle* (1905). See Hertzberg, *The Zionist Idea*, New York, 1986, p. 355

p. 127, *Therefore . . . production*: ibid., p. 356

p. 127, *most vital . . . production*: ibid., p. 357

p. 127, *If . . . to work*: ibid., pp. 357–8

p. 128, *all . . . determination*: ibid., p. 359

p. 128, *which . . . interests*: ibid.

p. 128, *There . . . struggle*: ibid., p. 360

p. 129, *National . . . group*: *Our Platform* (1906), ibid., p. 360

p. 129, *Anti-Semitism . . . masses*: ibid., p. 361

p. 130, *Two souls . . . co-religionists*: ibid.

p. 130, *Everywhere . . . masses*: ibid.

p. 130, *Its energy . . . emancipation*: ibid., p. 362

p. 131, *chained . . . on him*: ibid., p. 365

p. 131, *This land . . . Palestine*: ibid., p. 366

p. 131, *Political . . . socialism*: ibid.

p. 132, *The local . . . blood*: *Complete Works of Borochov* (Hebrew), vol. 1, 1955, p. 148

p. 132, *the indigenous . . . the Jews*: ibid., p. 283

p. 132, *So basic . . . guilty*: ibid., p. 287

p. 137, *Men . . . themselves . . .*: Karl Marx, *The Eighteenth Brumaire of Louis Bonaparte*

pp. 140–41, *One aspired . . . proletarians*: Quoted in Yosi Beilin, *The Price of Unity: The Labour Party until the Yom Kippur War* (Hebrew), 1985

p. 141, *Work . . . Nature*: 'People and Labour' in A. D. Gordon, *Selected Essays*, trans. F. Burnce, New York, 1973, p. 55

p. 141, *And when . . . everything!*: 'Logic for the Future', A. Hertzberg, *The Zionist Idea*, p. 371

p. 142, *not labour . . . culture*: *Selected Essays*, p. 51

p. 142, *Culture . . . culture*: ibid., pp. 54–5

p. 142, *In Palestine . . . our own*: Hertzberg, *The Zionist Idea*, p. 374

p. 143, *Let each . . . tongue*: 'Some Observations' (1911), ibid., p. 379

p. 143, *It is life . . . Homeland*: 'Our Tasks Ahead' (1920), ibid., p. 381

pp. 143–4, *a new people . . . creativity*: ibid.

p. 144, *We must . . . less*: ibid., p. 382

p. 144, *This has been . . . silently*: 'Final Reflections' (1921), ibid., p. 386

p. 144, *madman . . . improved*: ibid., p. 385

p. 145, *The workers . . . peoples*: *Our Work from Now On: The People and Labour* (Hebrew), Jerusalem, 1952, p. 244

pp. 145–6, *If mastery . . . stronger*: ibid., pp. 245–6

p. 146, *The Arabs . . . effendis*: *Letters and Articles* (Hebrew), Jerusalem, 1954, pp. 149–51

p. 147, *More important . . . improvement*: Hertzberg, *The Zionist Idea*, p. 385

p. 148, *the spirit . . . people*: 'The Jewish State and the Jewish Problem', *Ten Essays on Zionism and Judaism*, London, 1922, p. 44

p. 148, *What we seek . . . reverse*: 'Our Tasks Ahead' (1920), A. Hertzberg, *The Zionist Idea*, p. 382

p. 148, *the supremacy . . . leadership*: Antonio Gramsci, 'Notes on Italian History', *Selections from the Prison Notebooks*, New York, 1971, p. 57

p. 151, *I am for Bolshevism*: Quoted in Shabtai Teveth, *Ben-Gurion and the Palestinian Arabs*, Oxford, 1985, p. 41

p. 151, *the fundamental . . . reality*: David Ben-Gurion, *Memoirs* (Hebrew), Tel-Aviv, 1976–82, vol. 1, p. 245

p. 155, *man's . . . holiness*: 'The Land of Israel', *Lights* (Hebrew), Jerusalem, 1950. Trans. by and quoted in Hertzberg, *The Zionist Idea*, p. 421

p. 155, *The spirit . . . own will*: 'Lights for Rebirth', ibid., p. 430

p. 156, *It is not . . . evil*: 'The War', ibid., p. 422

pp. 156–7, *ignores . . . soul*: Quoted in *Encyclopaedia Judaica*, vol. 10, p. 1185

p. 157, *An individual . . . from above*: 'Lights for Rebirth', Hertzberg, *The Zionist Idea*, p. 430

p. 158, *Among . . . movement*: *Ha-Shiloah*, March 1907

p. 159, *These two . . . the other*: Quoted in Michael Assaf, *Arab–Jewish Relations in Palestine 1860–1948* (Hebrew), Tel-Aviv, 1970, p. 42

p. 160, *The Palestinian . . . smaller sects*: Y Ben-Zvi, *The Arab Movement* (Hebrew), 1921, p. 34

p. 161, *while the question . . . homeland*: Ha-Shiloah, March 1907

p. 161, *We must . . . benefits*: ibid.

p. 162, *And you shall . . . one kind*: Ha-Me'orer, London, 1906–7

p. 162, *for a single . . . fellow men*: 'In the Beginning', in *Meanwhile* (Hebrew), Jaffa, 1912

p. 163, *During . . . attached to it*: Ha-Olam, Cologne, 1911

p. 163, *we must . . . suicide*: Ha-Herut, June 1913

p. 164, *a binational state . . . rights*: Statutes of Brit Shalom Association, no. 1, Jerusalem, 1927

p. 165, *The formula . . . immigration*: David Ben-Gurion, *Memoirs* (Hebrew), Tel-Aviv, 1976–82, p. 299

p. 165, *We want . . . two thousand years*: Hugo Bergmann, 'On the Majority Question (Hebrew), *She'ifoteinu*, no. 3, 1929

pp. 165–6, *the task . . . peoples*: ibid.

p. 166, *we shall strive . . . party to . . .*: Martin Buber, March 1919. Quoted in A. Cohen, *Israel and the Arab World*, London, 1970, p. 241

p. 166, *What is . . . majority*: Judah Magnes, 'Like Unto All the Nations', Jerusalem, 1930

p. 167, *We want . . . society*: Robert Weltsch, 'Our Attitude to the Eastern Policy' (Hebrew), *She'ifoteinu*, no. 1, 1927

p. 167, *It is . . . minority*: Yosef Luria, 'Our Views on the Parliament' (Hebrew), *She'ifoteinu*, no. 2, 1928

p. 167, *This point . . . Arabs*: Rabbi Benjamin, 'Around the Issue' (Hebrew), *She'ifoteinu*, no. 2, 1928

pp. 168–9, *I could not . . . Bolshevism*: 31 December 1921, Alex Bein, ed., *Arthur Ruppin: Memoirs, Diaries, Letters*, Jerusalem, 1971

p. 169, *European . . . Palestine*: ibid., 29 April 1923

p. 169, *I think . . . Near East*: ibid., 30 October 1923

p. 169, *What continually . . . platform*: ibid., 31 December 1924

p. 169, *One of . . . side*: Ruppin to Hans Kohn, quoted in Susan Lee Hattis, *The Bi-National Idea*, Haifa, 1970, p. 48

p. 170, *the Arabs . . . for ever*: Ruppin to Hans Kohn, 30 May 1938, ibid., pp. 237–8

p. 170, *the way . . . self-righteous*: 'Like Unto All the Nations', pp. 15–16

p. 170, *What good . . . Arabs?*: 4 February 1932, *Arthur Ruppin: Memoirs, Diaries, Letters*

p. 171, *The situation . . . Arab state*: 31 December 1931, ibid.

p. 171, *Not negotiations . . . losses*: 18 March 1936, ibid.

p. 171, *In general . . . chauvinism?*: Arthur Ruppin, *My Life and Work* (Hebrew), Tel-Aviv, 1968, p. 149

p. 172, *He who . . . infant*: 'Politics as a Vocation', in H. H. Gerth and C. Wright Mills, eds., *From Max Weber*, New York, 1946

p. 174, *Jabotinsky . . . Jewish*: Chaim Weizmann, *Trial and Error*, p. 86

p. 174, *I have never . . . air*: Vladimir Jabotinsky, *Works* (Hebrew), Jerusalem, 1947, vol. 1, p. 16

pp. 174–5, *If I have . . . doctrine*: ibid., p. 27

pp. 175–6, *I have . . . my life*: 'Days of Mourning', Jabotinsky Institute and Archives (JIA)

p. 176, *Stupid . . . against all*: *Works*, vol. 9, p. 265

pp. 176–7, *he demanded . . . realized*: 'Reactionary', in Vladimir Jabotinsky, *Nation and Society* (Hebrew), Jerusalem, 1950, p. 106

p. 177, *What would . . . party . . .*: *Works*, vol. 1, p. 40

p. 177, *You may be . . . sort*: Joseph B. Schechtman, *Rebel and Statesman*, New York, 1956, p. 204

p. 178, *If this . . . proud of it*: 'On Militarism', *Works*, vol. 7, p. 43

p. 178, *a true . . . justice*: Schechtman, *Rebel and Statesman*, p. 369

p. 179, *I felt . . . defeat*: Minutes of Proceedings, XV Zionist Congress, p. 229

p. 180, *explosions . . . spheres*: *Works*, vol. 9, p. 140

pp. 180–81, *they show . . . nation*: ibid., p. 128

p. 181, *Every race . . . race*: ibid., p. 161

p. 181, *We Jews . . . French*: ibid., vol. 7, p. 221

p. 182, *traditions . . . east*: ibid.

p. 182, *to humiliate . . . Pan-Islamism*: ibid., p. 213

p. 183, *we cannot . . . break down*: 'The Iron Wall', *On the Road to the State* (Hebrew), Jerusalem, 1953, pp. 251–60

pp. 183–4, *But the sole . . . present*: ibid.

p. 184, *Zionism . . . truth*: 'Protected Jews', *On the Road to the State*, pp. 185–94

p. 185, *The Jewish . . . scattered*: Speech at the Va'ad Le'umi (National Council), *Collected Speeches 1905–26*, p. 291

p. 187, *it is . . . person*: 'The Idea of Betar', *Works*, vol. 2, pp. 319 ff.

p. 188, *I believe . . . pledge*: Confidential Memorandum to Zionist Executive, 5 November 1922

p. 189, *Moreover . . . belong to it*: 'What Do the Revisionist Zionists Want?', *Works*, Jerusalem, 1947, vol. 2, p. 293

p. 189, *In its eyes . . . peoples*: 'Zion and Communism', *On the Road to the State*, Hebrew (Jerusalem), 1953, pp. 65–6

p. 189, *My dear man . . . Mittelstand*: Joseph Schechtman and Yehuda Benari, *History of the Revisionist Movement*, Tel-Aviv, 1970, p. 222

pp. 190–91, *Not a fold . . . nations*: *Samson the Nazirite*, trans. Cyrus Brooks, London, 1930, pp. 179–80

p. 191, *. . . unless . . . Zionist Organization*: Letter, 20 March 1931, Jabotinsky Institute and Archives (JIA)

p. 191, *would not . . . the ZO*: Letter, 17 August 1931, JIA

p. 193, *I have no . . . culture*: Interview with Jewish Telegraphic Agency, Basel, 3 July 1931

p. 193, *If there is . . . know it*: Protocols of XVII Zionist Congress, London, 1931, p. 55

p. 193, *The aim . . . Jordan*: 'Report on the 17th Zionist Congress', *New Judaea*, July–August 1931, p. 210

p. 194, *I don't try . . . man*: Letter, 17 August 1931, JIA

p. 194, *It is hard . . . person*: *Herut*, 26 March 1933

p. 195, *The alphabet . . . shoot!*: 'By the Fireside', *On the Road to the State*, pp. 87–95

p. 195, *We see . . . Europe*: Abba Achimeir, *Revolutionary Zionism*, Tel-Aviv, 1966, p. 110

p. 195, *We are destined . . . kingdom*: 'Decay of the House of Israel', in Y. Yeivin, *Uri Zvi Greenberg: A Legislative Poet* (Hebrew), Tel-Aviv, 1938, p.6

p. 195, *I demand . . . work . . .*: Letter to Y. Yeivin, 14 May 1933

p. 196, *the obese . . . ideal*: Joseph B. Schechtman, *The Vladimir Jabotinsky Story*, New York, 1956–61, 2 vols., p. 240

p. 197, *Stavski . . . innocent*: Letter, 16 June 1934, JIA

p. 197, *I have always . . . Revisionists*: Letter to Paula Ben-Gurion, 6 September 1933

p. 198, *I felt . . . conflict*: David Ben-Gurion, *Memoirs* (Hebrew), Tel-Aviv, 1976–82, vol. 2, p. 186

pp. 198–9, *Whatever . . . his pain*: Letter to Jabotinsky, 28 April 1935

p. 199, *a work . . . monistic*: Letter to Ben-Gurion, 30 March 1935, JIA

p. 199, *the necessary . . . nation*: Y. Goldstein and Y. Shavit, *No Compromises: The Ben-Gurion/Jabotinsky Agreement and its Failure* (Hebrew), Tel-Aviv, 1979, pp. 147–8

p. 199, *If I were . . . established*: Letter to Ben-Gurion, 2 May 1935, JIA

p. 200, *I regret . . . Europe*: Joseph Schechtman, *Fighter and Prophet*, p. 340

p. 203, *I believe . . . believe*: Evidence Submitted to the Palestine Royal Commission, 11 February 1937. See A. Hertzberg, *The Zionist Idea*, New York, 1986, pp. 559–70

p. 203, *If you . . . Vistula River*: Official Summary of the Betar Congresses, JIA

p. 203, *the old-fashioned . . . lack*: Letter to J. Bartlett, 9 December 1938

p. 204, *For Zionism . . . Jabotinsky*: Quoted in Howard M. Sachar, *A History of Israel*, New York, 1976, p. 187

p. 206, *When I was . . . Dr Herzl*: David Ben-Gurion, *Memoirs*, vol. 1, p. 7

pp. 206–7, *The settlement . . . pastime*: *We and Our Neighbours* (Hebrew), Tel-Aviv, 1931, p. 9

p. 207, *The interests . . . the same*: 'Officialdom and the Workers' (Hebrew), *Yalkut Ha-Achdut 1907–19*, Tel-Aviv, 1962, p. 174

p. 208, *We are . . . brow*: Quoted in M. Bar Zohar, *The Armed Prophet*, London, 1967, p. 32

p. 208, *England . . . redemption*: 14 November 1917, in *My Talks with Arab Leaders*, Jerusalem, 1972, p. 6

p. 209, *Indeed . . . goal*: *Memoirs*, vol. 1, pp. 254–5

p. 210, *must . . . heart*: *Karl Marx: Early Writings*, trans. T. B. Bottomore, London, 1963, pp. 55–6

p. 210, *The very realization . . . self-sufficient*: *From Class to Nation* (Hebrew), rev. ed., Tel-Aviv, 1974, pp. 196–7

p. 210, *in all this . . . people*: ibid., p. 250

p. 211, *Our movement . . . community*: ibid., p. 220

p. 213, *and before . . . snow*: 'The British Administration and the Jewish National Home', quoted in Shlomo Avineri, *Arlosoroff*, London, 1989, pp. 78–80

p. 213, *Not because . . . work*: J. Goldstein, 'Anti-British Tendencies in Mapai in the 1930s', *M'asef*, Tel-Aviv, May 1976, pp. 122 ff.

p. 213, *The declaration . . . nullified . . .*: Speech at Jewish Agency Executive, 19 May 1936

p. 214, *England . . . lasts*: Letter to Jewish Agency Executive, 9 June 1936

p. 215, *The independence . . . state*: *My Talks with Arab Leaders*, trans. Aryeh Rubinstein and Misha Louvish, Jerusalem, 1972, p. 30

p. 215, *We did not . . . say it now*: Minutes of Evidence given before Royal Commission on Palestine, Colonial Office, London, 1937, para. 4539

p. 215, *England . . . fairly*: Y. Becker, ed., *The Teaching of David Ben-Gurion* (Hebrew), Tel-Aviv, 1958, vol. 2, p. 363

p. 217, *I saw . . . Jews*: *My Talks with Arab Leaders*, trans. Aryeh Rubinstein and Misha Louvish, Jerusalem, 1972, p. 5

p. 217, *Like . . . hostility*: *Ha-Achdut*, vol. 1, no. 3, 1910

p. 218, *Who is . . . workers*: Letter, 24 September 1921, Ben-Gurion Archives

p. 218, *The debate . . . movement*: Joint Secretariat, 10 November 1929, Beit Berl Archives

pp. 219–20, *an amulet . . . environs*: 'The Foreign Policy of the Jewish People', *We and Our Neighbours*, (Hebrew) Tel-Aviv, 1931, pp. 249–65

p. 220, *was merely . . . people*: Conversation with Fuad Bey Hamzah, April 1937, *My Talks with Arab Leaders*, p. 124

p. 220, *This time . . . respect*: Mapai Central Committee, 4 November 1933, Beit Berl Archives

pp. 220–21, *In this . . . people*: 17 April 1936, *My Talks with Arab Leaders*, p. 43

p. 221, *The legend . . . agreement*: 2 June 1936, ibid., p. 81

p. 221, *On the basis . . . settlement*: 13 August 1934, ibid., p. 25

p. 221, *If we . . . possibilities*: ibid., p. 31

p. 221, *I would . . . to us*: Letter to Shertok, 9 June 1936, ibid., p. 82

p. 222, *There is no . . . nation*: Speech to Inner Actions Committee, 12 October 1936

p. 222, *We are facing . . . fight*: Speech to Mapai Political Committee, 6 June 1938

p. 223, *The disaster . . . settlement*: *The Restored State of Israel* (Hebrew), Tel-Aviv, 1969, vol. 1, p. 57

p. 223, *We need . . . agreement*: *My Talks with Arab Leaders*, p. 84

p. 225, *a miraculous . . . problem*: Rony E. Gabbay, *A Political Study of the Arab–Jewish Conflict: The Refugee Problem*, Geneva, 1959, p. 110

p. 226, *The state . . . generation*: 'Socialist state "in our time" is foreseen by P. M.', *Jerusalem Post*, 23 March 1949, p. 1

p. 226, *A Zionism . . . exist*: 'The State and the Future of Zionism', Address to Zionist General Council, Jerusalem, 25 April 1950

p. 226, *The stories . . . Basel Congresses*: 'Terms and Values' (Hebrew), *Hazut*, 1957, p. 11

p. 226, *The redemption . . . redeemed*: 'Messianic vision', speech to the

Third World Congress for the Study of Judaism, Jerusalem, 25 July 1961

p. 227, *the creative . . . state-building*: *Our Stand: Programme of Mapai*, Tel-Aviv, 1949, pp. 8–9

p. 227, *What is . . .* ex nihilo: *The Restored State of Israel*, p. 429

p. 228, *the values . . . mankind*: 'State Education Law', *Laws of the State of Israel: Authorised Translation from the Hebrew*, vol. 7, 1952–3, p. 113

p. 228, *The Histadrut . . . control*: *The Histadrut in the State* (Hebrew), The Eighth Conference of the Histadrut, Tel-Aviv, 1956

p. 229, *There is no . . . character*: David Ben-Gurion and Nathan Rotenstreich, 'Israel and Zionism: a discussion', *Jewish Frontier*, December 1957

p. 229, *The people . . . headquarters*: Lea Ben Dor, 'Dayan takes "hard look" ', *Jerusalem Post*, 18 January 1959, p. 4

p. 231, *How could . . . rancour?*: Shlomo Avineri, *Midstream*, September 1965, p. 16

p. 232, *The law . . . country . . .*: *The Restored State of Israel*, pp. 428–9

p. 232, *In our country . . . affection*: *The Teaching of David Ben-Gurion*, pp. 496–7

p. 232, *Yesterday . . . were taken*: 'Ben-Gurion warns against IZL plot', *Jerusalem Post*, 9 January 1952, p. 1

p. 234, *not to know . . . to* do: 'Peres: living in a dangerous era', *Jerusalem Post*, 30 August 1960, p. 1

p. 234, *The world . . . fathers*: 'Israel as a way of life', *Jerusalem Post*, 9 October 1959

p. 234, *The last . . . come later*: 'The next ten years', *Jerusalem Post*, 23 April 1958

p. 234, *The ideology . . . created*: Interview with Mitchell Cohen, 2 August 1983, Tel-Aviv

p. 239, *in danger . . . character*: 'On Liberty', Marshall Cohen, ed., *The Philosophy of John Stuart Mill*, New York, 1961, p. 246

p. 250, *Jews . . . grief*: Philip Roth, *Operation Shylock: A Confession*, London, 1994, pp. 41–2

INDEX

READ MORE IN PENGUIN

In every corner of the world, on every subject under the sun, Penguin represents quality and variety – the very best in publishing today.

For complete information about books available from Penguin – including Puffins, Penguin Classics and Arkana – and how to order them, write to us at the appropriate address below. Please note that for copyright reasons the selection of books varies from country to country.

In the United Kingdom: Please write to *Dept. EP, Penguin Books Ltd, Bath Road, Harmondsworth, West Drayton, Middlesex UB7 ODA*

In the United States: Please write to *Consumer Sales, Penguin USA, P.O. Box 999, Dept. 17109, Bergenfield, New Jersey 07621-0120.* VISA and MasterCard holders call 1-800-253-6476 to order Penguin titles

In Canada: Please write to *Penguin Books Canada Ltd, 10 Alcorn Avenue, Suite 300, Toronto, Ontario M4V 3B2*

In Australia: Please write to *Penguin Books Australia Ltd, P.O. Box 257, Ringwood, Victoria 3134*

In New Zealand: Please write to *Penguin Books (NZ) Ltd, Private Bag 102902, North Shore Mail Centre, Auckland 10*

In India: Please write to *Penguin Books India Pvt Ltd, 706 Eros Apartments, 56 Nehru Place, New Delhi 110 019*

In the Netherlands: Please write to *Penguin Books Netherlands bv, Postbus 3507, NL-1001 AH Amsterdam*

In Germany: Please write to *Penguin Books Deutschland GmbH, Metzlerstrasse 26, 60594 Frankfurt am Main*

In Spain: Please write to *Penguin Books S. A., Bravo Murillo 19, 1° B, 28015 Madrid*

In Italy: Please write to *Penguin Italia s.r.l., Via Felice Casati 20, I–20124 Milano*

In France: Please write to *Penguin France S. A., 17 rue Lejeune, F–31000 Toulouse*

In Japan: Please write to *Penguin Books Japan, Ishikiribashi Building, 2–5–4, Suido, Bunkyo-ku, Tokyo 112*

In South Africa: Please write to *Longman Penguin Southern Africa (Pty) Ltd, Private Bag X08, Bertsham 2013*

READ MORE IN PENGUIN

RELIGION

The Gnostic Gospels Elaine Pagels

In a book that is as exciting as it is scholarly, Elaine Pagels examines these ancient texts and the questions they pose and shows why Gnosticism was eventually stamped out by the increasingly organized and institutionalized Orthodox Church. 'Fascinating' – *The Times*

Islam in the World Malise Ruthven

This informed and informative book places the contemporary Islamic revival in context, providing a fascinating introduction – the first of its kind – to Islamic origins, beliefs, history, geography, politics and society.

The Orthodox Church Timothy Ware

In response to increasing interest among western Christians, and believing that a thorough understanding of Orthodoxy is necessary if the Roman Catholic and Protestant Churches are to be reunited, Timothy Ware explains Orthodox views on a vast range of matters from Free Will to the Papacy.

Judaism Isidore Epstein

The comprehensive account of Judaism as a religion and as a distinctive way of life, presented against a background of 4,000 years of Jewish history.

Mysticism F. C. Happold

What is mysticism? This simple and illuminating book combines a study of mysticism – as experience, as spiritual knowledge and as a way of life – with an illustrative anthology of mystical writings, ranging from Plato and Plotinus to Dante.

Eunuchs for Heaven Uta Ranke-Heinemann

'No other book on the Catholic moral heritage unearths as many spiteful statements about women ... it is sure to become a treasure-chest for feminists ... Uta Ranke-Heinemann's research is dazzling' – *The New York Times*

READ MORE IN PENGUIN

POLITICS AND SOCIAL SCIENCES

National Identity   Anthony D. Smith

In this stimulating new book, Anthony D. Smith asks why the first modern nation states developed in the West. He considers how ethnic origins, religion, language and shared symbols can provide a sense of nation and illuminates his argument with a wealth of detailed examples.

The Feminine Mystique   Betty Friedan

'A brilliantly researched, passionately argued book – a time-bomb flung into the Mom-and-Apple-Pie image . . . Out of the debris of that shattered ideal, the Women's Liberation Movement was born' – Ann Leslie

Faith and Credit   Susan George and Fabrizio Sabelli

In its fifty years of existence, the World Bank has influenced more lives in the Third World than any other institution yet remains largely unknown, even enigmatic. This richly illuminating and lively overview examines the policies of the Bank, its internal culture and the interests it serves.

Political Ideas   Edited by David Thomson

From Machiavelli to Marx – a stimulating and informative introduction to the last 500 years of European political thinkers and political thought.

Structural Anthropology Volumes 1–2   Claude Lévi-Strauss

'That the complex ensemble of Lévi-Strauss's achievement . . . is one of the most original and intellectually exciting of the present age seems undeniable. No one seriously interested in language or literature, in sociology or psychology, can afford to ignore it' – George Steiner

Invitation to Sociology   Peter L. Berger

Sociology is defined as 'the science of the development and nature and laws of human society'. But what is its purpose? Without belittling its scientific procedures Professor Berger stresses the humanistic affinity of sociology with history and philosophy. It is a discipline which encourages a fuller awareness of the human world . . . with the purpose of bettering it.

READ MORE IN PENGUIN

POLITICS AND SOCIAL SCIENCES

Conservatism   Ted Honderich

'It offers a powerful critique of the major beliefs of modern conservatism, and shows how much a rigorous philosopher can contribute to understanding the fashionable but deeply ruinous absurdities of his times' – *New Statesman & Society*

The Battle for Scotland   Andrew Marr

A nation without a parliament of its own, Scotland has been wrestling with its identity and status for a century. In this excellent and up-to-date account of the distinctive history of Scottish politics, Andrew Marr uses party and individual records, pamphlets, learned works, interviews and literature to tell a colourful and often surprising account.

Bricks of Shame: Britain's Prisons   Vivien Stern

'Her well-researched book presents a chillingly realistic picture of the British sytsem and lucid argument for changes which could and should be made before a degrading and explosive situation deteriorates still further' – *Sunday Times*

Inside the Third World   Paul Harrison

This comprehensive book brings home a wealth of facts and analysis on the often tragic realities of life for the poor people and communities of Asia, Africa and Latin America.

'Just like a Girl'   Sue Sharpe
How Girls Learn to be Women

Sue Sharpe's unprecedented research and analysis of the attitudes and hopes of teenage girls from four London schools has become a classic of its kind. This new edition focuses on girls in the nineties – some of whom could even be the daughters of the teenagers she interviewed in the seventies – and represents their views and ideas on education, work, marriage, gender roles, feminism and women's rights.

READ MORE IN PENGUIN

The Jewish People: Their History and Their Religion

David J. Goldberg and John D. Rayner

'The handsomely produced and interestingly illustrated volume is two works in one. The first part offers a survey of Jewish history and literature. The second part presents what the preface describes as "a thematic analysis of the teachings and practices of Judaism"' – Israel Finestein in the *Jewish Chronicle*

'Fluently written, with an admirable fair-mindedness in surveying both history and belief, this book faithfully conveys the insistence of Jewish tradition on meaning, on mission and on responsibility both individual and collective. The very compression of their survey allows the authors to see broad trends, the force and sweep of a cultural heritage that links the passion of contemporary secular Jews to improve the world with the "holy impatience that stems ultimately from Sinai"' – A. J. Shermann in *The Times Literary Supplement*

'They provide many of the clues in a wide-ranging account of things Jewish that one can truly recommend to intellectually curious Gentiles, as well as to the majority of modern secularized Jews who know relatively little about their complex tradition' – Louis Marcus in the *Irish Times*

'The intelligent non-experts gets a clear picture of Jewish life, letters and history and it will be an endlessly useful reference book for people working in the religious field' – Julia Neuberger in *The Times Educational Supplement*